I0764029

MEMOIR

OF

ABNER KINGMAN NOTT,

LATE PASTOR OF THE

First Baptist Church in the City of New York;

WITH

COPIOUS EXTRACTS FROM HIS CORRESPONDENCE.

BY HIS BROTHER.

"For we are His workmanship, created in Christ Jesus unto good works, which God hath before ordained that we should walk in them."—EPH. ii. 10.

"Bringing every thought into captivity to the obedience of Christ."—2d COR. ii. 5.

NEW YORK:
SHELDON AND COMPANY.
1860.

R. CRAIGHEAD,
Printer, Stereotyper, and Electrotyper,
Caxton Building,
81, 83, *and* 85 *Centre Street.*

CONTENTS.

MEMOIR OF

REV. ABNER KINGMAN NOTT.

INTRODUCTION.

Abner Kingman Nott, at the age of twenty-three years, having just completed his course of theological studies, entered upon the pastoral charge of the First Baptist Church in the City of New York. In this position he labored with rare fidelity and success for a period of one year and ten months, when he was removed by a sudden death.

It might be doubted whether a career thus brief, whatever may have been its promise, could present any actual achievement worthy of public review.

But the value of a life is not to be measured by its length; nor even altogether by its deeds, however famous or useful. A life-history affords topics for study in what it may exhibit of individual character; of purity and tenacity of purpose; or of processes and laws of mental action. A life neither conspicuous nor especially eventful, may yet involve problems for the philosopher and lessons for the Christian.

In its facts as well as in its moral significance, the short career of Kingman Nott exhibits much that is attractive and valuable. Its peculiar *success*, indeed, presents questions of curious interest for consideration. In early manhood, he had been chosen for a position which presented almost every advantage that could be imagined or desired by one whose aims and aspirations were for the widest field of usefulness as a minister of Christ. The active use of his talents brought his name into unexpected prominence. Liberal means were placed at his disposal; the best culture and the "luxury of doing good." In his social relations he enjoyed that implicit confidence and warmly affectionate regard, which can only be called forth by unaffected kindness of heart, and an appreciative genius, chastened and governed by tact and good sense. As a speaker, he united clear reasoning, fervid rhetoric, and a winning manner, all inspired by earnest conviction and deep feeling—which gained alike the hearts and intellects of young and old, of the critical scholar and of the most unlearned. Not merely in his own society and in New York, but in other cities he began to be eagerly sought for on account of his attractive and effective eloquence in the pulpit.

Yet this kind of popularity apparently did not elate or dazzle him. All who knew him best, testify that he never lost the simple directness of his character, nor the undivided earnestness of his consecration to the higher objects of his ministry. Power and influence were of little account in his esteem, except as means for practical usefulness.

But to complete his happiness, the most cherished aims of his life seemed to be on the full tide of prosperity. His earnest desire was to see his large church trained up to the highest standard of Christian efficiency; co-operating with the pastor in all efforts of beneficent influence, and for the salvation of souls; not merely in the congregation but in the "region round about." The conversion of nearly two hundred persons during the short term of his ministry gave evidence that these labors were not in vain.

Passing from these features and facts in the brief record of the subject of this memoir, we are naturally led to inquire whether his success was a fortunate accident? Shall we rather say, succinctly, that it was the special favor of God? or, reverently recognising His supreme control, shall we descend to the human plane to seek for second causes? Among these, perhaps, were the following:

(1.) He was favored by a peculiarly excellent constitution:—the intellectual, emotional, and moral natures being equally healthy and active:—well-proportioned, and harmoniously adjusted to each other.

(2.) The circumstances of his childhood and early youth were such as to encourage, and through the grace of God, effect the development of virtuous impulses, and to educate intellect, taste, and conscience. Thus he was preserved in mental and physical vigor comparatively untouched by the evil influences which lurk in the path of so many young men, and prepared for the reception, in due time, of a concentrated, energetic "motive power" into his soul.

(3.) The key to the ultimate harmony of his character—to his endeavors and to his success, may be found, perhaps, in the fact that he was thus early arrested and absorbed by an ambition far higher than that which is apt to seize upon a buoyant youth on the threshold of life. Instead of a thirst for distinction, or wealth, or pleasure, or even the nobler desire for mere learning, or power, or fame, or any selfish or sordid achievements, he became, while a mere boy, the loyal and devoted servant of Jesus Christ. He chose the Saviour as his dearest friend—his captain and leader—a being to worship and glorify—and yet one to imitate. Possessed—animated by this all-absorbing and controlling affection, he was at once led to a great Work to be done—the noblest and best. All his faculties, developed to their greatest activity and strength, were devoted to this work, and these faculties became harmonized into symmetrical proportions.

The "philosophy of a life" thus outlined, is delineated circumstantially, though in an imperfect and informal manner, in the following pages. The simple incidents of Kingman's history, and glimpses of his spiritual experience, are revealed chiefly in his own letters and memoranda. These have been connected, with such brief explanations and comments as appeared needful. If the reader of these pages has heretofore questioned whether love to Christ be a safe and worthy motive, and a sufficient power to develope power, and to purify and elevate the entire character, perhaps a fair consideration of the aims and results herein imperfectly pictured, may solve these doubts—may cast an additional ray of light on the pathway of Christian duty and the road to the reward of those whose duty has been done; and may possibly incite some, here and there, to pursue the investigation, and test for themselves the value of the gospel. It is to be hoped that some good lesson may be learned from the brief history of one who, under a divine impulse acting on his soul, seemed to make the most of himself, and "the most of two worlds."

CHAPTER I.

CHILDHOOD, UP TO CONVERSION.

Abner Kingman Nott was the son of Handel G. and Lydia C. Nott. His paternal ancestors, a century and a half ago, emigrated from England, and established themselves in the old town of Saybrook, Conn., taking their stand firmly at the same time on the "Saybrook Platform." It was a stock robust and thrifty. From it came "Old Dr. Nott, of Franklin," President Nott, of Union College, Samuel Nott, D.D., the original companion of Judson, and other well-known names. The ancient family homestead still remains, though it has passed into the hands of strangers.

His mother's family also were of Puritan descent. Her father, Mr. Abner Kingman, was well known forty years ago as a prosperous merchant in the city of Providence, and was greatly respected for intelligence and piety.

Handel G. Nott, born at Saybrook, in the year 1800, was graduated at Yale College in 1823, studied Theology at the same institution, and in 1826 was ordained to the work of the Christian Ministry, and to the pastoral office in connection with Congregational Church in Nashua, N. H. During the nine years of his ministry in that place, there was an almost uninterrupted revival.

The subject of this memoir was born at Nashua, on the 22nd day of March, 1834. He was the fourth son in a family of fifteen children, six of them the fruit of a second marriage. Two, of tender age, had been laid in the churchyard before the birth of Kingman; two others were taken away before his death, also in infancy.

Only two years of Kingman's life were passed in Nashua. Indeed his childhood saw many changes. In the spring of 1836 Mr. Nott began the pilgrim life, which is the lot of so many clergymen. . . . Having changed his opinions upon the subject of baptism, he resigned his charge at Nashua, and removed first to Buffalo, New York, where his field was the wharves and a Seamen's Bethel Church. Three years later, returning to the East, he became pastor of the Federal street, now Rowe street, Baptist Church, in Boston. Thence he removed to Bath, Maine, about the close of 1840, and eight years later to Kennebunkport, Maine, where he still preaches.

Of the fourteen years preceding Kingman's conversion (Jan. 1849), no minute account need be attempted. *That* was the great epoch—the time when his history, properly so called, begins. Previous to that he had nearly the usual tastes and habits of moderately "good" boys, was fond of play, tolerant of books, an attendant on schools. Yet some details may illustrate what were his natural qualities, and what the influences that aided to mould him.

His body did not, up to his sixth year, promise the vigor it afterwards possessed. He had a large and noble head, and sufficiently broad shoulders; but a slender frame, and legs scarcely able to support the weight of the slight superstructure. His parents, indeed, had much anxiety for him. But in '39 he was sent to pass the summer on his grandfather's farm in Saybrook; and being here encouraged in free, out-of-door sports, barefooted rambles over the breezy hills, and such gentle labor as a child might mistake for play, he rapidly gained strength, and laid the foundation for permanent and robust health. This was his physical salvation; who shall say how much it had to do with his moral preservation.

Kingman early displayed an affectionate and tender disposition—loving his friends ardently, being quick to sympathize with their distresses, sensitive to rebuke, easily moved to tears. He was very independent of companionship, and even when very young would amuse himself contentedly in solitude by the hour.

Yet he had a most wholesome love of the usual sports of boyhood, and was enterprising and fearless, if not to a fault, at least to the discomfort of those who had the charge of him. Some anecdotes show this:—Upon his third birthday, in Buffalo, he was suddenly, after dinner, missing; and an anxious search, continued through the whole afternoon, failed to discover any traces of him. At last, near sundown, the city crier was summoned, who went forth, with jingling bell and the cry "Child lost!" and finally succeeded in capturing the infant adventurer, two miles from home, on the bank of a small pond, where he was still placidly delighting himself, in the departing twilight, with experiments in the navigation of chips. He rode home on horseback, exulting in his enterprise and his exploits.

The town of Bath, where much of his boyhood was spent, lies upon the Kennebeck River, there nearly a mile in width. On, *in*, and about this river, he found his chief amusements, swimming, boating, clambering about the frames of ships on the stocks, or the masts of ships at the wharves. Several times he was near drowning. Once he slipped into the water between a ship and the wharf to which the tide was rapidly drifting her in; he was unable to extricate himself, and was with difficulty saved by others from the double danger of drowning and being crushed.

Having become accustomed to sailing in company with older persons, he was filled with ambition to voyage on his own account. The first attempt proved unmistakably premature. Venturing out in a high wind, with an unwieldy, two-masted boat, he found more than he could manage and was soon drifting at the mercy of wind and tide. These dealt tenderly with him, however, and brought him to the shore a mile or two below the town, with no loss but of the ship and lading. He came safe home, but the boat was found next morning with torn sail, and oarless and bilged.

In the sieges and assaults of the mimic warfare in which boyhood delights, he exhibited more skill than for elementary navigation. In winter it was the custom with the boys to build great snow-forts, with massive walls. Two of these, occupying neighboring elevations, would sometimes bombard each other for a whole afternoon, varying the dread scene with the "circumstance" of sorties and assaults. The ammunition employed was not always of a safe sort. Snow-balls, dipped in water and frozen—and intended to effect breaches in the walls of the enemy, would sometimes do execution among the unlucky garrison. A few "casualties" resulting in this way caused the "new arm" to be abandoned.

Another source of frequent amusement, was rambling in the woods and fields. About Bath there were extended "pastures," not soft and rolling, but rugged, with great rocks and deep dells, with frequent brooks, and woods of oak, maple, and pine. These rough fields afforded inexhaustible pleasures. There were berries, squirrels, fish, maple sap,—and the mere delight of roaming. The love of nature here acquired, and nursed afterwards on the wild sea-coast of Kennebunk port, was one of Kingman's strongest passions.

Kingman was not, in the ordinary idea of it, a precocious child. That is, there was no premature and eccentric development of any kind. The intellect had not been unduly stimulated, and was not excessively active, to the disadvantage of physical, and finally of mental health. He had a symmetrical nature in body, mind, and soul. He possessed always a certain spirituality, but was tangible and loved tangible things. He was "of the earth—earthy" in a proper sense, and to a healthful degree—for a dweller on earth.

Yet he early displayed great native intelligence and aptitude for learning as well as for doing. An old sobriquet, clinging to him from childhood—"The Little Old Man"—suggests some of his peculiarities. It was grounded partly on his appearance; since the large head on small body, his great forehead, and almost white hair, caused doubts often as to his real age. But what was particularly noticeable at this very early period was, not merely the propriety and ease of his conversation (for his "talk" deserved that name, with its curious mingling of simplicity and adult wisdom) but the *large diction* that he used, yet with perfect unconsciousness of its singularity. He seemed to comprehend the length and breadth of our language, almost by intuition.

Kingman had quick apprehension, a retentive memory, self-possession resulting from self-unconsciousness, and, as has been said, great fluency of speech. With these gifts, he rarely failed to make a good appearance in his class at school. An art in which he early excelled was declamation. His whole elocution was remarkably good; the articulation perfect; the inflections instinctively correct; voice full and sweet. In his fifth year, during the visit at Saybrook, he was wont to astonish his grandmother with borrowed eloquence, and frequently assured her of his intention to become a minister. He visited the A——s once, when seven years old, and during his stay entertained them regularly with speech-making. It was at a time when the papers were filled with political addresses. Kingman would be put upon a table, newspaper in hand, and set to pronouncing some fiery harangue; he would enter fully into the spirit of it, make the heat his own, and shout with a vehemence of passion that in a real contest could not have failed to make the day his own.

Kingman was fortunate, again, in being constituted with a comparatively sound and vigorous *moral nature.* There were no strong tendencies to vice, as there are in some, ready to be developed at the first occurrence of temptation, and either to betray soul and body to ruin or to be finally conquered only after severe conflicts. He was morally healthy. It is true that God kept him, counterbalancing inevitable temptations with gracious interferences, yet much is due to this original blessing. It is certain that his purity throughout boyhood was uncommon. Grossness seemed utterly foreign to his nature. His faults were chiefly of a superficial order. This was part of God's plan concerning him,—to constitute him healthily, to preserve him from ruinous habits, and thus to save him in manhood from the dreadful expenditure and waste of strength, necessary in so many to restore and keep the lost balance of appetite and moral sense.

Religiousness is to be distinguished as another characteristic of Kingman in his early days. He was often deeply affected by thoughts of his own sinfulness, God's greatness and condescension, and the Divine love in Christ. Particularly was this the case during a great Revival that occurred in Bath, in 1842. It was a work of extraordinary power. During the months of its continuance, multitudes thronged the churches daily, hundreds were converted. A brother and a sister of Kingman's, older than himself, were baptized. Kingman's sympathetic nature responded to the influence of these scenes; and unexpectedly one day, in a crowded meeting—having mounted a bench, he was heard exhorting the multitude, confessing his sins, and begging for prayers in his own behalf, and for a dear friend, "who was an infidel." He was then seven or eight years old. His interest at that time was really deep and genuine. He himself says of it, writing several years afterward: "I have no doubt the Spirit wrought upon my young heart, though, of course, much of my *manifestation* of feeling was the result of sympathy; and how much connection this may have had with my subsequent awakenings and final conversion, six years later, I cannot say. I talked and prayed constantly and zealously. I exhorted sinners to repent and believe, and urged my playmates to come with me. I remember my special interest in some converts' meetings for children. I remember C.'s coming home one day, and saying, 'I fall into Jesus' arms,' or some such expression, to signify a newly found Saviour. Especially do I remember a Union Prayer Meeting in the 'Old South,' where so many hundreds were present, and my trying in vain to be heard, till Captain L. put me upon the seat, and I spoke. On my way home from church, I went into the house of a playmate, W. G., and we prayed together. I was quite disconcerted, on coming out, to find a considerable collection of people, who, in passing, had been attracted by the sound. With the excitement my feelings wore away, and nothing shamed me more in after years than an allusion to that time."

An old playmate says, referring to a time just subsequent to this: "We all felt there was something in Kingman *superior*. He was earnest enough in play, but his *mind* seemed at work all the while on higher things." He relates also this anecdote:—"Once several boys, with Kingman, had been playing an afternoon in the woods, and had chased squirrels and climbed trees till they were tired. 'What shall we do next?' said they. Various proposals were made, to no purpose, when at last Kingman offered his: 'Come, boys, let's go and pray.' So all went, good and bad, moved by a strange impulse, into a grove where the ground was smooth with the fallen verdure of the pines—and all prayed."

What influence from that singular prayer-meeting perhaps followed some of those lads through the succeeding years into their manhood! Thus the religious spirit in Kingman was from its beginnings a spirit that sought to communicate itself to other minds.

Amusements, schools, religious meetings—all these, in Kingman's childhood, contributed to the formation of his character. There were other influences that might be named. Among them, certainly, the *parental discipline* ought not to be omitted. Christian parents, consecrating him at his birth to the Lord, honestly regarded him thenceforth as not their own but the Lord's, and themselves as the Lord's servants employed to train him, and responsible for the trust. Never was there a child for whom a greater amount of earnest dedicatory and supplicatory prayer ascended. All possible religious restraints and inducements were kept around him, yet without severity. Whining, hypocrisy, and cant, which creep into many so-called religious households, were far from this. Cheerful piety and consistent lives recommended religion to this boy, as a fact and a power, and, with the kind enforcement of reasonable law, the parents were to him as all parents should be to their children,—God's representatives. Home was rendered happy and sweet. Not that there were no storms, but these did not effect the atmosphere, and were speedily dispelled. Cheerfulness and healthful merriment were here: conversation, reading, singing. Morning and evening there was singing at family-prayers. The words and music of how many of those old hymns are now laden with the dearest recollections, and bring tears of hallowed sadness, or "thoughts too deep for tears!" Kingman's attachment to home, during his whole life, was remarkable; its bonds were never loosened. Next to love for God, indeed, the strongest affection in his heart was love for his father.

An extract from a brief private record, dated 1855, says:—

"One object of my writing now is to trace out the hand of Providence, which makes all things, I believe, 'work together for good to them that love God.' Here I must mention first—that I have received just such a home education as I have. I know enough of my own character to assure me that no other man I have ever known, beside my own revered father, could have made me even what I am—little as that is. No living being—thank God—will ever know what I should have been without him."

Kingman's mother died when he was in his tenth

year, on the 9th day of February, 1844, after a linger ing and painful illness. This is not the place to record her virtues; though there are hundreds who recollect her as an accomplished and noble Christian woman, intellectual, well read, and herself a graceful writer, but most of all devoted to the attainment of close, personal communion with the Holy Spirit of God, and to the elevation of others as well as of herself to a high standard of Christian living. She died most peacefully, commending her six young children to God, with a calm trustfulness that was always her characteristic, and saying, "They will be converted;" "E—— also," a dear friend, "will be converted—I am certain of it." The response to her faith is evinced in the fact, that all her children became members of the church before the age of sixteen, and her two sons became preachers.

On a bitter winter's day Mrs. Nott was taken to her grave, where already her infant of but a few months was slumbering. Together their bodies sleep, till the resurrection shall bring mother and child again to a living embrace.

The two years that succeeded her death were necessarily full of trial and temptation to Kingman. The good hand of God preserved him unharmed. In 1846 Mr. Nott was married to Sarah Louisa Smith, of Bath, Me. This lady proved a mother indeed to the motherless children, and became speedily the centre of their love. Kingman's warm affection for her is indicated by numberless references in his letters.

In the summer of 1847 Mr. Nott, resigning his pastoral charge at Bath, removed the family to Waterville, Me., for a few months, previous to fixing his residence at Kennebunkport. In Waterville Kingman attended the Academy kept then by Mr. J. H. Hanson, now of Portland, an efficient teacher, under whose direction Kingman made good progress. The facility with which he rendered Virgil into shapely and sonorous English, used especially to excite the wonder and hopeless emulation of his classmates. Yet he was a favorite from his good-nature and gayety.

Here he received new religious impressions. He says—"Here my feelings were once more deeply wrought upon. There were some prayer-meetings in private houses which I attended. I talked with father, anxiously examined the Scriptures to know what I must do to be saved; prayed and resolved, and did my best to make myself a Christian, and persuaded myself for a time that I had succeeded."

In July, 1848, the removal was made to Kennebunkport. Here by far the most important year of Kingman's early youth was spent. It was important as the time when he first began to obtain some thorough mental discipline (in distinction from the mere acquirement of information), and when, above all, that great moral revolution took place in his soul that made him a "new creature."

Kingman at this time had little power of mental concentration. A "fatal facility" sufficed to put him in possession of the form of knowledge, at little cost of exertion and small gain of power. It began to be feared he would grow up a superficial scholar and an idle thinker.

Mr. Nott himself accordingly resolved to undertake for a time the business of his son's education. And now began a course of training such as few boys of fourteen ever experienced, and which with many might have proved ill-judged. The Greek and Latin grammars, with portions of Virgil and Cicero, Tytler's Universal History, and a little French, constituted the routine part of this drill—the machinery that other instructors would have employed. But the great engines of discipline on which his father relied were Locke, Butler, and Crabbe. Large portions of Locke's Essays and Butler's Analogy were required to be thoroughly read, analyzed, discussed, and written about; and there was a daily recitation in Crabbe's Synonyms. The former studies were expected to cultivate acumen and a logical mode of thinking. The latter had special adaptation to the needs of a boy whose natural fluency threatened, when he wrote or spoke, to overwhelm and hide his ideas with a flood of verbiage.

Both objects were gained. Kingman learned to think—to think with precision and clearness, and rapidity; and the power of nice discrimination in the use of terms that he gained, was such as to warrant the declaration of his theological instructor afterwards, that "Nott always pounced by intuition on the right word." Not altogether by intuition, but by training.

This discipline was the making of Kingman. To nothing, except his conversion, was he accustomed in after years to look back with more gratitude. All that he became in the pulpit, beyond a noisy declaimer, was due to the training he received from his father, in his fifteenth year, followed by a subsequent course of instruction, managed with equal philosophy and skill, in school and college. But how small, comparatively, might have been the results of a school and collegiate education, had he not gone to school and college with a mind already "put in order," and faculties trained to know and do their work.

We have now approached the time of Kingman's conversion, the account of which is reserved for another chapter.

CHAPTER II.

Conversion—Journal, etc.

On the 1st of January, 1849, Kingman Nott had before him only ten years of life. In that short space his earthly destiny was to be worked out, and whatever he did in the sight of men, and for men, achieved. Awake, young dreamer!—only ten years to live! Ten years to gain a fortune! ten years to become great. Ah! the appeal must be in vain, for death at twenty-five will be premature; the years will have been spent in learning how to live, or a course of honorable toil commenced only to be, without reward—cut off! Such would have been the prophecy, and such might the fact have been, but for a revolution that at this juncture took place in his soul.

The manner of the origination of his new life would be best described in his own words, if these were on record. The *growing* life may be through this medium watched, for in his letters, which immediately after his conversion begin to be numerous, his whole heart, to the last, is copied out, and over long periods little is left for the biographer, but to transcribe this epistolary autobiography. But the only sources of information respecting the first decisive operations of the Holy

Spirit upon his heart are the recollections of friends, and an incomplete memorandum of his own, made several years later. The last is the paper from which extracts have already been taken, relating to his religious awakenings in Bath and Waterville. It continues:

"This interest"—in Waterville—"was of short continuance, but it was of use in its restraining influence over me. After one year we moved to Kennebunkport, where I lived along for several months in growing neglect and sin. I well remember the day of fasting and prayer which opened the year '49. Olive M——, then living in our family, was under deep concern of mind. My own attention was gradually drawn along to the subject of religion, I hardly know how. News came from L—— (a younger sister), then in Buffalo, that she had become interested in religion, and mother remarked, 'O Kingman, that we might know the same of you!' I made myself very busy, so as not to betray the feeling I really had.

"Sunday morning, January 21st, I attended our little prayer-meeting as usual. Brother H—— made some ordinary remarks on the importance of attending to personal religion, and that without delay. Though I had heard him speak again and again with utter indifference, his words at this time, for some reason, seemed to carry conviction to my heart, and I then and there resolved to become a Christian forthwith.

"All this time I was supposing that the power was all with me, and that whenever I concluded, as I now did, that it was best to live no longer in sin, but begin to serve Christ, I could do so. With these determinations, then, I silently left the meeting, walked home, went to my room, and tried to pray. I sought with—"

Here this interesting account abruptly breaks off, and was never resumed. The sequel of the story is told by his father, substantially as follows:

He did seek, in earnest. Several days passed; little was said, for I saw that the Spirit of God was guiding him. One day (Jan. 26th) he came with a happy face, telling me he had found the Saviour, and his sins were forgiven. He was full of joy and praise. His instant clearness of spiritual discernment was remarkable. A revelation in his soul had rendered truths before dark now luminous and beautiful. The plan of salvation was completely opened to him. He apprehended most distinctly the person and the work of Christ, relied with conscious faith on Christ's atoning sacrifice, and was filled with holy ardor to serve his newly-found Redeemer. He was new-born *complete:* as if a bird should burst through its shell not merely into life, but full-fledged and ready to soar. He displayed immediately the same qualities that were long afterwards the characteristics of his religious life: the same quick decision, the same simple honesty of purpose, the same spirit of allegiance to duty, the same exhaustless enthusiasm, and all comprehended in the one idea of serving the *Master.* Love for the Saviour, love and pity for the souls that slighted Christ, were his impelling motives.

The letters written by his father and mother at this time, confirm the soundness of the change.

For instance:

"Kingman has of late been under very deep impressions. Sabbath eve he seemed in agony of spirit—brought to feel his sinfulness, weakness, and utter dependence. He reads his Bible much, prays often, and seems very much changed. I can but hope this is the work of the Spirit, and will be carried on and perfected."

"You will be pleased to know that Kingman gives pleasing evidence of conversion. He is a greatly changed boy—more and more so. I wonder more and more at what the Lord has done for him. I want to magnify the mercy and praise God much for it. He has taken a part in prayer, as well as in speaking, at our social gatherings. May the Lord sanctify him for His service!"

"The spiritual change in him is as manifest as I ever saw in one, for so short a time. At present he gives promise of some useful activity in the cause of Christ. He seems almost a perfect character in some respects."

Once more he began to "exhort sinners," and "urge his playmates to go with him." Witness the following brief tale—given in the words of the original narrator, a young lad converted through Kingman's influence:

4

"On the 1st of June, 1849, as I was coming home from a prayer-meeting, I overtook Kingman Nott, whose heart the Lord had opened; who spoke to me, and asked me if I was wholly unconcerned about these things. I told him I supposed I was. We walked along, and he asked me if I believed the Bible? I told him I did. He spoke to me of the importance of coming to Christ at that time, and asked me if I would not try to come. I told him that I hoped I should. He encouraged me, and told me not to put it off.

"I thought a great deal about what he had said, and the next week I went to prayer-meeting again. He spoke to me, and warned and entreated me to come to Christ. I saw that I was a great sinner in the sight of God. My friend came to me again, and explained to me the way of salvation through a crucified Redeemer. As he saw tears in my eyes, I believe it gladdened his heart, for I told him that I had tried to pray. I took Christ for my Saviour. I even dared to hope the Lord had forgiven my sins. A feeling came over me which I had never before experienced; it was a feeling of joy, thanksgiving, and praise."

The youth who wrote thus charmingly, Howard Wildes, a few months after these occurrences, suddenly died. Upon his grave-stone is this inscription:—

"Amiable, beloved; a Christian, devoted and humble; his race run—his death peaceful: he has a crown of joy."

This was Kingman's first trophy. The first year of

his Christian course was signalized by the winning of a soul to Christ—a soul that soon was safe in heaven. Young Christian, go and do likewise!

Kingman kept a journal during the greater part of the year 1849, of which a few scraps have escaped destruction. From these we quote:

"*March 22d*, 1849, my 15th birth-day.

"How can God be suitably thanked for His great mercy and long-suffering in sparing my life for these fifteen years. I, all the while rebelling against him, and grieving His Spirit by putting off the day of repentance, which I well knew should be *now*. I know that His Spirit was continually knocking at my heart. Not a day or a night passed without my hearing the 'still small voice,' urging, 'now is the time;' 'you are growing harder every day, and every day you are increasing your condemnation.' But still I endeavored (thank God, without success), to repel this voice, and live at ease in sin *a little longer*.

"But how is God to be rewarded for His mercy? If I could begin now, and spend an eternity upon this earth, laboring in His cause, and never doing one act displeasing to Him, I never could pay the slightest recompense in comparison with what is due.

"Is it not, then, my solemn duty to consecrate all I am to God; to labor with all my might, to pray without ceasing, to watch, guarding every thought and word? May God help me to do this! In Christ I can do all things."

"FRIDAY, 23*d*.

"I feel deeply oppressed with my weighty responsibility, since I have named the name of Christ, *not to listen to the offers of another leader*. [This was his motto through life.] I feel, also, anxious to keep very strict watch over my *little* actions, that my light may shine *purely* among men. May God take me, as the potter the clay, and mould me after his own image! But I can do something. I can pray."

"SUNDAY, 25*th*.

"Is it possible! How fast the Sabbaths come round! And what a solemn, yet delightful thought to the believer, that every Sabbath brings us one week nearer eternal happiness. Is it so with me? Thank God for the answer I can give: I have confidence that God will enable me to conquer, and so shall I be for ever with the Lord."

"MONDAY, 26*th*.

"R. and C. are eighteen to-day, and I, as Capt. L—— would say, am two months old."

"TUESDAY, 27*th*.

"The subject of baptism was brought up by father to-day. I feel, as I have for some time past, that it is my duty to make a profession of that religion which, by the grace of God, I hope I possess.

"I have read the Declaration of Faith, and think I can subscribe to every article. *Election* seems hardest! [Yet he hoped God would take him as the potter the clay! The trouble was, the *word* Election stunned him. As is liable to be the case with all technical terms, the idea had fled out of the word; and the great, empty husk, as he handled it and pondered it, was a very wonderful and mysterious thing to him. The *idea* lay naked and unnamed in his mind and heart; for it is of necessity born into the heart of every Christian, and the mind of every thinker.]

"FRIDAY, 30*th*.

"Father received a letter from L—— [an absent sister], in which was contained the precious and joyful news of her conversion. Bless the Lord!"

"SATURDAY, *March* 31.

"I lack energy:—sometimes when I see my duty clearly I shrink from it. I must study the Bible more."

"TUESDAY, *April* 10.

"I think I discern some, at least, of the devil's methods of endeavoring to draw me into temptation. He endeavors to take me off my guard, when not under the influence of prayer; and then such is my disposition and weakness — he leads me almost anywhere he chooses. God help me to resist him."

"THURSDAY, *April* 12.

"I sometimes think it almost sacrilege, and a thing abhorred in the sight of a pure and holy God, for me to attempt to come before Him. I see so many things I ought to correct, that I hardly know how to begin the work. Do not I harbor sin in my heart, and thus prevent my supplication from being heard? Do not I sometimes fall into a snare laid for my pride, and desirous of making a prayer approved of men, keep this before me, rather than the fear of God, and my own simple wants? It is a horrible sin, I know, but one easy to be guilty of. May God preserve me from what I know to be so heinous."

"SUNDAY EVENING, *September 2d.*

"I took out my old journal this evening for the purpose of recording the baptisms that have taken place of late. I have put on Christ by a public profession (Aug. 19th) and to-day another has followed, Howard Wildes. He was first awakened under the slight means which God enabled me to use. I write this that I may often read, and never be discouraged in performing my duty, especially in employing the means which God has appointed for the salvation of souls."

These serve as specimens. They show us what are the thoughts, and hopes, and aims of this boy of fifteen. Noble thoughts, hopes, and aims, if he can but persist in them.

It is not greatly to be regretted, probably, that the journal was not continued. A journal of emotions and states of mind is very likely to degenerate, becoming occupied with "vain repetitions," and encouraging a habit of too minute self-scrutiny. Kingman was too busy and too happy to keep a journal of this kind.

One or two extracts from letters of this period follow:

TO HIS ELDEST SISTER, THEN ABSENT IN THE ISLAND OF CUBA.

"April '49.

"Here I am, seated at my desk, in my pleasant little room, and—where I suppose you would very much like to be—at home. I know not what time it is, but it must be quite early, for father only has gone down stairs. From the window before me I have a beautiful view: three or four fine houses, a grove of evergreens, and many large, splendid trees; while in clear weather I can catch a glimpse, over the low hills, of that wide waste of waters that separates you from me. . . . . How kindly God has watched over and cared for you thus far. And I doubt not that just what is best for you and all of us will be done; for the apostle, you know, says in that most beautiful and comforting verse, 'We know that all things work together for good to them that love God.' What more do we want?

"I am prospering in my studies. The Greek Reader &c., and the *wood* occupy my attention at present. Soon I shall exchange the saw and axe for spade and hoe. These I say occupy my attention, but do not misunderstand me. I mean as my secular employments (!). But I have far more important duties, which I fear I am too lax in performing. Still I keep them up and am conscious of a strong and fixed determination to serve my Saviour; and I have confidence that I shall be enabled to press on in the name of the Lord of Hosts. Pray much for me; all our strength lies at the mercy-seat," etc.

TO THE SAME.

DECEMBER 31, 1849.

"My dear young friend and brother, Howard Wildes, was, as you already know, suddenly and mysteriously separated from us. I said *mysteriously*, but would recal it. How weak are we to call that a mysterious dealing of Providence, which calls a saint to that blessedness for which he has prayed earnestly.

"The first time I ever entered his house I prayed with him an anxious sinner. The second time I entered with tears to behold him a corpse! Excuse me for dwelling so long on one topic, but my heart is full," etc.

During the whole of 1849, and until the summer of 1850, K. remained at home, engaged in a variety of occupations; rambling in the woods, fishing, exploring the mysteries of the rock-piled and caverned sea-coast, managing the garden and the wood, studying Locke, Butler, and Crabbe, and *preaching* in his own way, *i.e.* privately, among his companions, as he worked and played. He was gaining strength of body, mind, and soul, for the Lord's service afterwards.

CHAPTER III.

GOING TO SCHOOL—DIFFICULTIES—SCHOOL LIFE—REMINISCENCES BY A TEACHER.

KINGMAN had now (Spring of 1850) reached an age when it became important to make some decisive arrangements with reference to his future profession or business. It was at least necessary to determine in general whether books or trade, or some labor of the hands should employ him. The question was placed entirely at his own disposal. He consulted his father. "Follow your own inclinations, if you can obtain God's approval of them; any useful business is honorable," was the response the oracle gave; and Kingman, much to his father's joy, decided for books. Not, probably, that he had an ardent love of learning for its own sake, but partly because he could not easily forego the pleasures he had learned to relish in the companionship and associations of books, and partly because he heard, as almost every youth does, his *destiny* calling him. Happy he who has the gift of interpretation, and can understand the mystic summons.

It is interesting, moreover, to observe how frequently in his letters the word *duty* occurs. "I am sure it is my *duty* to get an education." For he was true-hearted: his question honestly was, What will God have me to do? Accordingly, when he resolved, in the face of great difficulties, to go from home and devote himself to the business of procuring an education, he felt as confident of acting by divine command, as Moses did when he determined to cross the Red Sea.

The *difficulties* were all comprised in this: The want of money.

He had to "begin the world" without a dollar and without the promise of one. Literally, his only outfit for his first venture away from home, besides the endowments nature and grace had bestowed, was a few books, the passage money to his place of destination (with fifty cents surplus), and a somewhat generous supply of second-hand clothing. For his raiment had this peculiarity, that each individual article of apparel could be referred to a different, original owner. "This was my uncle's," "this my cousin's," and "this my father's." His boots and his cap were the only parts of his dress he could properly call his own; and these were of compulsion so, because his head and his feet were in a peculiar sense his own. It will be inferred that Kingman's father was not a man of large means. Such was the truth. He had nothing on earth. But he had large possessions in the Kingdom of Heaven, and these his son—a fact in strict agreement with God's promises—did distinctly find available. Kingman himself also possessed what proved sufficient for every emergency, a brave heart, buoyant temper, indifference to little inconveniences, an unflinching will, faith, and good muscles. These last, it will soon be perceived, were a most important auxiliary.

The school selected was "The Connecticut Literary Institute," located at Suffield, Conn., a classical and English Academy for both sexes, then under the charge of Mr. William Woodbury. Few men better qualified to be educators of youth have appeared in this country, than Mr. Woodbury: a premature death alone, in the opinion of many, prevented his attaining a celebrity as wide-spread though not altogether of the same character, as that of Dr. Arnold in England.

With sufficiently extended and exceedingly accurate scholarship, he joined the habit of absolute self-government, keenness of penetration into the minds and hearts of others; tact in management, and decision in enforcing law—the very qualities of a great executive officer. Although a martinet in his drill, yet he understood how to *educate*, not only in the popular sense of cramming in, but in the more important, etymological idea of drawing out. He succeeded, except in obstinate cases, in teaching his pupils to think as well as to acquire. He did much for Kingman, and Kingman in return gave him both respect and warm affection. Such tributes as the following are frequent in his letters.

"I cannot help loving and respecting Mr. Woodbury more and more every week. His aim in the increase of advantages, intellectual, moral, and religious, seems to be nothing short of *perfection*, and I find myself surprised at the constant onward march of improvement in every department."

The following affords a glimpse of Mr. Woodbury's methods:

"Thoroughness is the thing chiefly insisted upon. For instance, our Greek. Three times a week we translate and parse Xenophon—one page at a lesson in advance, and one to three or four in review. After we have read and thoroughly reviewed a chapter, we present a *written* translation of it. The three other days of the week we take our written translations and, independently of book, translate back to Greek—then take Greek and translate to Latin.

Such a variety affords great interest, and one cannot help gaining some knowledge of these languages."

Professor E. C. Hamlen, now of Waterville College, then at Suffield, was a teacher to whom Kingman was also strongly attached.

Kingman remained at Suffield from June, 1850, to the summer of 1851, a little more than one year; at the expiration of which time he was excellently prepared for college. His expenses were met chiefly by his relations in ways unanticipated by them and himself.

Assistance was given him, especially by an uncle, Mr. Abner Kingman, of Boston, who also aided him in the most generous manner throughout his college course.

But Kingman contributed something himself; pittances now and then earned at large expenditure of time, labor, and ingenuity. Besides, his expenses were reduced to half their legitimate and expected amount, through his pinching economy. As for earning, no honest labor by which he could gain a dollar for the "sacred purpose," was too hard or too mean for him. He would sweep, saw wood for anybody, dig gardens—anything but beg. As for economy, he wore any clothes that would keep him warm, and he could get. But Providence took care of his apparel: he was never but once destitute of a decent coat, and that was when he had left the garment at a tailor's for repairs, and for two weeks could not procure money to redeem it. But he saved in another way. When ordinary economy was insufficient, and earnings and donations both were inadequate, he abandoned his boarding-house and all civilized modes of living, bought Indian-meal, milk, and crackers—descending slowly, but fatally, to pork—and did his own cooking. And ever and anon from his drudgery he looked up, and his cheerful tone rang out, "It is my *duty* to get an education!" Often he saw no ray ahead; but he pressed forward with a "no matter" for every inconvenience, a "trust God" for every perplexity, and a "thank God" in everything, and he got through, and the whole discipline did him good.

In all his books at this time was written the motto: "Nil desperandum!—never despair!"

We say, the discipline did him good. It did. But be it remarked, that with a less buoyant temper, or less physical robustness, he might have been disciplined to death.

REMINISCENCES FURNISHED BY PROFESSOR HAMLEN.

"Kingman Nott entered the school at Suffield, shortly after the opening of the Summer term of 1850. He had been a pupil of Mr. Woodbury at Bath, and I suppose, was drawn so far away from home by a high regard for that admirable and lamented teacher.

"He attracted much attention in the school from the outset, giving at once the impression that he was a youth of much more than ordinary talent, and quickly standing among the foremost in the classes which he joined. The most striking features of his mind, as it then exhibited itself, were a tenacious memory, quick perception, and active fancy. His fellows sometimes thought he saw things intuitively. Probably the truth was only that he completed the mental process necessary to the result more rapidly than they.

"His command of language was quite unusual. Whether called upon to translate a passage, to recite a grammar lesson, to give his views upon some passage of an author, to speak in the students' meetings for debate, or to take part in a prayer-meeting, he was always ready to express his own or another's thoughts, as the case required, in copious, appropriate and tasteful phraseology.

" His readiness of allusion showed a range of reading much wider than is common for one of his age. His mind was stored with varied information upon many subjects, and these stores were very ready at command in description, in which he was sometimes exceedingly apt. I well remember an instance of this, in an account which he gave me of a vacation visit to the venerable Dr. Samuel Nott, of Franklin, Conn.

" In respect to his habits of study, he was remarkable for rapid mastery of his tasks rather than for continuous application or very carful preparation. He was constant and punctual in his attendance at all exercises, and in recitation was prompt and attentive. He was what would ordinarily be termed a faithful student, but he had not as yet those habits of consecutive and industrious study and careful preparation which are essential to the highest scholarship, and which, by a remark of one of his later instructors, I am led to suppose he afterwards formed.

" He maintained throughout his residence at Suffield the character of a consistent Christian. He was active in the meetings for social worship, often showing great warmth and tenderness of religious feeling, and never, so far as I am aware, setting before them an example at variance with his professions.

" In disposition he seemed to be mild, amiable, sincere, and affectionate. His beaming countenance and expressive eye were always lighted up with kindly feeling. I never saw them clouded with ill-humor or passion. He was at all times obedient and respectful to his teachers, and grateful for their exertions in his behalf.

"He was conected with the school, I think, until the end of the Summer term in 1851. He left upon the minds of his instructors, the impression that he was a young man of unusual promise, who was destined to pre-eminent distinction and usefulness in whatever walk of life he might enter, if he should be able to endure the ordeal of popular favor, and attention which evidently awaited him.

"C. E. Hamlen.

CHAPTER IV.

School-life—Ups and Downs.

We now proceed to take from K.'s correspondence such extracts as shed light on his character, and its development, with occasional comments, to render the narrative intelligible or call attention to its lesson.

TO HIS FATHER.

"Suffield, *June* 25, 1850.

"Dear Father:

"How difficult to comprehend that I am really settled at Suffield, and separated from my home by a distance of nearly two hundred miles! Yet it is even so; and when I bring myself to the stern reality, it is impossible to resist a feeling of sadness and sickness of heart. . . . Mr. Woodbury has placed me in the boarding-house for the present—my room-mate, I am happy to say, is a pious young man. . . .

"Pray much for me, as I feel confident you will, that I may be 'diligent in business, fervent in spirit, *serving the Lord*.' Ask the children to write me speedily, for I am already beginning to speculate on the contents of eagerly anticipated letters. Give Georgie a kiss, and charge C. and L. not to let him forget me.

"Your aff. son

"K."

TO HIS ELDEST SISTER.

"*July* 1.

"DEAR C.

"I had indeed been compelled to turn away from the Post-office here with bitter disappointment and useless conjectures. I finally suggested to the Post-mistress that my name began with *N*, and not with *K*. Soon after, one of the boys called me and displayed a letter with the beautiful motto, *Hope*. But I, not knowing the letter was for me, but supposing that he had perceived my disappointment and wished simply to encourage me to 'hope,'—replied, 'True, but hope deferred maketh the heart *sick*.' Judge, then, of the eagerness with which I perused the precious contents of that envelope!

"I am now fully established as a member of the 'Connecticut Literary Institute.' Bell-ringer—sweeper—woodsawyer, by profession and practice—and ready for any kind of work by which I can earn ten cents an hour! Yesterday I took my initiatory lesson in *haying;* raking up the 'trails' and 'stowing.' The duties of this afternoon (a holiday,) will be, first: to sweep the chapel thoroughly; second, to wash five or six huge blackboards, and third, to go and hoe a garden.

"A week ago I attended what is here called, and most appropriately, the 'Covenant Meeting,' corresponding to our 'Conference.' . . I have not yet heard Mr. I. preach, though I have seen enough of him in prayer-meetings and other places to become very much attached to him. . . . . The pious members of the Institution form a church almost by themselves, holding three weeklv prayer-meetings.

"We have here a Debating Society, called the 'Calliopean.' I made my first attempt last week, and of course our side gained the decision of the question! I think it is very well conducted."

In the next letter a great light shines upon him. He describes a "*very marked providence.*" He has surely seen the burning bush. Witness the sincerity of his trust in God.

TO HIS FATHER.

"*July* 18.

"Once more have I been called to witness the truth of the promise, 'Commit thy way unto the Lord, *trust* also in him, and He shall bring it to pass.' Listen to what has been done since I came here.

"1. My chum, who had intended to remain through this term and had engaged the bell-ringing and sweeping, etc., for the year, was led to the determination of leaving, and thus that occupation passed into my hands, affording me means for paying my board.

"2. Mr. Woodbury spoke to me of two individuals, with one of whom he thought I might possibly work my board—both farmers, and some distance from the Institute. One of them was spoken to, but could give no definite answer, though he held out some encouragement. But yesterday, after I had inquired for letters at the post-office, and was going away; the post-master abruptly inquired my age, etc. The result was, that after talking some time with him, and conferring with Mr. W., a bargain was concluded, and yesterday morning I entered on my duties and board here. My duty is, to have some care of the *office*. I sit at my studies, with only occasional and short interruptions. My employer holds out encouragement that soon he may provide me with a room of my own. I know not what you think of all this. For my own part, I cannot but consider it a *very marked providence*—so unexpected, so adapted to my want. I forgot to mention that I have the garden and horse to care for, wood to split, and numerous other chores.

"I did not intend to write you fully at present, but could not help informing you of this new favor—so *marked*—and also desiring your prayers that I may be enabled to keep a thankful, trustful heart, and receive grace to conduct myself properly and satisfactorily to my employer."

Is this the delusion of a simple child, or is it the very feeling which God loves to recognise, and names *Faith?* If it is Faith, very likely it will be put to the test to try its *strength*. See the next :—

TO HIS FATHER.

"*July* 29.

"I have but a few moments to write, but wish you to know of another change in my prospects. It is very easy to see the hand of Providence and feel that all is for the best, when things are to our own eye prosperous and we move on swimmingly. So I have found it, and I have seen too, how difficult it is to feel so when the reverse is the case.

" One week from the evening on which my engagement was made with the Post-master, I was informed by him, to my complete surprise, that he had concluded to employ some other person: he wanted some one who was of sufficient *age* and experience to assume the responsibility of the whole post-office, when necessary. The reason was, that he could not be tied to the post-office himself. And so this matter is ended!

" I had indulged too strong expectations of finding there a good home and pleasant employment for a long time. I returned forthwith to board at commons. The sweeping and bell-ringing, my *chief dependence*, and Mr. W.'s wood, have both been placed in other hands. Thus things look rather dark; but I do not despond, nor, above all, complain. No doubt all will come out straight yet."

" In all this Job sinned not."

"*August* 20.

" On Thursday morning large teams were on hand, to convey the joyful students to their happy *homes*. Oh, how *I* felt!"

" *September* 3.

" Vacation has now very nearly passed, and very swiftly has the time fled. To-morrow school once more commences.

" During the four weeks I have read, worked, and travelled. I have not found so much work to do as I should have been glad of; my earnings have amounted to between three and four dollars. . . . . . Several little necessary articles are drawing on my resources. I do not know about my prospects for next term. I have made several applications for a '*place*,' but am unsuccessful in every quarter. Still I hope I may yet succeed. Even if I do not, still I hope that by being as economical as possible, and improving every opportunity for earning, I may be able to cancel my board. If not, of course I shall be obliged to be out the winter term, which will hinder my progress in study. Rather dark at present, but the way may be clearly opened yet. If I had now about three dollars to clear up my debts here (!), I could go ahead for some time at least. I will let you know how I prosper, speedily. *Don't be anxious for me.*"

Later, his difficulties increase, but he finds a solution of them.

"I have thus far forborne mentioning some things, which I feared would cause you unnecessary anxiety. When the last vacation approached, I saw that my board in commons during the four weeks—which would amount to six dollars—would be more than I could earn, and I was already behindhand about four dollars." . . .

Has any rich servant of Christ ten dollars to give this boy of noble heart and great talents, who struggles here to prepare himself for usefulness? If, remembering what he afterwards accomplished in the Lord's vineyard, one feels his heart involuntarily grow warm and generous, look about! There are scores of young men this day, contending with even greater discouragements, but manfully combating them, because it is *duty*. Some fall: some exhaust their energies in climbing up upon the "wall of Zion," and have little strength to "blow the trumpet."

But let us see what a youth does, who has no way to earn six dollars, yet will not starve, and yet is determined not to leave his post.

"——— I therefore concluded to board myself, as the only alternative. This I did, occupying my room in the Institution. I had no conveniences for cooking, (!) and therefore lived upon *crackers and milk.* Kept a good appetite, and enjoyed perfect health. This term I was in doubt what to do. I made unsuccessful efforts to obtain a 'place,' hesitated till the last moment, and finally—am boarding myself." . . .

He evidently feels that his course requires some apology.

"It seems utterly impossible for me to keep up my studies, and at the same time earn $1.50 a week; especially at this season of the year, when scarcely any work is to be had but wood-sawing—which, at 75 cents per cord for sawing twice and splitting, does not pay very well. I cannot tell how I am to pay my way, and extricate myself from debt, though I now board at half the expense of commons. I have no one here to rely upon. *I must be independent.* . . .

"My advantages I now feel to be uncommonly good,

and I should be loth to leave the school at present. I can pay at least half my board—perhaps more. .

" Thus you have everything, and I shall wait anxiously to hear what you shall think best. If I remain, I shall endeavor to gain all I can of knowledge, money, and grace. If I leave—I know nothing." . . .

The conclusion is, that he determines to remain, eating crackers and milk—(with pork now added, probably requiring a small expenditure for cooking utensils) and trusting in Providence.

Meanwhile he thinks he is "much prospered—health good—studies interesting"—he himself "more interested in maintaining religious exercises"—and full of affection for his "priceless home."

November 12th he gives the statistics for the term then closing. His board has cost *eight dollars.* He finds attending school "more expensive than he had expected, and to one situated as he is, involving vastly more responsibility and anxiety." "Sometimes," he adds, "I get down-hearted and almost discouraged, when I think how great a burden I am to my friends, while I ought to be independent, if not aiding them. Still I do feel that I am following the path of duty, and it is my hope and prayer that I and my friends may live till I shall be able to repay, in some slight measure, their unmerited favors."

"The fact that I am deprived of some enjoyments, causes me to realize for what object it is that I am placed here: not to occupy time merely, but to gain an education. I just begin to feel this as I should. I have golden opportunities, and I do feel desirous"—now he is ambitious—"that *the world* may receive some benefit from it. I know *God will require this.*"

More, perhaps, than was important, has been allowed to appear concerning K.'s struggles with pecuniary embarrassments; but it has been with the purpose that the religious reader may have the opportunity of seeing precisely *how young men, in many instances, are educated for the ministry:* through what hardships many of them find their way to the pulpits of churches, where critical congregations demand polish as well as piety in the minister. Help them to obtain the culture you demand.

CHAPTER V.

RELIGION IN SCHOOL—A REVIVAL.

In answer to inquiries respecting his own religious condition, he thus writes:

"September 11.

"My Dear Father.—You wish to know my religious state of mind. I will endeavor to inform you as exactly and honestly as I can.

"I endeavored, when I came here, to take my stand at once boldly and openly as a Christian, both in the Institution and in the public prayer-meetings: I thus *pledged myself*, and have not regretted it since. . . . . The three meetings in the Institution I have invariably attended, and in one of them have always taken part. I also attend the weekly church-meetings, and the covenant-meeting on Saturday. In the last I have invariably endeavored to present a correct view of my growth in grace. . . . . I fear you will think I am contenting myself with these *dead forms*, and introducing now these statements for the purpose of justifying myself, while my heart is cold and indifferent. You will say, I have not yet come to the *heart*, from which proceedeth good or evil. . . . . I cannot help feeling verily *guilty* before God. I know that I am exceedingly cold. I fear that I have not been making any great advancement, if any, in grace. The Christian cannot remain stationary—then where am I?" [How could he know, *then*, that God was carrying on the work of grace within him, by the very process of discovering to him his imperfection? "Men may rise on stepping-stones of their *dead selves* to higher things."]

"Much depends, in such circumstances as mine, on the character of one's room-mate. For a few days I was with a true Christian; afterwards with one who professed the name of Christ; but more than profession was not to be found, and I heard irreligious young men *laugh* at the idea of his calling himself a *Christian.* They *saw through* the thin veil. At present I room with a young man half a dozen years my senior, and not a professor of religion. I however pursue my own course, as if I were alone, and he is never in the least disposed to ridicule or question the propriety of my exercises.

"Many things I have had to learn by *experience:* one is, I must be *independent.* In pursuing a course of study, I must *make myself*, and not expect to be made; and so, also, if I am ever saved, I must *save myself;*—and I may with propriety add the words, 'from this untoward generation.'

"I thank you for your letters, and the character of them. I need to be reminded and stirred up. Since the first night that I attended meeting here, not an individual has expressed to me a word on the subject of religion; nor *would* any one, if I were to remain here for years, unless there should be a great change in the state of affairs." [Was he himself equally negligent? His schoolmates answer that no such guilt attached to him.]

"I find pleasure—satisfaction—in taking my Bible; so in prayer too; still I cannot find that *warmth* and *fervor* and *zeal* that the Christian doubtless may enjoy."

There is much in that letter that deserves attention. Perhaps the whole deserves to be read again by any young man—especially any young Christian—away from home. Depend upon it, in that letter is revealed the key to success; and in it also is a warning of the way to disgrace, contempt, and ruin. Ye true-hearted Christians, in the midst of temptations and discouragements, take courage; be "independent," and work out your own salvation. Ye *half*-Christians, weak, vacillating, conscious of secret hypocrisy, take warning. Your "thin veil" will be "seen through." And how is it in schools and colleges? Shall young men enter them and be able to remain "years" without being addressed on the subject of religion? Religion ought to be *the power* in such places. It might easily be so, with conscientiousness, resolution, and faith on the part of its professors.

Who can estimate the difference between looking back, as Kingman could, upon a school and college course in which the great aim of glorifying God was not lost sight of, either in monkish devotion to books and solitude, or in the reckless pursuit of ungodly excitements and frivolous pleasures; and the gloomy remembrances which haunt many, of time worse than wasted, influence given for Satan, and habits contracted which fetter and drag down the soul ever after in its efforts to rise towards Heaven! Hear also a few words from the next epistle:—

TO HIS MOTHER.

"SEPTEMBER 18.

"I think that father's letters, with yours, have been instrumental in awakening in me a much better state of religious feeling. We have among the many new students this term several who are professors of religion, and of them one young man who is an *active Christian*, which is saying a great deal for Suffield.

"I can thoroughly bear you out in your remark concerning *lifeless, back-slidden professors of religion*. I have myself *seen* that they are a *withering curse* to the cause of religion; and I have heard irreligious young men *ridicule the very idea* of such and such a one being a Christian. God grant that I may be saved from such inconsistency!"

After a short visit, in a vacation, to his friends in Saybrook, he writes:

"Reluctantly I left the place where I had spent a week so pleasantly, in the midst of friends, to become once more an outcast from friends. However, I felt that I was called once more, by the voice of stern duty, to *work*. And I resolved that I *would work*, and so far from allowing my mind to be turned aside by pleasure and new friends, I would work the harder, that I might merit the respect and approbation of friends. The path of duty is what I wish for. . . . . My chum has come this term filled with the Spirit, having been in the midst of a revival. There is a better state of things in this church—a spirit of prayer.

"I have formed a resolution to be second to no classmate in *any recitation.* How well I fulfil it, it is not for me to say. I don't want to prove entirely unworthy of the favors showered upon me."

He writes again:

"Alas! if I could only *fully realize* what I *know* to be true, that there is *no time for action like the present,* nor any situation in which I can expect to be placed more favorable for glorifying God!

"I could wish that my mind were in a more devoted state. I need a revival of religion in my soul. My lamp burns but dimly, so many influences are there to diminish the brightness of its flame. It is in some degree as we feared, the world occupies too large a portion of my thoughts. I am determined to do all I can in study, but I would rather give up everything else than not maintain my piety. I would not, *I dare not lose that,* even though all else go. You know how apt I am to be the mere creature of impulse and feeling. I must learn to look more at the state of my soul in general, and less to my feelings at any particular moment. Thank you heartily for your inquiries and remarks. I need to be often reminded of these things."

Hitherto none but gloomy representations have come to us of the state of religious feeling at Suffield. But now, suddenly, a new day dawns. We need only K.'s account to bring the changed aspect of affairs distinctly before us.

TO A SISTER.

"MONDAY, *Dec.* 16*th.*

"DEAR C.—I write with very different feelings from those I expressed Saturday evening. *The Spirit of God is among us.* Yesterday we had solemn preaching, especially in the afternoon. The previous Sabbath Mr. I. commenced a series of sermons on the Reception of Christ, answering the three great questions—*why*, *when*, and *how* sinners should receive Christ. Yesterday was the *when*, and he indeed seemed, as it is expressed in the words of an eloquent preacher, to have prepared the discourse 'continually hearing the surges of eternity beating against his study door'; for, as matter of fact, the preparation was constantly interrupted by the cries of a dying friend in the next room. After the evening meeting I was in my room. Who should enter but two young men with whom I was more familiar than with any others, companions with whom I had spent many an hour of lightness and trifling mirth. They are youths of fine appearance and high talents, and we have formed an inseparable trio. But on what an errand were they now come! Almost the first words that saluted my ears were—'Well, Nott, we feel solemn to-night; here's S. and I have become very much interested in the *subject of religion*, and as we've always been together, I thought I would come and talk with you a little: I find nothing does so much good as to be perfectly *frank*.' O, the thrill of joy and surprise, mingled with a deep sense of guilty neglect, that shot through my soul! That night was spent by us, with some others of the Institution, in prayer, and *such prayer!* We heard also the voice of *one* who never before had prayed, beseeching mercy on his companion and himself.

"The other could not yield—declared himself perfectly insensible. Satan was busily at work, and though I reasoned, and plead, and prayed with him until near the midnight hour, *he* could not *pray*. His impressions, however, have not by any means left him, and I pray with *great faith.*

"So you see those social prayer meetings I desired so much, but as I thought almost in vain, are likely to come, after all.

"I cannot forbear looking forward to a few years hence, and seeing these young men employing their talents and education in turning the souls of men to God. Both are preparing for Yale."

A prophetic faith! One of these young men is now the Rev. Theron Brown, who preaches the gospel at South Framingham, Mass. The second who "could not pray," was not converted till years after, but is at the present date, 1860, a student of theology in the Union Seminary in New York. Both, therefore, are giving "their talents and education" to the work of "turning the souls of men to Christ."

REMINISCENCES FURNISHED BY REV. THERON BROWN.

"It was during the early part of the summer of 1850, while a student at Suffield, Connecticut, that I observed a young stranger, plainly but neatly dressed, and with blue eyes and luxuriant brown hair, seated upon one of the front forms in the Academy Chapel, at evening prayers.

"I did not seek his acquaintance at first, for he was more than a year in advance of me as a scholar, and I supposed he and myself could have nothing in common. But chance soon brought us together, and it was not long before an intimacy sprung up between Kingman Nott and me, which deeply influenced both our lives, and gladdened eight years of mine with the dearest privilege in the whole history of my friendships.

"I wonder how we could have been so familiar; for, when I first associated with him, I cared very little about religion; while he, though two years my junior, was an experienced and consistent Christian. We read and wrote together; we worked and played together; we kept 'bachelor's hall' together, and together we rambled over the country on foot between the school terms: but there was one thing in which I could not join him. I could not pray; and I now remember with peculiar emotion when he used to kneel by the bedside at night, and ask God to bless him and me, while I indifferently went to sleep. Kingman loved me, but I could not know *then* how much he longed to see me a Christian. I trust he had the desire of his heart. During December of 1850, a sermon was blessed to my awakening, and in Kingman's room, after a week of struggle and helplessness, I heard one night the forgiving voice of a Saviour. Overjoyed, my impulsive friend led me to Mr. H.'s study, and there, at that late hour, three glad hearts, teacher and pupils, offered up each a thankful prayer to God."

The following is from the friend who "could not pray"—now a student of theology. It is part of a letter addressed to Kingman, dated *New Haven, Feb.* 1, 1857.

"My Dear Nott.

"Do you remember writing to a certain friend one year ago last November, and in that letter saying, 'Flee to Christ.' That friend *has done it!* And you asked too, 'Are you a pardoned sinner?' I answer, 'Yes!' and I 'look forward to a higher, happier future,' and 'with a hope well grounded in Christ Jesus.' O Nott, that I could see you an hour only, if no more, and talk with you as a Christian brother! I know not whether you remember me as a friend, on account of my long neglect; but I *must* write, for I know you well enough to believe that you will be *happy* to greet me as a *brother in Christ.* . . . Suffice it to say, that the Spirit of God has shined into my heart; His love has melted me to repentance, and His mercy has pardoned me. Love, peace, and joy, are welling up from a purified fountain; and I pray God that from these may flow out a pure life.—Yours etc.,

S———."

We append to the chapter one or two letters.

Here is a letter to his youngest sister, then eight

years old. The characters are printed so that she can read them. The words, moreover, are nearly all Saxon, and of one syllable. More than that, his heart is in it.

"*Oct.* 17.

"DEAR LITTLE LIZZIE.

"I want you to tell father and mother, C. and L., and little Georgie, that I have not had a word from home for more than two weeks. Now, since all the rest seem to have forgotten brother Kingman, I thought, perhaps, I had better write to you, and I want you to try to get some one to write for you to me. You can tell me all about home, and whether darling Georgie is stouter and plays better since his visit to Bath. Tell me what you are studying, and how you like it; whether you get all your lessons well, and try to help mother all you can. When I come again I must teach you how to write, so that you can write to me whenever you please.

"Last Saturday was a holiday, and I went to Hartford. I visited the 'Antiquarian Hall,' where I saw a vast number of very curious things. I have also got some acorn cups for you and Cordie from the famous Charter Oak.

"I sometimes feel very sad when I think that you are not a Christian, and not prepared to die. If any of the others should die, I could feel that they were happy in Heaven, where you know we have a dear mother and four darling little brothers. But this is not all or the most. There is a precious Saviour there, who is perfectly holy, and all who enter that place must be holy too. Are you holy? Perhaps you may think that you may be good enough; that you have never done anything very wrong; but you do not know your own heart, and it is enough that Christ has said you are a sinner, and that unless you repent you cannot be saved. Perhaps you want to know then, how you are to repent. Christ died for you, and you have only to cast your sins upon Him. If you do not understand, know, and feel, you have only to ask him, and he will grant you his Holy Spirit to teach you all things."

[The whole Gospel is summed up in that paragraph, reader; everything needed to save—not the righteous —but a sinner.]

"I hope and pray that you will think a great deal of these things, and will pray a great deal for Christ to show you your sinfulness, and make you a true follower of Him and an heir of Heaven.

"Now I have something for you to do. Give a kiss for me to all, give Georgie at least a dozen, if the rest will not be envious; then take for yourself as many as you give all the rest, if you can add it up yourself.

"Your affectionate brother,

"KINGMAN."

TO A DEAR FRIEND.

"*January* 2.

"For a week or two past I have been almost wholly absorbed with the study of my own character, and the nature and requirements of true Christianity. . . . It is with a heart melting with penitence and with gratitude, that I tell you that the Holy Spirit is in the midst of us. I fear, dear ——, that I may incur your censure for what you may consider a stepping out of my place. I wish not to reprove or advise, but I must say that my anxiety for your spiritual welfare has been, at times, intense. Where are the resolutions you expressed in your last? I know you cannot be actively engaged in the service of our Master, nor is your spirit refreshed by the light of our Saviour's countenance. Yet you are acquainted with all the motives which urge to Christian activity; you know their number, their weight; and what can I say more? I shall continue to be earnest and frequent in prayer for you; and shall do so with more freedom, when I shall be sure that *you know* I am endeavoring from day to day to pray in your behalf.

"For my own part, I desire to be found at work. I have been idle long enough. O how glorious to me is the thought of doing something for the glory of God, and of being made the instrument of saving deathless spirits from everlasting woe, and raising them to communion with the infinitely Holy God; God nerve *me* for the work."

In a memorandum under date of Jan. 26, 1851, the anniversary of his conversion, he writes: "'Tis to-day two years since I was enabled by the grace of God to surrender my helpless soul into the hands of Him who formed it, and who died to redeem it. I have recalled the vows made at that period, and entered into a renewal of them, consecrating myself afresh to God.

"In a review of the past year, I am excited to great gratitude, on the one hand, that I am still in the exercise of a *hope*, founded, I trust, on Christ, that should

I now be called to the spirit land, my soul could greet her Saviour with heavenly rapture. 'Oh! that *hope*—how bright, how glorious!'

"On the other hand, I am compelled to confess that I have made but little advancement in the divine life. My circumstances have been completely changed. Removed from my beloved home and church, I have come among strangers. I have been freed from many restraints, and thrown among very different classes of associates, etc. O, I need to pray without ceasing! A great work is before me. Christ himself displays the glittering crown.

"The prime antidote to declension and coldness will be found in communion with God. I wish to guard well this point.

"O for more entire consecration to God! Let me devote *all* to Him. May I guard against idleness, as the avenue to every vice, and strive to fit my soul for the service of God on earth, and His praises in Heaven."

CHAPTER VI.

CALL TO PREACH—A PILGRIMAGE.

KINGMAN had not yet decided upon his future profession, but simply held himself at the disposal of his Master. But at this time he received his "call." The account is given in the following letter to his father:

"*March* 24, 1851.

.... "You will no doubt be glad to hear that your absent son is enjoying the influence of the Holy Spirit more fully than for some time. I must again thank you and mother for that New Year's gift [Life of Taylor]. I fully believe that its precious pages have been a means of increasing in some degree my religious strength, and confirming my principles.

"A week ago yesterday was perhaps one of the most eventful Sabbaths I ever passed. I never listened with more intense interest to the preaching of the word. In the afternoon we were addressed by Mr. Bertram, a missionary from St. Helena. He told us his tale briefly, and made an earnest appeal to the young men; but nothing spoke so loud to me, or forced such weight upon me, as the facts and my own reflections."

[There follows an account of Mr. Bertram's missionary operations in St. Helena.]

He continues:—"It is wonderful how much God may be pleased to accomplish by the instrumentality of a single man, unaided, except by divine power!

"You well know that my mind has never been settled upon any vocation for life. Though I have for some time been bent on acquiring an education, and have felt desirous of employing it for the service of my Master, yet I have never decided in what particular way to employ it—simply because I was unable to determine whether it was my duty to preach the gospel, or to engage in a secular calling; and thus I have been always waiting for some future event, in God's own time, to direct me right. For a week past my mind has been occupied with these thoughts. Saturday morning, bright and beautiful, ushered in by the familiar notes of the returned robins, was a solemn and yet joyous time for me. An hour and a quarter before breakfast was spent in a grove in prayer and reflection with reference to my commencing the eighteenth year of my life. *What constitutes a call to preach the Gospel?* My notions are changed, whether for right or wrong you can determine. Is it a special, and, to the uninitiated, a mysterious revelation, that it is the will of the Deity to constitute one an ambassador for Christ? If so, I am yet in the dark. Or, does the command to the Apostles, 'Go ye into all the world and preach the Gospel to every creature,' make it binding on every Christian to do all in his power, in his own sphere, to further the execution of this command, until it be accomplished? If so, then, let him who has love for souls and love for Christ, and intellectual and physical abilities, and who, the cost being counted, comes to a deliberate and firm conclusion that he is *ready* to endure the cross, relying on God alone for support, go forward and preach the Gospel as a door shall be opened! If this is it, then I do think I can firmly say, '*Here I am, Lord, prepare and send me.*'

"Great and self-denying is the work; and I suppose, too, that my present conceptions are but faint compared with the reality; but *great also* are the motives for undertaking the work, and great the Power on whom we may lean, and to whom look for guidance."

The subject is continued in another letter, and his own aspirations more exactly defined.

TO THE SAME.

"*April* 14.

"I was very glad to receive your kind letter, and to find that your views upon the subject introduced are similar to those which I had somewhat timidly entertained.

"I had not considered that in giving myself to the work of an evangelist, or preacher of the Gospel, the office of *pastor* was included. In fact, to speak freely, I have not by any means decided upon *that*, or been led to look upon it as the office which I am to fill. I do not think it adapted to me, from this consideration; it affords too great temptations to my *pride* and fondness of display. I am very fond of speaking; and a pulpit and pastorate at home would not offer a safe position to me, in this age of worldliness and formality. I have often thought of the colporteur's work as an intermediate step; but if my present views do not alter, nor something unforeseen oppose, my course shall be to seek out some dark—darkest corner of this planet, where the light of revelation has never penetrated. This is *my ambition.*

"The thought of the stupidity of men in this country, whose slumbering consciences give them no trouble, nor awake at the sound of the revelations of God's word, affects my heart; but when I think of human beings created on a level with the rest of mankind, who know not even that there is a God, that there is a Saviour, or any need of salvation; nay, nor that they *have souls*, and are to exist after death, I cannot rest. . .

"I hope I may be guided aright—kept both from erroneous views and sinful practices. That this may be so, I ask, and know that I shall have your prayers."

These expressions of longings for a distant and difficult field of toil, were not the vague language of youthful and uninstructed enthusiasm.

If a romantic fancy gave unreal coloring to the pictures he drew of future self-sacrifice and labor, yet the outlines of these sketches were traced with a firm and true hand. His zeal was genuine and holy: and though differently directed in after life than he had anticipated, it burned as purely and warmly in New York as it would have done in Burmah.

The Spring vacation was occupied with a pedestrian tour—a sort of pious pilgrimage: *i.e.* a visit to a venerable relative, the late Rev. Dr. Nott, of Franklin, Conn., a brother of Dr. Nott of Schenectady. At the time of the visit he was considerably past ninety; he died at the age of ninety-nine. The letter descriptive of the visit is so graphic, and intrinsically so interesting, that we quote portions. See his hearty, honest enthusiasm, not afraid to express itself, and compelled to resort to plentiful italics and triple exclamation points!

"*May* 12*th*, 1851.

"DEAR FATHER,—

"I have seen him! that most venerable patriarch! My long-cherished desire has finally, in the good providence of God, been gratified, and I have looked upon, conversed with, and received instruction from, the reverend man, Dr. Nott, of Franklin!!!

"But perhaps your first inquiry may be, 'How came you here?' Do not be displeased with your runaway son, and all shall be explained. With umbrella and carpet-bag I left Suffield last Wednesday morning with *the crowd*, but though I strove to make it seem like *vacation*, and leaving school for home, and to appear like the rest of the company, I could not help realizing the *sad difference*. While others were indulging in *unbounded glee*, 'Oh, I'm going home! home! home!' my lot was different."

He spends the night in Hartford, and next morning, to continue his own account: "I slung my carpet-bag on my umbrella over my shoulder, and set out for Franklin, thirty-six miles distant. 'Labor *improbus* omnia vincit, nec aspera terrent,' and when these mottoes did not suffice, *Dr. Nott* did. At last I actually reached the top of the everlastingly long hill, stood by the neat little meeting-house, and was soon, with a burning face and quick-beating heart, trudging up the old lane, till I came in sight of the old mansion."

He enters, and "Soon the door opened, and in came the oldest man I had ever seen. He walked with a tall cane, his hair was literally white, he wore the old small-clothes, etc. I met him in the middle of the room and shook hands. 'Well, I don't know who you are,' he said, in a shrill clear voice, very pleasantly. I told him my name was Nott. He *seemed mightily pleased*, and said, 'Well, I'm *glad* to see you for your name's sake. Pray, to what family of the Notts do you belong?' 'I'm son of *Handel* Nott.' '*Oh, we all know Handel Nott!!*' This news pleased the Dr. very much. 'I'm glad to see you for your *father's sake*, and for your sake. Then he told of his boyish days (before the Revolutionary war); his father's house burning, and his mother pulling him out by the hair of his head and throwing him on the green, etc. 'Why,' said he, 'it seems but a little while since I was a boy, running about Pettipaug.' As soon as I had satisfied his inquiries about Handel, and he had got to talking, he would forget the whole, and again ask me the same round of questions, 'Whose son are you?' etc.

"The Dr. is in his study as much as ever. *Reads much of the time and without glasses!* Selects his texts and *writes parts of sermons!!* Pores over his old manuscripts a great deal. He still attends meeting twice on the Sabbath *rain or shine;* sits in the pulpit; often makes the last prayer. He kneels and prays with his family daily. His prayers are the *most pointed* and excellent I ever heard, and as *varied in form and expression as ever!*

"He thinks he preaches now constantly. What astonishes me as much as anything is his *constant good-nature* and flow of spirits. He exhibits ten times the life and energy in his talk that one half of our young ministers do. *Nothing* ruffles or displeases him in the least. He always turns off everything unpleasant with some pithy hit and a laugh. He waits on himself in almost everything. If he wants more fire he will hobble off, get wood and fuss about the stove at a great rate.

"The Dr. seemed quite brisk last evening—telling about his long life, ministry, great changes, etc.; and as he spoke of 'fitting a great many for college,' I took this opportunity of introducing myself again, by saying, 'You fitted my father for college.' 'Ah, I don't know whose son you are, I'm sure,' he said, laughing. 'Handel Nott's.' He took my arm in his withered hand and shook it long and heartily, at the same time laughing for pleasure and saying, 'Ah, I did not know I had one of my cousins here!' Then he wanted to know how I came, etc., etc. Being told I came the day before, he said he did not remember it, and referred to his '*bewildering cold*.' Poor old man! this has been his complaint for a long time; to this he refers the wasting away of his once powerful mind.

"This afternoon I had the most lively conversation with him of all. He asked me the customary round of questions. When he inquired about your occupation I varied my usual reply of 'a minister' and said, '*A Baptist minister*.' 'A Baptist! well, that's a rarity! that's out of the line! I wonder how he came to be a Baptist! Well I hope he will make a good one!' . . . . He likes to tell of the changes he has passed through in his long life:—blacksmith, shoemaker and tanner, school-master,—'went through College, and, as the Irishman said, had to work my own passage;—then, after I got through, I put my brother Eliphalet through;—fitted a great many for college, and been a minister a long time.'

"*A long time indeed!* Seventy years has he been pastor of this church! He says, 'It seems but a short time to look back when I preached my first sermon here. The text is now in mind, "I ask, therefore, for what intent ye have sent for me?" The people all stared a time, for I announced the words before I told them the place. Those who were then here have passed away. Not one of those who asked me to settle here is now living. The present senior deacon of my church was born the same year I came here. Well, we must all die, or *grow old!*' . . . .

"To-day he asked me, 'And what are *you?*' The question took me wholly by surprise—I laughed, and told him I was a *student.* 'Fitting for college, hey?' I told him I was. 'Well, I hope you will do better than any of your predecessors.' This I felt set my mark high."

On his return from his pleasant excursion he thus expresses his resolutions for the next term.

TO HIS FATHER.

May 23, 1851.

"I suppose you may wish to be apprised of my safe return to my 'post,' and entrance upon the duties of another quarter. . . . . I never entered upon studies with more ardor. I have a definite object now in view (the ministry), my purpose is fixed—and it is the most worthy and noble that ever fired the breast of an ambitious youth. I delight in my work, and in the consciousness of God's assistance and grace, in answer to my unworthy prayers. I hope I may be kept by His grace, directed by His Spirit in the path of *usefulness*, and finally taken to Himself.

"I am disappointed in each letter from home, not to hear of a revival in my church at home. I feel attached to that body and that people, and it is my prayer that my father's labors there may be blessed by the conversion of souls. . . . .

"Mr. Woodbury tells me he wants me to do something *transcendental* this—the last quarter! . . . .

"Let me hear from home each week; and with studies and work, the changing weather and exciting scenes, the eleven weeks will soon flit away, and the 7th of August arrive to bear me through the Old Bay State to rocky K—port. *Provided* that God's good providence shall so order."

CHAPTER VIII.

RESOLUTENESS—"I MUST HAVE AN EDUCATION"—THE ANNIVERSARY—RECOLLECTIONS.

As the end of the school-year approached, the question began to be discussed, whether it would be possible for Kingman to continue his course, as he had intended. Would not a partial course suffice? Would not a year or two more at Suffield answer the necessary purposes, without incurring the expense and pecuniary risk of going to college? No doubt, the most thorough training was desirable, but how if it could not be procured?

To all this, Kingman replied by reiterating his unconquerable determinations; and the correspondence on his part displays so remarkably the resoluteness of his character, his enterprise, and happy faculty of looking on the bright side, and making the best of circumstances, that we quote liberally.

There was involved in his project, the wish to go to Yale. This was overruled: the other portions of his plan he carried by main force.

"*June* 6, 1851.

"MY DEAR PARENTS,

"I have for some time been desirous of talking with my friends with relation to my future course; still, as your wishes were not known to me, I have refrained. Of late, I have been inquiring and pondering with relation to the advantages and expense of various colleges, compared with each other, and with the advanced course at Suffield.

"A letter received to-day damps my spirits and discourages me not a little. But pray consider..... I stand with my occupation for life now *immovably fixed upon.* I can say *immovably*, because my purpose seems to grow stronger and deeper daily; and it is a source, too, of constant satisfaction and pleasure.

"It is *dear* to me, as the lofty-laid plans of any aspiring youth. Now, I propose to express to you my own desires, and leave it with you to see whether my plans are, in your opinion, practicable. In a word, I am bent on obtaining a thorough and complete collegiate education....

"The difficulty, the main obstruction in your mind, I suppose is—*expense!* Now, I cannot believe that it will cost more to go to college than to remain here:—at any rate, but very little more...

"I have my denominational prejudices, to a certain extent, regarding colleges; still, colleges are not, I suppose, practically different to the student. To Yale College I have very strong attachments. I know not what your views and wishes are. Mother's remark, I shall never forget; it awakened a thrill. 'You can then go [after teaching a year or two, as was then proposed] to what college you please; you can go to Yale.' Not only the long standing and lofty reputation of this institution move me; but its shades seem very peculiarly sacred and endeared, because previous Notts, not with-

8

out distinction, and my own father dwelt among them.

TO THE SAME, A FEW DAYS LATER.

"Thanks for your letter; but I must confess, that I had some hopes of hearing something more conclusive. However, I felt the reasonableness of the considerations you urged; and when I had read your letter and mother's, I half concluded that it was best to give up all my fond plans for going to Yale, yielding without a word to the wishes and advice of friends.

"The most important point, however, seems to me to lie back of all that has been said; and having pondered your inquiries, as I am able, and prayed for the directing influences of the Spirit, I shall endeavor to state to you as freely, and as candidly as I can—*just* my state of mind, my hopes and desires, and what they are founded on.

"I am not my own. I owe a debt of gratitude to my Redeemer, greater than it is in my power to repay, and I feel desirous of doing what I can to promote his glory. This end, I believe, I can most effectually attain by preaching the Gospel. I love the work. I glory in it. I am determined to engage in it. This point is, in my own mind, firmly settled, and my prayer is, 'may God nerve and fit me for it, and make me instrumental in the salvation of dying souls.' I believe I am a Christian; I believe I have been led by the Spirit; I believe God has called me to this work; and my *present* work is, to prepare my mind and heart for engaging most advantageously in it.

"Accordingly, I am anxious to obtain a thorough

education. How, and where can I best accomplish that? The *heart*, I believe, can be cultivated at one college as well as at another. Then, how and where can I best cultivate what intellectual faculties God has given me? An important inquiry!—because, supposing the heart to be right, I can accomplish the more in proportion as my *mind* becomes trained; for, my powers of *doing* will thus become greater; and certainly my influence among men of the present age will, in no small degree, depend upon my standing as a *man*, independently of my religion.

"With these views, I endeavor to stand—waiting as patiently as possible to discover an open way—the path of duty.

"Yet, I have a word or two to say about colleges, or I shall not have told you all. I do not wish to go counter to your wishes, or to reason, etc. etc. . . . . Now the *point* in my own mind is *this*—Can you give me your consent to go to Yale, and provide me with a hundred dollars a year, as you mentioned? [Through the aid of his uncle.]

"Is it unreasonable to suppose that, with this assistance, I could get along for one year? I really think not. Let me at least make a trial. Of course all will depend on my doing well. If a student gains the confidence of the Faculty, he will not be obliged to leave on account of poverty. God has, I believe, given me the powers to excel, or at least to do well, and I *will*.

"My 'spending money' would not be a large sum. My clothing will, in considerable part, come from my predecessors. I can board myself, if necessary. In the vacations, I can do something as book agent.

"But besides all these things, my opinion regarding one point has changed within some months. I *used* to think that I never should be willing to be connected with the *Education Society.* It cut my pride to think of being dependent on strangers, and *bound* to pursue a certain profession. Since I was led to form the purpose of preaching, my feelings, directed, I trust, by the Spirit of God, have changed. Anxious to serve him, I desire to lay hold of the best advantages he presents me, to fit myself most adequately for the work.

"It seems as though I had almost been but *dabbling* till within but a short time. I know young men are apt to be impatient to enter upon public life. I wish not to be hasty or unreasonable.

"But, parents dear, my work of intellectual preparation will be a *long one.* God has given me *some mind*, and whatever it is, I mean to cultivate it as much as is in my power.

"I have myself the fullest confidence and faith that, could I but gain your consent to start, I could get through, by kind Providence.

"I am fast passing to eighteen;—the time seems *too short* which will make me a *man.*

"O! I need every moment, and every advantage I can gain, to prepare for my arduous work. If I am wild and unreasonable, tell me and check me. The subject is not presented without previous study, close calculation, reliable information. If my friends deem it *absolutely necessary* that I keep out another year, I shall strive to acquiesce without murmuring. I would not have my parents do more than they have done. I trust not to manifest the least ingratitude or want of appreciation of their exertions. May I prove worthy of them."

Here strong hope comes to him:

"*June* 17.

MY DEAR FATHER,—

"Thank you for your kind letter, advice and encouragement—which so far exceeded my expectations that I almost wept tears of joy. I feel now a good degree of hope, and have set about the work of reviewing and preparing in earnest; for if I go, I do not want to be lost among the vast crowd of youthful aspirants, and the time is very short. I am waiting in suspense to know whether you succeed in your kind endeavors on my behalf; if so, I have no fears as to getting along. I have been making liberal estimates of expenses at Yale. There are young men there who have sustained themselves entirely during their course by teaching classes in New Haven," etc., etc.

And here is disappointment:

"*July* 15.

"I now hasten to reply, as the matter seems settled for the present.

"So I must give up my too fondly cherished plan for going to Yale, and retracing my father's steps. I am willing to yield to the better judgment of my friends, anxious not to appear bent upon my own course, or ungrateful for favors shown."

It was settled, however, that he should go to college, and that without delay.

The "Anniversary" now came, with its scenes of excitement and, to Kingman, of bewildering delight. The poor student, who had had little but industry and faith, and that word of power, which was better than any talisman, DUTY, had prevailed. He had fought his way through.

Now he is a "graduate!" He has a seat, for the first time, upon a public platform, and—novel experience—is a public speaker! He stands before the great audience—in his queer and threadbare coat—the loveliness of his soul making itself radiant upon his face—himself forgetful of himself. Soon he holds the people by an unexpected spell—there is applause—and he has the joy of a *first oratorical triumph.*

In a crumpled old Programme we read thus:

" . . . .

" MUSIC.

"11. . . . .

" . . . .

"12. The Classics the Foundation of English Literature.

"A. KINGMAN NOTT, Kennebunkport, Me."

. . . .

Underneath is written, in a stranger's hand,

"You do Nott need praise, but you merit it."

And a torn, irregular scrap of paper, that was found

tucked carefully away in the pocket of a much be-scribbled little memorandum-book for 1851, evidently was precious for a lady's compliment.

"I am very glad that my native state has produced one of the best speakers on this occasion."

Now good-bye to Suffield. The expected 7th of August "rolls him through the beautiful Old Bay State to rocky Kennebunkport." The friends are all there whom he has not seen for more than a year, "and now," he exclaims, "are we not *almost happy!*"

Now there is a long vacation and rest:—rambles, swimming, boating, berrying again, and preaching too, after the old fashion which he has not forgotten.

Kingman's friend, Theron Brown, thus continues the "Reminiscences" from which we have already quoted.

"I need not say how much more intimate and precious was my fellowship with Kingman after this change. Our intercourse was now entirely without restraint. . . . . Kingman went to College and left me alone, for I did not find another friend like him—so tender, so sincere, so generous to all my faults, so perfectly genial in temper, and refined in taste. . . . .

"Kingman never alluded to Suffield in his subsequent letters without expressing the strongest affection for the scenes and persons that he remembered there. It was there that he, the scholar, the orator, and the youthful Christian, exhibited a picture of his life of single purpose.

And though I saw him in the winter of '55–6 more manly in appearance, and more keen in the use of his many acquirements, yet he had not materially changed. It was at Suffield that he learned self-dependence amid the praises and the little envies of schoolmates, and it was here that he exercised his boyish eloquence in the excitements of youthful debate, and his scarcely less impassioned exhortations to impenitent associates. It was in Suffield that I formed the estimate of his character which I still cherish after the confirmation of six years' correspondence. I never saw a man of so much meekness. He seemed to me to be utterly incapable of revenge. I never saw a man wear honor with a better grace. I never saw a man who at so early an age had so much singleness of heart joined to so much polish of mind. In brief, I never saw a man who commended himself in so many points to my affection and esteem.

"I feel his loss—I loved him.

"—'But my Lord and his
Had loved him long before,
Weeping, I turn me where he is,
And wish—but will not murmur more.'"

The great topic of family discussion, for the few weeks following K.'s return to Kennebunkport, was, "to what College can the boy best go?" The new and thriving University of Rochester was the institution which, after much debate, was fixed upon, and it was a choice which K. never had cause to regret.

CHAPTER IX.

College History.—General Characteristics.

Up to this point we have been able to trace distinctly the shaping power of *circumstances* in Kingman's development. Not without constant pressure and direction from the external, have the processes of spiritual and mental growth been carried on—an honest heart and right will keeping the soul open and susceptible to the good, that infallibly resides in all circumstances, for the well-disposed.

When we now behold the subject of this history, while his character is yet only partially formed, removed into a new sphere, and subjected to influences before untried, we at once infer that God has a special design in the transfer, and we look with interest to see what are the new forces brought to bear, and what their effect.

Kingman first set foot in Rochester about the beginning of September, 1851. Fresh from the Academy, a provincial and narrow world, he found himself under the more expanding and generous influences of a College. Fresh from the country, too, with its staidness and quiet, he was now in a bustling city. But the change was advantageous. Rochester, distinguished for pleasantness of situation, and for grand scenery as well as softer rural charms within the very limits of the solid town—"The Rural City"—offered to him still the real sweetness of a country home, while it added this, that it brought him into contact with a mass of men sufficiently numerous to constitute together an epitome of the race, and sufficiently dense to feel without abatement or long delay the vibration of events and of changing opinion in the great world. The book of nature was still open to him, while that of human nature, unabridged, was spread wide. This may appear an important advantage, if it be reflected that to one intending to devote his life to the persuasion of men, knowledge of men is a good preliminary acquisition; and, certainly, to study human nature in the original, is more efficacious than ever so careful pondering of the renderings of it given by philosophers, theologians—or novelists.

It was another advantage of dwelling in a city at this period, that, by mere contagion of the general activity, though in material concerns, the mind even of the scholar was quickened to a more perpetual liveliness, and thus grew to be more prompt, quick, energetic, and versatile, if not actually more powerful than it might, in greater seclusion. Is it not to the causes now mentioned that we should trace, in considerable degree, many of the traits that afterwards contributed to make the young pastor a favorite—the brisk and animated manner and urbane polish—as well as the knowledge of affairs and familiarity with the intricacies of the human heart, which qualified him for a leader?

The University of Rochester, of which Kingman now became a member, had been recently founded, and possessed the vigor of healthy youth. It was a consequence, perhaps, of the recentness of its origin, that among its hundred and thirty or forty students, a spirit of order and of wholesome emulation was more prevalent than usual in colleges. High scholarship was common, and a rare value was set on excellence in composition and in extemporaneous speaking. A young man felt himself bound to excel in something; if not, by some chance out of his own control, in mathematics or Greek, then certainly with the pen or in the accomplishments of an orator: and an idler, or a "good fellow," found no toleration. The Literary Societies were sustained with uncommon enterprise. The debates, which were publicly held, and attracted considerable audiences, called out usually the whole power of the disputants; and the bi-weekly "Paper" in each Society was certainly conducted with an ability which would have won reputation to any public literary gazette. A similar animation reigned in all the departments of the college. Industry, alertness, enterprise—these were the watchwords. Nobody was allowed to be dull. A professor felt the same obligation to be vital, as learned.

Such was the practical spirit in both the institutions —the University of Rochester, and the Rochester

Theological Seminary. It is easy to see how suited to interest and stimulate our young student.

There was, similarly, an active religious life; demonstrative and outgoing, but not yet so occupied with merely radiating, as to forget the essentialness of maintaining central, intrinsic heat. In the city and the suburbs there was abundant opportunity for missionary enterprises. Though a "City of Churches," at least one-third of the population was papist, and more than a handful infidel. Mission Sunday-schools and mission preaching establishments occupied a portion of the leisure Sunday hours of almost every religious student in College.

Kingman himself, the very week of his first arrival, enlisted in a Sunday-school held in a school-house at the "Lower Falls," on the Genesee River two miles below the city, and occupied faithfully the post, soon adding familiar preaching to teaching, until near the end of his course—and until after a church (Presbyterian) had been formed, and a comfortable meeting-house substituted for the school-room as the place of assembling. Two or three other students, to whom equal credit is due, were colleagues of his in the enterprise.

Kingman's conduct and scholarship are described, and many traits of his character as at this time exhibited and developing, are pleasingly illustrated, in the following sketch by Dr. Anderson, President of the University:

"I first knew him," says Dr. Anderson, "in childhood while his father was pastor in Bath, Me. During my college vacations I frequently met him, then a child of eight or nine years, at my father's house. He was a model of childish grace and vigor, overflowing with the buoyant animal spirits which are the sure indications of a healthy moral and physical constitution. Even then he gave indication of that capacity for ready and elegant expression, which he seems to me to have acquired from his mother, whom all her friends remember as a woman of high culture and extraordinary conversational power. Cicero said of the Gracchi that they acquired their mastery of Latin in the lap of their mother. Kingman's ear and tongue were trained from infancy to the discrimination and utterance of elegant English. That mastery of words which enabled him to adjust words to thought with such mingled rapidity and exactness was the result, not merely of natural power, but of assiduous training.

"After these early years I knew little of him until my removal to Rochester, where I found him a member of the Junior Class in the University. My early religious obligations to his father, and the memory of his own early years, naturally led me to take a personal interest in his success as a student. I found him conscious that certain public efforts in which he had engaged during the previous year, had somewhat interfered with his prescribed course of study, and he voluntarily expressed his determination to permit nothing within his control to set aside the great object of furnishing and disciplining his faculties for future labor. The pledge thus voluntarily made he most fully redeemed, and I never had occasion to complain of his failure in duty. He had special facility as a linguist, but he was able to master easily any of the scientific studies which were put before him, and in the metaphysical department to obtain marked distinction.

"Not having been able, by reason of absence, to obtain a satisfactory understanding of a portion of the Mathematics of the Sophomore year, he reviewed carefully the Analytical Geometry of the course, attending the recitations of the Professor in that department, after he had graduated and entered upon his professional studies in the Theological Seminary. Though pressed by the severe labor required in the Seminary, he found time also to join a class of resident graduates for the reading of Plato, and another in German. I am the more careful to allude to these facts, because the idea has been entertained by some that Kingman owed his success to genius alone, independent of scholarship and long-continued mental discipline. Taking as a standard the best class of graduates from American colleges, it is bare justice to say that Kingman entered public life a sound and accurate scholar, and no one was more ready than he to recognise the value of both liberal and professional education.

"Genius is the power of rapid working in one or many different directions. Kingman's mind naturally moved with extraordinary rapidity. By intellectual discipline and culture, this rapidity acquired systematic direction and orderly movement. He was often able to look upon all sides of a complicated subject, and search out all its relations, during a time in which another mind of equal soundness, but with slower rate of movement, would hardly have seized upon its most obvious bearings. He brought more to pass intellectually than other men, because he was able and willing to do more work. Those instances of rapid combination and facility of language and illustration, which seemed so like inspiration, were the result of the same process through which ordinary minds pass, varying in his case only in the velocity with which the results were accomplished. This power of rapid mental action was accompanied by the impulse to its exercise. Hence the fertility of his mind and his capacity for meeting the many and various drafts which were made upon his resources during his public life. Many thoughtful men predicted that a man so young could not meet, for any considerable time, the intellectual demands of the place to which he was called. Those who knew his mental habits and constitution had no fears in this respect. A mind so well furnished and active is a living spring, and not a reservoir. Its power of literary production is measured only by the body's capacity for endurance.

"His mental activity was not of that disorderly and unproductive kind which reaches no tangible result, and leaves no clear and positive impression. His most rapid thinking was analytical and orderly. It was for this reason he was never confused. His thinking, when obliged to speak with little time for reflection, might not have been equal to his highest capacity, but it was never wanting in system or clearness. Whatever ideas he had, on a subject were always under his command, and compelled to array themselves in the best possible order for convincing and impressing other minds.

"The religious development of his mind, while in the University, was marked and striking. In the course of the Junior year, and especially after the day of prayer in behalf of institutions of learning, he seemed to have acquired a new and very decided impulse towards a higher Christian life. This was manifested by no abatement of his habitual joyousness of mien, but rather by a more careful and conscientious attention to the discharge of all duty, both secular and religious. A college friend of his lately informed me, that at this period he formed the habit of rising at an early hour, and spending a specific time in reading the Scriptures and devotion. In the exercise of reading he placed before him the Greek of the New Testament, or the Septuagint, and by its side the Latin, German, and English versions, and examined them in turn, carefully comparing the shades of expression in each. This practice was faithfully continued during his remaining course as a student.

"His earnestness of religious life was especially shown in the religious labor which he performed among his classmates and acquaintances in the University. He was very constant in his attendance upon all the devotional meetings, and gave much time to personal religious conversation. His remarks and prayers in these meetings were marked by spirituality of tone and the most intense exhibition of personal allegiance to the Saviour. Doubtless some of his most effective effusions of natural eloquence were thrown off in these class and college prayer-meetings. I have an abiding conviction that his extraordinary success as a pastor was in great part due to the training which he gave himself in the performance of pastoral duties among his associates in study.

"A large part of my confidence in his success, when he became a pastor, was founded on my knowledge of the conscientiousness of his religious labor while a student. In many years' experience among students I have never seen his equal in the judgment, perseverance, and fidelity with which he performed this personal religious labor. Marked as was his success in the service of his Master, in New York, it was but the natural result of the religious discipline of his student life. His capacity for this too much neglected part of a pastor's duty was due to some elements that are worthy of a moment's notice. In the first place, this work was done, not from a goading sense of duty, but from a love of the work and from a confident expectation of doing good to those whom he addressed. Hence there was a reality and heartiness in his representations and appeals, which rarely failed to reach the conscience. Connected with this was a living faith in the promises of God and the present agency of the Holy Spirit. More than any young man whom I ever knew, he realized that Christ is a living and present Saviour, actually moving among us, and sympathizing with our woes and wants.

"Again, he always labored for a direct and immediate practical result. This gave directness and simplicity to his language and address. He was never willing to utter vague generalities about religion, in the hope that in some unexplained way they might at some time produce a good effect. He strove for results at once, knowing that he who would reach the future can do so only by impressing the minds of men in the present.

"These facts of Kingman's history seem to me more important from the fact, evident to all who knew him, that his style of oratory was formed on the model of elevated and serious conversation. Hence was derived the peculiar individualizing power by which he made each hearer in a large congregation feel himself personally addressed. His public style was concrete, personal, and dramatic, because he had trained himself thoroughly in addressing men one by one in private.

"In this work, which Dr. Watts somewhere calls 'parlor preaching,' Kingman illustrated another of the virtues which entered into the formation of his character. I refer to personal courage. This I am aware does not often rank high among clerical accomplishments. But it may be seriously questioned whether a minister or any other man can honestly do his duty without it. It was a remark of one of his college acquaintances that Kingman was constitutionally indifferent to physical danger. He was certainly largely imbued with moral courage. In the discharge of religious duty he feared no rebuff, or outrage, or opposition. He never shrank from conflict with any kind of error, or any amount of hatred for truth in the minds of those whom he personally addressed. This element of character gave a calmness and regularity to his mental action, a tone and force to his public utterance, which added greatly to his power to sway and control the minds of men.

"I have followed out a few only of the manifold suggestions which have come unbidden into my mind. My personal interest in Kingman must be my apology for lingering fondly over his memory. His robust health and vigor of constitution gave the promise of a long life.

"With our short vision of futurity such a death seems inscrutable. But in the light of immortality there is no waste of power. God has taken the departed to a higher sphere of existence where the 'larger movements of the unfettered mind' have their natural place in the grand economy of heaven. He has left the example behind him of an elevated and earnest Christian life, which speaks with an eloquence which even his living voice could not equal."

This judicious sketch needs small supplementing—but remarks on a few points will not be superfluous.

From the first he showed a remarkable genius for writing, and a still greater for public speaking. Gay, sparkling, or satirical, or easily decorating a closely jointed argument with the drapery of illustration and metaphor, he was, in the "Society," a favorite essayist and "editor." In debate, he was a champion. He did not commonly, it is true, by instinct, burrow straight down beneath the whole superficies of a subject, and through all the accumulations of dust, soil, drift, to what was ultimate—the beams of rock on which all rested—to "first principles;" but he took in the whole superior landscape at a glance, appreciated it with a military eye, encamped on positions from which he could not be dislodged, and concentrated from every strong point a fire on the enemy that blasted him where he stood.

Thus he could be overthrown only by the art of undermining, and before this slow and secret process could be effected, he was commonly, after a rapid evolution or two, exulting over a field swept clear of foes.

The remarkable qualities he united were, this quick appreciation of all the strong points in a case, with perfect command of all his faculties, a mastery of words, and the power of constructing perfect sentences in rolling succession, extempore and endlessly, a fancy that easily took fire, and a most attractive and bewitching voice and manner. "Nott had less logic than some," said a contemporary "Delphian," "but he carried everything before him by his eloquence." All this is, of course, reckoned on the scale of a Young Men's Debating Society.

President Anderson has spoken in adequate terms of Kingman's religious activity in college. He was, in truth, during the last years of his course, "college pastor." For the delicate functions of that assumed office his disposition aptly fitted him. He was no grim, morose religionist, feeling solemnly accountable for motes in the eyes of others, while ignorant or vain of beams in his own; but he was light-hearted, clear-visioned, unsuspicious, frank, and sincere, as a child. With a many-sided nature—and windows on every side, so that his mind looked out fairly on every aspect of life and character, detecting the element of genuineness, and therefore, of good, that lies in everything, not vicious, that humanity on the large scale loves to be and do; free from bigotry, therefore, and prejudices, and not mistaking gladness for levity, nor a gloomy countenance for the proof of a pious spirit—his soul radiating light and beauty from his sunny face, he could go where he pleased, disarm suspicion, attract confidence, and make his way to every heart.

Yet he accomplished even a greater amount of religious work outside of the college than in it. Accounts of the various enterprises in which he engaged for doing good, particularly in the long summer vacations, will be given in their proper places. Only this now—that whatever he undertook for God, if only to preach a single sermon, he must needs do *earnestly*. Everywhere he was driven to personal conversation with men. A power also went with him. The cloud of God's presence stood constantly over him, and blessings descended wherever he came. It is safe to say, that as large a number of souls was converted through his influence while he was a student, as afterwards during his pastoral labors in New York.

It is by no means meant to be intimated that his conduct in college was always perfectly consistent with his religious professions and with his intentions. He was developing now—and developing from a depraved being *into* a holy. Yet his departures arose chiefly from the influence of a temperament that—in itself—was admirable, and was the ground of some of those traits which ultimately were his best. His temperament was extravagantly gay. Perfect health of body and mind—and a spirit, in fact, that chains could not have dragged down, made him *glad* to exuberance. Among his companions he "kept the table in a roar," not at all by cool *witticisms*, but by the infectious spirit of humor and drollery. In recitation he compelled the Professor sometimes deliberately to "suppress" him. "Your brother," said President Anderson to the writer once, when in Rochester, "is mad with fine health and gay spirits. I think of ordering for him a strait jacket."

No words could describe his grotesqueness at times. No one could be near him sometimes without being filled with laughter. Yet this disposition had no alliance with any low tastes: he was no comedian, or foolish inventor of petty mischief. He could be severely sarcastic when he chose; yet he was unaware of this power until he was told of it, much to his astonishment, by a friend whom he had often unintentionally wounded, and he never deliberately exercised the fatal gift (fatal to easy, confidential friendship) with any malign or selfish purpose, and was as tender of the feelings of others as he was respectful of any of their natural rights.

It is easy to see that gaiety like this would hurry him often into culpable extravagances. "I am fearfully light and frivolous again," he writes on one occasion; "these are my besetting sins. The fact is, I do not know what to do with my *surplus*. I shall have to open a vein!"

Yet the wrongfulness of errors arising from this cause, would naturally be exaggerated in the eyes of persons of an opposite temperament, or who did not know him thoroughly. Beyond any other individual the writer ever knew, he was able to pass suddenly from one occupation or course of thinking to another, most opposite, at the shortest warning, and to pour the whole forces of his energies equally any way on demand. He played one hour as if he was made for nothing else, and studied the next with the abstractedness of a bookworm. From the most vivacious conversation or uproarious (healthful) mirth, he could go at once to his closet, and thence ascend the pulpit, if called, when the suffused eye and the indescribable, sweet solemnity that seemed not so much *expressed from* his face as to *bathe his face*, like a subtle ether, were warrant enough for the genuineness of his feeling.

But persons did not always understand this, and such individuals he often shocked severely. Whenever he ascertained that he had done harm, whether through inattention to "avoiding the mere appearance of evil," or through positively indefensible levity, he repented with the deepest self-reproaches, and often with humiliating confessions.

And it is here that the thought that he was *developing*, has a special and interesting application. Dispositions and tendencies, latent to a great degree before, were now revealing themselves. Thus his conduct for a year or two in Rochester was probably not so undeviating from the strictest lines; his deportment was less exact, less severe, than it had been in Suffield. He now saw the world in a different aspect; there were new and broader revelations of life; there were more varied appeals to different aptitudes; and he became at once *more natural.* That is, parts of his nature, which before had been hidden, not conquered, now burst into activity. Part of the character he possessed while at Suffield was unreal—not implying the slightest wilful insincerity—the farthest from it—but this: he had an ideal, and strove to live it without having grown up to it. This was a right attempt, he could do no otherwise,—only that he *must* grow up to it. Or, to represent the fact in different language, his religious character was partially unsubstantial, because resting upon pillars here and there of special qualities, and not upon his whole nature as a basis. Part must come down, and before it could be rebuilt, the foundation must be made uniform—marshes reclaimed—sand removed down to the solid stone.

But it must also be remembered that the development was going on under the care of religion. Religion demands the whole of a man; she will leave no native capability to slumber for ever in the germ, nor, on the other hand, suffer it to grow untrained. In Kingman she had already, out of his noblest traits—sanctifying them—woven a firm web of holy character; but she would interweave with it now, as intrinsic components, other capabilities, to render the web both more complete and more beautiful, and that in the figure, when perfected, might appear the genuine hue and form of every quality in the soul. Development and *transformation*, then, comprise the process. Religion restores a man to the image of the perfect archetype.

In New York, therefore, K. was not more holy than in Rochester, or in Suffield. A *greater part* of him was holy. Additional capabilities had been called into exercise, had passed through their period of wild and erratic development, and now, chastened, sanctified, and wrought into harmony with all other traits, they made up, together, a combination of superior symmetry and completeness. Nature had become, in more of its parts, developed, transformed, and consolidated into holy character. More "thoughts" had been "brought into captivity to the obedience of Christ."

How essential were *all* his qualities to what he ultimately was! Without that elasticity of spirit that made vain the buffets of care, that cheerfulness unconquerable by the worst discouragements, that versatile sympathy with men which gave him the key to hearts, what could he, in the peculiar work destined him, have done? Yet these traits are so allied to gaiety and a humorous disposition, that they can scarcely exist without—not that gaiety in itself is not a good; only extravagance is to be rebuked.

It ought to be remarked, finally, that K. maintained throughout his college course, the strictest rules of morality, without any deviation. He never weakly yielded even to doubtful indulgences. At the close, he had nothing to regret, except occasional slight indiscretions resulting from the sometimes too free effervescence of high animal spirits.

The lesson of his college course, is threefold; that sincere rectitude of aim, ensures the final conquest and subjection of opposing wrong tendencies; that the time for religious usefulness, is *now;* and, that religious usefulness now is the best pledge of, and preparation for, high usefulness in the future.

The sketch that has now been given, will be filled up, according to the plan hitherto pursued, chiefly with letters, with such narration as seems needful.

CHAPTER X.

THE FIRST YEAR—WILLIAMSON.

NOTT arrived in Rochester, it has been stated, about the 1st of September, 1851. His first impressions are thus communicated :

"UNIVERSITY of ROCHESTER, *Sept.* 6, 1851.

"My DEAR PARENTS :

"Examined—tried—condemned—to four years' imprisonment within these brick walls ! I feel contented, yes, happy : convinced that I am in the path of pleasure and of duty. I do not regret my choice of college, nor do I think I ever shall. Last evening, I called a few moments on the pastor of the First Baptist church, and then attended the Monthly Covenant meeting.

"I am greeted with a warm Christian cordiality, which makes my heart glad. Persons, whom I have never spoken to, take me by the hand and give me a hearty welcome.

"I feel that my privileges and blessings are very great, and my opportunities for growing in both intellectual and religious culture most excellent. My prayer to God is, to grant me grace for a faithful improvement, etc.

"Yours," etc.

"*September* 18.

"I feel thankful that I have been directed here. Of the

whole number of students in the Theological Seminary and University, more than one hundred have the ministry in view. By contact with so many young men of talent and piety, in private life, in the prayer-circle, etc., I have been *humbled.*

"I never was led before to look upon myself as so insignificant, upon my religious exercises as so cold and formal,—in fact, to feel so much my inferiority as a Christian. I find a higher standard of piety, which I am far below, and am now aiming to attain. There is great opportunity both for getting and for doing good here. Let me give you the occupations of last Sabbath. Prayer-meeting at 9 A.M. in the University; the usual church service in the forenoon; Sabbath-school in the afternoon, followed by a teachers' meeting; church in the evening.

"My Sabbath-school is an absorbing interest. It is held in a school-house two miles distant—at the lower Falls of the Genesee. We gather into the room a considerable assembly of both young and old; one of the students usually preaches familiarly, and after other good religious exercises, we have a Sunday-school in the usual manner. By such labors, I am refreshed and strengthened. Thus I do not lack for exercise on the Sabbath—walking six miles.

"I have taken my stand boldly as a professor of religion, and candidate for the ministry, and feel that I have thus incurred no little responsibility. I hope and pray that the Lord will spare me from dishonoring my master. There seems to be a strong desire on the part of a few students that God will favor this institution with an endowment of His Holy Spirit, and thus manifest His approval of the undertaking."

He thus alludes to his first attempt to preach, probably in the Mission school:

"On Sunday I did what I never attempted before. I felt almost ready to sink, but there was no alternative; the Lord sustained me very graciously. Our field is peculiarly excellent, the audience containing a large proportion of children—thus demanding the study of *simplicity*."

From this time he appears to have preached frequently in this unofficial manner.

In the winter of this year, oppressed with pecuniary wants, he left college for a few months, and engaged in teaching. The school was in the town of Williamson, Wayne Co., New York, about fifty miles from Rochester. The history of his connexion with this school illustrates in a singular manner the force of his allegiance to religious principle and the sensitiveness of his conscience.

At first he writes:—"My situation is one of uncommon responsibility. I have to fill the place of an infidel who has taught here two winters, and left an indelible stamp upon the community. The people are full of 'notions.' I shall do the best I can, leaning on the Almighty for support." So his first thought was of his religious obligations, involving here, as everywhere, some "uncommon responsibility."

The history proceeds:—

"WILLIAMSON, *Dec.* 8, 1852.

"DEAR FATHER:

"Here I am this pleasant evening, tired and dull, under the hospitable roof of Mr. B——. All around me are engaged in the absorbing occupation of paring and coring apples by the bushel. I have come here to-night for the first time, and am to spend a week. . . . .

"Teaching is harder labor than I have been accustomed to, but I hope it will do me good. . . . . I have opened my school with *prayer*, a thing which has never before been known in the district! Of course it seems very strange to many, and some, I suppose, hate it; yet I have met with no public opposition.

. . . . "I am surprised to find how little practical knowledge I have had of real life, and especially how poorly prepared I am to meet the attacks of the enemies of religion. Yet I am brought to realize more deeply the privilege of being a Christian. Oh, how I thank God that He has not left me to wander through the mazes and labyrinths of unbelief, trusting to no guide but unassisted reason. The sentiments of bold infidelity fall strangely and grate harshly upon my unpractised ear. . . . . I am of course under the necessity of being very careful as to what I say. On local questions, sectarian or unimportant, I maintain comparative indifference; but when I am called out by a challenge from the skeptic to defend the principles of my religion, I try to respond, prompt and unyielding. Pray for me, that I may be able to take to myself the whole armor of God."

"*January*, 1852.

"I exceedingly regret that I did not, while opportunity was afforded me, become acquainted more fully with the various objections commonly urged against our religion, and prepare myself to oppose the deadly errors which now meet me. Deists, Universalists, Andrew-Jackson-Davisites, Parkerites, etc., abound. . . . . Yet my school is one of a thousand, and my various homes uncommonly pleasant. Thus far I have found imagined difficulties vanish away like smoke, both in the school and with the people of my district. I think I have succeeded in gaining the affections of my scholars. . . . .

"The boys in the entry (it is recess) are making themselves exceedingly merry over an old hand-bill: having succeeded in metamorphosing the words 'Yankee Notions' into 'Yankee *Not!*'"

Enough has been quoted to show that K. emphatically "stood up for his religion" in this place of strange heresies, and was chiefly a noticeable object in the district, in fact, from his bold attempt to carry religious principle into practical life. Few young men, coming from a warm religious atmosphere, could have sustained so abrupt a change of temperature without growing torpid under the chill.

Are we prepared, then, to anticipate a letter of exactly the character of that which follows?

"WILLIAMSON, *March* 6, 1852.

"DEAR PARENTS:

"My heart is so occupied by conflicting emotions, that I hardly know what language to employ in writing.

"I have sad news to communicate. Still, perhaps it is not *news*, for you have doubtless already grieved over the same thing, having inferred it from the tone and spirit of my few hurried letters home. If so, you will not be shocked when I confess to you, that my life this winter has but poorly accorded with the professions I have made here and elsewhere. True, I have outwardly in many respects performed the duties of a Christian.

"I have constantly attended church, and usually the prayer-meetings, and have taken an active part in these. But closet religion and *secret prayer* have been too far neglected, and of course the killing consequences have ensued. My heart has been amazingly cold; lightness and frivolity, my besetting sins, as you know, have had the mastery, and my heart has seemed steeled to the emotions of true piety. I look back with mingled surprise and deep regret.

"But the past is past. I trust it is repented of;—nay, more, I trust it is forgiven. Still the question, What have I been doing? seems to come again and again with force enough to break my heart. Last night I conversed with a young man, with whom I had formed a very pleasant acquaintance: I confessed to him my feeling, and entreated his forgiveness for my levity, etc. Shall I tell you the reply? His heart seemed to break and flow forth. He confessed that he had sometimes been constrained almost to think that, if what I acted was the religion I professed, *he didn't want it!* This I know will pierce your heart, but oh! not so deeply as it already has mine. I never till that moment realized the guilt of *carelessness*. He forgave me fully, attributing all to the natural buoyancy of my disposition. That night bore to Heaven the joyful tidings of a repentant sinner, and my friend rejoices in the hope of sins forgiven.

"O pray much for me, that the work of grace may be deepened in my soul. O that I may have grace enough in my heart to overcome those *dangerous elements of character* which make my besetting sins. Shall I ever be a constant, consistent Christian?

"My heart is not alone in this work of repentance. There is a mighty work commenced here. The waters have been troubled for more than a week. . . . Christians are coming forth, a strong and numerous body. Last evening twenty manifested their anxiety for salvation, and begged the prayers of God's children. . . . .

"O mother, I wish you had been able this winter to write me such letters as in time past, urging so strongly the deep guilt of inconsistency. Why, O why is it, that my religion is not a constant religion? What security have I myself, or can I give to others, that in a few months I shall not relapse into the same apathy and worldliness? And a minister!—a minister at least in anticipation. How this aggravates my guilt! Shall I ever be fitted to occupy that awfully responsible station? . . . . . . Yet it has pleased God to hear prayer. I wish I could feel as thankful as I ought. A number of my dear scholars have been feeling deeply. Last night I was permitted to bow in prayer with two of them. We plead for mercy, and God, I trust, had mercy upon them. They are young men of sixteen and eighteen. Another found peace the same day, so that three of my scholars have entered the school of

Christ. Shall I not praise him? I cannot as I ought. I cannot be happy. My past inconsistencies seem to stare me in the face, and charge me with dreadful guilt. . . . . . My soul goes out after one and another, and longs to see them born of God. I have talked with some of the men in my district: my mouth seems filled with arguments and persuasions, and my heart burns to *reason* the matter, and to beseech men, in Christ's stead, to be reconciled to God. In a few days, you know, I shall enter on my nineteenth year. Is it not time to work more publicly for God? I have longed for the time when it shall be prudent.

"Your affectionate son," etc.

The next is from Rochester.

"University of Rochester, *April* 8.

"I closed school on Tuesday, 23d ult., the day after I completed my eighteenth year—closed it successfully and triumphantly, without the slightest mark of dissatisfaction or ill-will, but on the contrary, with manifest signs of regret on the part of my pupils and their friends.

"Williamson will always remain holy, consecrated ground to me. It was a hard and tearful separation, for I had some dear young friends bound to me by the closest ties of true Christian sympathy. I have been made glad by the conversion of some for whom I had agonized in prayer. Yet I rejoiced with trembling. I trembled for them, and I trembled for myself, lest on either side we should ever prove false to our religious vows" ———

The question may suggest itself with interest to the reader, to what extent was there real foundation for these laments and repentings? What degree of guilt actually, in the opinion of competent observers, attached to this vehement self-accuser?

Answer: None at all, as men commonly reckon their sins. So reply candid persons of whom inquiry has been made. He was free from any other faults than those arising from an extravagant gaiety.

Shall we say, then, that in this instance K.'s grief was excessive? Not as God reckons sin.

The remainder of the year had no incidents of importance. A few extracts from letters will serve to dot the passing months:

"*April* 17.

"My tendency to *levity* has done much to injure myself and others. I am trying to govern, in this respect and in others, my 'unruly member.' I wish I could have it said of me, for instance, as I have known it to be of some, 'he was *never known to speak evil of another*.' How much to be admired is that pure spirit of charity which 'thinketh no evil.' I think there is no one characteristic of the Christian more peculiar, and striking, and desirable. Pray for me, that I may not *idly wish* for these Christian graces, but strive for them by self-denial and earnest prayer."

The hungering and thirsting for *this* grace—of charity—was certainly satisfied in his case to a rare degree.

"He never spoke evil of others," has been the free testimony of a multitude of individuals respecting him. He that seeketh, findeth.

"SAME DATE.

"Our students, on parting, agreed to consecrate each twilight hour during the short vacation, now in progress, wherever they might be, to offer up at least a *silent* petition in behalf of the University—its meetings—its unconverted students. If this pledge be faithfully fulfilled, who can doubt that we shall receive a refreshing from the Lord? The little prayer-circle of our class, also, agreed each one to make some particular class-mate the subject of special prayer during the vacation.

"How little do we suspect how much God may be pleased to perform by us, when we are only willing to be His instruments."

"*June* 28, 1852.

"DEAR FATHER:

"I was fairly rejoiced by the receipt, and still more by the perusal of your last. Nothing can be dearer to me than the will of my earthly, save that of my Heavenly Father. I very often think of my dear mother's words to me, in anticipation of her departure and my bereavement: 'Why, K., how rich you are! a father on earth and a Father in Heaven!'

"I have been arranging for the coming long vacation. Not having money to spend in visiting, and knowing you would not wish me to be idle, I have offered myself, with the advice of friends, to the American Sunday

School Union, as a Sunday School Missionary, and have been accepted, although my field has not yet been assigned me.

"Yours," etc.

We quote from the last letter of the college year:

"ROCHESTER, *July* 6, 1852.

"DEAR FATHER:

"The business of the University is suspended; the badge of mourning is decreed; stillness and gloom are upon us. My own heart is sad, for *death* has been among us. For the first time he has entered our University; yes, and my own class; the name next to mine is struck from the list. *George J. Newell.* He died very unexpectedly. He was talented, pious, much beloved, promising much usefulness in the church; designing to enter the ministry. His loss is severely felt by us, and will be a terrible stroke to his parents and friends. They were in joyous anticipation, and may still be, if the telegram has not reached them, of seeing him at home next week. Poor fellow, he had talked much of going home, and meant to leave next Monday.

"*Why was it not your son?* I think with tears how my parents would feel to receive the telegraphic news that their son was dead—would be buried to-morrow! He was much stouter, stronger, and manlier than I am. I hope I, and we all, may take warning to work *now*.

"My Sunday-school field has been assigned me, that is, if I wish to labor in it. It lies at the base of Mount Agamenticus, if any one knows where that is. 'It cannot be lucrative,' says the Secretary of the Union in his letter to me, 'a region of great darkness! You must be able and willing to meet the rudest of our rough population, and labor amid scenes from which a missionary to Burmah might shrink!'

"Well, I shall at least learn some useful lessons for the future, and obtain some partial insight into the real nature of the *fight*.

"If I cannot earn money, I may do good, and doubtless shall get good. Pray for me."

CHAPTER XI.

AGAMENTICUS.

The vacation accordingly was occupied with Sunday-school and Missionary labors in the region round about that mountain, known—among those who know it—as Agamenticus. How can any just idea be communicated to the reader of the strangeness of that region! A district belonging nominally to civilization, but left on one side fifty years ago by the course of "progress," and, worse than fossilized, relapsed into semi-barbarism. Agamenticus is the name of a mountain upon the coast of Maine, just within the line where that State joins the limits of New Hampshire that reaches down to the sea. The traveller eastward from Boston, by the "Lower Route" enters Maine, passes through flourishing villages, views the rich city of Portland, perhaps advances into the well-cultivated and charming country that extends far to the North and East, or to the romantic wildernesses about Moosehead or Schoodie, and returns, totally unaware that on his very introduction to the State, he was borne along the edge of the wildest, most unique, and, to the curious, perhaps, the most interesting portion of its territory. It is a district resembling Cape Cod in some of its peculiarities, but not yet secularized by worldly cranberry growers and prying tourists. It is an old country, long settled. The farms, whose soil is substantial granite, were first tortured for their scanty products by, perhaps, the great-grandfathers of the present occupants. The houses, of unpainted wood, and "many of logs or rough boards," are black with age. Forests of dark, stunted pines extend unbroken for miles, and cover the uninviting lands with a gloomy thatch. Roads, which were only rocky lanes, climb the rough hills, and wind endlessly through mazes, bewildering only through their monotony. It is Agamenticus, the stern mountain, that controls the character of the region. Civilization under his shadow dies. Even if "the age" had not swept by, and left the people on their sea-washed cape, isolated from the stir and movement of men, still they could not have resisted the frown of Agamenticus. Lifting his three-headed peak to no great height, he yet domineers inexorably over all he looks upon, and impresses his own rudeness upon fields, dwellings, and dwellers alike. The race that flourishes along the secluded portions of the New England sea-coast, is indeed everywhere peculiar.

Of the character of these particular inhabitants it is sufficient now to say, that while they have many rough virtues, yet irreligion, gross ignorance, and superstition sadly prevail. "There is little interest in common schools, still less in Sabbath schools," writes K.; "while many oppose both." "They have living among them a set of 'preachers,' who are on a level with, or a little below the common people, who work their own farms, and go about preaching in the school-houses. Some of them are good men—*some are not.*" "I find some Lots in the Sodom—really good men; and once in a great while a whole-souled, warm-hearted, *interested* man." "This is a strange, dark region. The people know scarcely anything about religion, care less, and do nothing. For the most part, they are 'twice dead, plucked up by the roots.' They need a *great power* to raise them to the condition of an enlightened, Christian community." I find them hospitable enough."

Here, amid "scenes that might have discouraged a missionary to Burmah," K. labored for several weeks with enterprise and good success. "I entered the field under additional discouragements," he writes, "from the fact that the persons on whom I first depended for support, direction, and encouragement, advised me not to go, and presented some very plausible arguments. For a time I was sorely tried, and was on the point of surrendering the plan. Thus I was foolishly detained for some days. I then mustered all the grace and courage possible, reproached myself for my folly, and determined to go at once where the Am. S. S. Union had sent me with their eyes open, do what I could, and thus relieve myself from responsibility. I am glad enough that I took this independent course.

I doubt not, the Lord helping me, I can accomplish some good here. My confidence in God is firm—my heart sometimes light and sometimes heavy—my hopes great."

"Last Sunday I talked four times. Some of the people became quite stirred up, and asked me to come again and lecture; and some even followed me a mile or two to the next school-house (though they had already come as great a distance), to hear again, though I told them I could give no new story. 'Well,' said they, 'let's hear the old one again—don't want no better.' "

Aug. 17th he thus writes :—

"It is two weeks to-day since I came to this region, and notwithstanding the fears of some at the outset, I cannot help thinking that *good* has been accomplished. I have set on foot two Sunday-schools, each furnished with a $10 library, and disposed of $10 worth of books by private sale. I have given six addresses, besides attending several other meetings, have travelled ninety-two miles, visited hosts of families, etc., etc. I have succeeded to some degree in awakening an interest in the S. S., and I pray God that His good Spirit may nourish and bless the word sown, that it may bear fruit to the praise of His name.

"I hope by His grace to accomplish as much the fortnight ensuing, and by that time I shall be glad enough to return *home*. Yet I cannot leave this region without sadness and anxiety. I shall have time to touch only one corner of it. I cannot go on the sea-board side of the hill (York, Wells, Ogunquit, Cape Neddock, etc.), as I wished."

"SOUTH BERWICK, *Aug.* 21*st*, 1852.

"MY DEAR FATHER,

"Did any of you glance at Agamenticus, yesterday? I then found out, satisfactorily to myself, the *location* of this notorious place; for I climbed its rocky summit. The view is very extensive and varied: land, river, and sea; hill, valley, and mountains; fields, villages, and towns, are spread out in fine array.

"Agamenticus Woods, Witch-Trot, Tatnick, etc. etc. form a rough rocky country, indeed. The 'roads' are almost covered with rocks, often as big as a half-bushel, with now and then a huge ledge extending quite across from side to side. Sometimes in coming suddenly upon a 'road,' I have mistaken it for the stony bed of a mountain stream. Then, they are so full of twists and turns, that I scarce ever know where I am. Once, in attempting to go to a house three or four miles distant, I tramped no less than sixteen or seventeen miles.

"Though somewhat tired yesterday, after accomplishing Agamenticus, I came down to Bro. R——'s, in South Berwick, as he had earnestly requested me to be present at his *Inquiry meeting* in the evening. It was a precious season. Nineteen presented themselves to inquire, 'What must I do to be saved,' or to rejoice in their newly found Saviour.

"I feel, and have felt, that I am getting good this vacation; and I would fain hope, also, *doing* good. My mind is more than usually exercised on the importance of Christian activity, particularly in the sphere of the *ministry*. How much grace I need! The subject presents itself to me in almost a new light.

"Your kind letter was received an hour or two after

I mailed mine. It has been a *great* comfort to me, and given me new strength.

"I wish I could get another to-day, as I may not see a post-office again in some time. Thank mother for her little note. Much love to all."

"Your affectionate son,

"A. K. N."

A FEW EXTRACTS FROM A JOURNAL, KEPT DURING THIS TOUR.

"*August 5th.*

"Walked several miles. Found one woman who had not attended meeting, or read a word in the Bible for years. I offered to read her a chapter . . . . . read the fifth of Matthew. Soon the old lady dropped her work, then her eyes began to redden, then the spectacles came off, and the tears dropped. Tried to persuade her to attend church," etc.

"SUNDAY, *Aug. 5th.*

"Awoke this morning, feeling that I had a great work before me, and one for which I was in every way poorly prepared. Was enabled to depend on a higher power to aid me, and found much satisfaction in so doing. At 'Emery's Bridge' found a very pleasant S. S. under the superintendence of a young man of true piety and intelligence. He, with the assistance of only one or two others, organized the school. Spoke in several places. In the evening, went to the L— school-house: after reading and prayer, I felt just in the right mood for speaking; and knowing that if I accomplished anything among this people, it must be by hard labor; I strove to make some impression, and was not altogether unsuccessful. Before I got through, was hoarse and tired."

"*August* 11.

"Am spending this week in scouring the L—— district. Families mostly poor and ignorant. Found one grog-hole—gave them a little Temperance—got twenty-five cents from a rum-seller for a S. S. in his neighborhood. If Satan be divided against himself, how shall his kingdom stand?"

These labors were a providential test of Kingman's *endurance.* He stood the trial—gained experience and blessing. This was the beginning of an active interest he ever afterward maintained in Sabbath Schools.

From a letter written to him afterwards by Mr. Hoyt, agent of the Am. S. S. Union, the following extract is taken:

"BOSTON, *September* 13, 1852.

"MY DEAR BRO.

"On my return from Troy to-day I found your letter. . . . . You have labored in *heathen* soil for a month, and have succeeded far beyond my expectation. Nurtured by prayers of faith, I trust the seed thus scattered may yield fruit to the glory of Emmanuel. The missionary work thus done, though often of a cross-bearing nature, may perhaps be of some little service to the missionary himself. It is good for a man to bear the yoke in his youth, and if perchance it gall the pride of the flesh, still the fact itself is worth not a little to him whose life's work it shall be to preach the cross to others.

"Yours truly,

"H. HOYT."

CHAPTER XII.

Second Year.

The first week in September finds our missionary again a student, and glad to be once more in Rochester, where, however, he declares, "the world seems only half alive, extravagant reports having been circulated respecting the cholera, in consequence of which not more than half the students have returned."

Pecuniary troubles are harassing him again, the slender proceeds of the summer's toil having been immediately melted away by the expenses that met him on his return. He is even less willing to starve now than when in Suffield. "I could," he says, "if my nature would let me, become one of those pinching, scrivening, close, calculating, hard-fisted men, who stint themselves to *absolute* necessities, and make it a principle to beat down on everything they buy. I don't mean to disparage true economy, but I hate the 'haggling' way of some, who borrow books or go without; and besides establishing an unenviable reputation for meanness, reap not half the benefits of a college course? Well, I must hope for the best, and without doubt the best will come. I am, in one sense, independent; I need not starve, for I have youth, and health, and mind, and part of an education."

Again:

"I am just convalescent, after an attack of despondency, the most severe it was ever my lot to experience. It affected my physical, mental, spiritual, and every other organization. To be, or not to be!—that is the question. To mope along, always in debt, and poorer than poverty, unhappy, and disheartened; or to go only half through college—spending the best portion of each academic year in teaching; or to leave entirely, and return only when I have earned money enough to ensure a full and thorough course of education. These are questions which it is difficult to leave with Providence, and which I have foolishly and fruitlessly endeavored to decide for myself."

At last he writes:

"I confess I have borrowed much unnecessary trouble. I have at last given up the thought of teaching. . . . . . I have concluded that my duty is to stay, and I ask no more."

He adds: "I have much to reproach myself with; my ingratitude, unbelief, and neglect, are heavy burdens. I cannot be what I would—I would not be what I fear I might! May God have mercy upon me! . . . . I am surprised to see how little religion there is in the world. Are there few that be saved? Shall I be? If not, how great my condemnation! I sometimes doubt whether I am advancing at all, intellectually or spiritually." . . . .

But so seldom is it that he gives way to gloom, that this dark mood moves our smiles, from its strange contrast with his natural temper, even more than it excites our sympathies for the despondency more deeply penetrating, because unusual. *Hopefulness* is decidedly his characteristic, and his buoyancy of heart floats him easily over all shallows and reefs.

Respecting his pecuniary support in college, it is sufficient to say, that, taking all things into consideration—the cheerfulness that made difficulties slight, and his need of some discipline to faith—he passed through college easily: perplexed enough to keep him consciously dependent on Providence, and compelled to exert himself in earning money sufficiently to teach him the value of money, and educate self-reliance. His uncle, Mr. Kingman, assisted him most kindly and generously, and, at some late period in his course, he became a beneficiary of the Education Society. Aid came occasionally in other ways, too; often in some great exigency, and from wholly unexpected quarters. "It was a matter of remark in college," says one who was then a student, "how invariably Nott's wants, whenever they became urgent, were supplied—often from sources least anticipated. He used to say, 'I need this or that—I shall surely get it—it will come in some way;' and come it always would."

EXTRACTS FROM LETTERS.

——— "At our 'Lower Falls' Sunday-school station, the burden is suddenly thrown upon my own shoulders. My associates have all left but one, thinking their labors unappreciated, and unblessed. That *one* will not preach. For my part I could not resist convictions of duty to persevere. I thought that if we were willing to labor in encouragements, we certainly should be so in discouragements, since there was then so much more need of labor. Such difficulties affect me differently from many. They *drive* me to more zealous exertion. For the last two Sabbaths I have tried to preach there, and intend to follow it up. I believe the Spirit has influenced me to take this course, has aided me, yes, and blessed me. Several are already pricked in the heart, and manifest deep feeling. My effort has been to present the plainest subjects in the most direct way. . . . O pray for me that I may be endued with power from on high, and by a godly walk and conversation be an instrument of good."

"O how good—*how good* to have such early tokens of God's peculiar favor to me in my contemplated calling. It has done me good every way. I feel aroused, have something to labor for, something to pray for."

"*December* 8, 1852.

"It is all over—our dear H. M. has breathed his last, and been consigned to the ever open grave. His race was not without glory, but was quickly ended, and we mourn the loss of a second classmate. I loved him as a brother. . . . . A few months since he was converted

12

and baptized. . . . . His sickness was short and violent, and sudden in its termination. . . . Never, since darling Franky's death, have I shed so many tears, or thought myself so sorely wounded. Such events make me weary of living—I wish to die. Indeed, I have sometimes thought, before this, that my career might be brief. If I *should* die before you, mother, know that death cannot come unexpectedly to me. Often have I in imagination gone through the closing scene, and when called upon to do so in reality, it will be no new thing to me. How strange it is that we live! I used to think thus when Franky and Howard died, and often prayed with the impression that it would be my last prayer, and went to sleep thinking I never should awake; and when in the morning I was aroused in full health, I wondered and almost lamented. But life is earnest and active," etc.

——— "Last Saturday E. and I went on a mission to 'our parish.' We visited the families, etc. The effect was apparent next day in a larger school and audience. There is still much interest. They will have a church before long; then, if living, we intend to go somewhere else to rear a foundation on which other men may build. What immense responsibilities I have assumed! Why here I am, pretending to preach the gospel, visit families, and pour words of consolation into the ear of the afflicted. I am almost frightened sometimes to think of it, for I so poorly and superficially discharge these duties that I fear I abuse the trust and the office. My intentions are good, and yet mixed with so much that is impure!"

CHAPTER XIII.

SECOND YEAR CONTINUED—ALBION.

IN March and April of this year, there occurred a remarkable episode in his history, the events of which exercised both an immediate and a permanent influence upon his habits and character.

In the town of Albion, a beautiful village lying forty miles west of Rochester, on the railroad to Niagara Falls, lived at this time the Rev. Silas Ilsley, pastor of the Baptist church in A., who, from a former acquaintance with the father, Rev. H. G. Nott, now invited the friendship of his son, the young student at Rochester.

The following letter will now be understood:—

"ALBION, *March* 4, 1853.

"MY DEAR FATHER:

"Your first thought at seeing my date may be, that I am 'rusticating,' in the technical sense of the word; but not so bad as that, though perhaps I have so tried my tutor by my 'boyishness,' as long ago to have deserved it.

"I am with Mr. Ilsley, spending a week or two for reasons I will speedily unfold. . . .

"Last Friday I received a note from Mrs. I., stating

that they have a large society of ladies in their church, who 'wished the privilege of furnishing me with aid in the article of *clothing*, during my course.' . . . . I resolved to visit Mrs. I. on Saturday, intending to return Monday morning. . . . On Sunday Mr. I. would have nothing but that I must preach—the church wanted to hear me—and in the evening I tried to do so, from that solemn text, John v. 28. There had been for some days an unusual interest, and I had a full and solemn house. This was, you know, my *first sermon in a pulpit*, and I did not by any means satisfy myself, though I trust good was done.

"Mr. I. had arranged to hold meetings every afternoon and evening of the present week. A minister whom he had expected, was detained from coming, and as God was pouring out His Spirit, there seemed to me to be a call to stay. . . . I returned to Rochester, and made arrangements for a week's absence. Tuesday night I preached on the *Cost of Salvation*, as a *motive for securing it*. The church was nearly *full* of *young people*, and much feeling prevailed. Next day came the news of a ball to be held on Thursday night, a great temptation to the young who were serious. I tried to preach from Deut. iii. 18. I felt deeply, and God gave me unwonted strength. The house was filled, and we had a time of solemnity and power."

"*March* 11.

"I have not found a moment's time to complete my letter. . . . You will want to know what I am doing with myself, and what the Lord is doing with me and with this people.

"Thursday I spoke on *A Time to Mourn*. . . . Saturday was the regular covenant meeting. The large vestry was crowded full, and we had a blessed season. The next day was indeed 'the Lord's.' Five were baptized. I have spoken every evening this week except Monday. The church pray mightily for me, and the Lord accordingly blesses wonderfully. The house is *thronged* every night—even the *aisles*. My own soul is abundantly blessed. I have given two sermons to youth, from '*Show thyself a man*,' and, '*Save yourselves from this untoward generation*.' Last night I took up the excuses of the unawakened, from *Lord, I will follow Thee*, BUT——. To night, the excuses of the awakened; to-morrow night, the excuses for delaying.

"The Lord of Hosts is with us. You may think I am 'off on a tangent,' and unwisely, but I couldn't help it. I think it has done me *permanent good*, and I will return to college as soon as I can, much better fitted, I trust, to improve its privileges. . . .

"You will fear that I am becoming *intoxicated*; pray that I may not; but I never saw myself so little, or cared so little for externals, etc.

"The Lord is reviving His work in all this region. O for a like blessing with you.

"Pray much for 'the stripling'—'David and his sling' are in great requisitions in the good people's prayers.

"Your affectionate Son," etc.

The result was, that Kingman was persuaded to stay, with occasional flights to Rochester, for a period of *seven weeks*, preaching, with few exceptions, every evening. Part of the time was vacation; for the rest, leave of absence was procured from the Faculty, through the representations of brethren at A.

How large the draft upon the resources of a youth of hardly nineteen, may be understood by those who have made, or witnessed similar experiments. That he was sustained at all, is only explained by the fact of his remarkable mental activity, and rapidity of working, and by the earnestness of his heart, which forced his intellect along in an equal race. This, from himself is to be added:

"I have been surprised at the *elasticity of my mind.* Deep feeling and solemnity have immediately brought on their reaction of lightness, against which I have been obliged to guard, but without which I could not have kept up with such ease as I have."

We quote other brief extracts of interest.

"ALBION, *March* 22 (his birthday).

"I hardly know how to characterize the emotions of a youth just entering his twentieth year! Though I indulged in a hearty laugh at the first thought of the 22nd of March, yet I cannot say I feel particularly glad. I am beginning to be frightened, lest I should lose boyish prerogatives, to which I would cling for many a year yet.

"I feel surprised at myself—not at the extent of my capabilities! or the progress I have made! but at the way in which the Lord hath led me, and the goodness which crowns my days.

"The interest still continues here, with new cases of convictions and conversion each day. . . . Mr. I. has been full of the impression that God sent me here, and that I had a mission to perform, and could not go until it was accomplished.

"This may be so; but I feel now that every day I remain, and every sermon I preach, is injuring me in many ways. Next Monday I shall fly back to Rochester—dig into my books, and prepare for examination." . .

Speaking of certain temporary and slight annoyances, he says:

"I assure you I have not been slow to wish myself fifty years old! However, I congratulate myself that the faultfinders have been very rare, and obliged to strain at a gnat.

"As for my manner of life, I have had none: so far as the public knew, I have visited nowhere. As for my preaching, I was not at all molested. I regarded it only as complimentary that some should say I 'drew on my father's barrel' (strange idea they must have of my father!); or that, as I got rather excited in discoursing on 'And thou, Capernaum,' etc. etc., I should so move the indignation of some, who thought themselves at least 'almost Christians,' that they made loud complaint about their harsh usage, etc.

"But, oh! how have I wept tears of joy, as I have listened to the voices of one after another, who have spoken of this sermon, or that, as having awakened them, or set their anxious souls at rest!

"The church have given me the heartiest co-operation. It would do you good to hear them pray for your son. 'Good God! he's but a stripling! but Thou hast done great things by a stripling,' etc. Borne up by such prayers, one can hardly help preaching.

"On Sunday the right hand of fellowship was given to sixty individuals. You may judge of the impression made on my mind by such a scene, especially when I could not but know that God had made me instrumental in the salvation of many of these. I shall never forget that scene. It opened a new life to me. I learned to realize, as never before, the grand object of my ministry and my life. I see how I should make everything subservient to this—laboring with zeal and watching with care if by any means I may save some.

"By the way, speaking of *feelings*, I am a strange creature. You know I have always been able to raise *tears* at a rather slight emotion—I have not during all my preaching shed one! I could not . . . . . . I have sometimes been wrought up to a high pitch of nervous excitement—sometimes have felt *tenderly*, and just ready to gush out in tears—but *never a tear in preaching*. All my emotion has a very different effect upon me when I stand up to speak. It seems to throw itself *all* into my speaking. I have sometimes thought that I had not much feeling; but I have wept in preparing sermons, and by myself." . . .

"*April* 26.

"I do not know what to think of myself sometimes.

I do not know what God has meant by carrying me through the scenes just transpired. In one moment I am frightened at myself, thinking I never could do the like again, and condemn my foolhardiness. But I was gradually and unsuspectingly drawn into the work, and I am constrained to think it was of God and none else. The results prove the same, and I tremblingly praise the name of the Lord.

"About ninety have been baptized at Albion. You fear 'a sad reaction.' But there is no unusual cause for fear. The work has been almost a silent one. Very rarely has a meeting been continued beyond nine o'clock. No extravagances—no flights of transport—but the young, many after a long conflict indeed, giving themselves away to Christ. It may be that public professions have been made in some instances too early—this is about the only cause I have to fear.

"I preached my last sermon on Sabbath evening: 'He that saith he abideth in him, ought himself also so to walk as he walked.'—Physician heal thyself!—Every available spot was occupied, even to the entries.

"I have wished amidst all that I might gain a spiritual blessing to my own soul; that my principles might become more settled, and I become rooted and grounded in the faith. Rochester University is not the most fruitful soil for the Christian graces to grow in —it is *too rich*."

Mr. Ilsley sends the following notes: —

. . . . "When I first invited him to preach, he promptly refused, and urged many reasons for that decision. But I plead my extraordinary labors, etc., and at last prevailed. . . . . . . His first sermon was decidedly a success. The conviction was immediately impressed on many minds, that God had a work for him to do with us. . . . . .

"From his youthfulness (he was but eighteen) the curiosity of the whole community was aroused, and the sanctuary was always crowded. Some declared it impossible that his sermons could be original . . . but all were finally compelled to admit that his ability to preach and pray were from God. . . . His preaching from the first was brilliant, but then less pointed and doctrinal than it soon became. In preparing for the pulpit he had little to do with books. Prayer and the study of the Bible were his chief reliance." . . . .

Mrs. Ilsley also sends the following most interesting communication:

"The remembrance of that revival," she writes, "and of Kingman's labors, has ever been delightful. In a letter received from him just before the acceptance of his call to New York, he says, 'I shall ever look back to that time with the same interest as to the hour of my conversion, and as stamping my character as a minister of Christ.' He learned at that time, that it was the presentation of the *simple truths* of the Gospel, with strong faith and prayer, that drew down those influences of the Spirit that resulted in the salvation of souls. This explains his great success; for often did he say to me, 'if the church keep on praying for me as they do now, I shall never tire in preaching, and I shall always expect glorious results.' And he said that many times while preaching he would have more *thoughts* and *words* to express them, than he had time to utter during the hour allotted to preaching. Some of the sermons he preached at that time have been remarked upon often for the strength of argument and reasoning in them which, indeed, sometimes seemed more than human, and which would have been considered *great* from an old divine, but coming from a youth of eighteen, astonished the wise and learned among us. His youth attracted crowds to hear him, and many went away spiritually blessed. One hundred and twenty-five were added to the church as the fruit of that revival, of whom many ascribed their first religious impressions to words that fell from his lips, and will be stars in the crown of his rejoicing through all eternity. During that time he preached almost every evening, and attended the afternoon prayer-meeting, and enjoyed uninterrupted good health. The forenoon of every day was devoted to preparation for the evening work. He never took anything written with him into the pulpit but twice, and then a small card contained all. He rode horseback every morning, which exercise he enjoyed much. He was abstemious in diet, and took no other drink than cold water. He loved the Albion church and they loved him much, and contributed much to his personal comfort."

It may well be questioned whether this episodical proceeding was judicious and justifiable. Was it wise and safe, and a proper thing, for a young man in course of education, to absent himself from college, and, with untried powers, plunge head foremost into the work of an evangelist, and for six weeks give himself to public exhortation and preaching? Is a similar course to be recommended to other young men? Are students to be encouraged to seize the earliest opportunity of rushing before the public, and to seek in the pulpit, as well as the recitation-room, their school of preparation?

Decidedly not; the experiment in this case was doubtless hazardous. Only "success vindicated the attempt;" but disaster was imminent. The greater number of the so-called "boy-preachers," prematurely fledged, stoop quickly from their first ambitious and sun-aiming flight, and, exhausted and thenceforth stunted, remain ever afterwards waddlers on the earth instead of soaring eagles. In this instance, the hand of God was manifested, as was *proved alone by the results.*

There is every reason to believe that the following testimony is true. It is what Kingman writes after his return to Rochester:

"If the query had been soberly raised beforehand as to the propriety of my leaving college and going off to preach six weeks in a revival, I should have looked upon it not only as a dangerous experiment, but almost as an absurdity. I was led in a way that I knew not. And I do not think I have been injured. The large drafts that have been made upon my capital have showed me how poor my resources really are, and made me feel the necessity of laying a deep and broad foundation if I would build largely."

He adds :—Prof. —— called me to his house and had a friendly talk with me a few days since. He seemed fearful that I might *run away*, or take up with a partial course. I assured him that I had only been led to see more than ever the necessity for a thorough education; and that, so far from limiting mine, I would prefer rather to extend it beyond the ordinary bounds. He did not know—what he was very glad to discover —that I had a good and wise father to counsel me.

"I have done preaching for the present, except at my mission post."

There can be no doubt that this experience at Albion was of the greatest utility, in quickening his emotions, deepening his piety, and, as Mr. Ilsley has most truthfully remarked, *teaching him the most effective mode of preaching*. He formed his style in Albion.

This was, then, his third great lesson, in College: Williamson inculcated *deeper conscientiousness;* Agamenticus called out *endurance;* Albion taught the *art of preaching*.

One or two extracts close the records for this year.

The following letter to a convert of the Albion revival, Harding Ilsley, a son of the clergyman, gives a good example of the tenderness and tact with which Kingman drew to himself, and led always to the Saviour, the hearts of the young. The lad was only eleven years of age when baptized. The letter was written two or three years later:

"My Dear Harding:

"I am glad to hear that you still love to pray, and are still trying to live like a Christian. No doubt you sometimes find this hard; and so must every one, a man as well as a boy. I hope you still remain *firm*, and full of love to Jesus. I hope you are gentle, patient, obedient—always just as you think Christ would be if he were in your place. That is the way to live, the only way to be happy. Thus you can show to others the beauty of religion, and win them to Christ.

"I am afraid you get cold sometimes, and feel tired of praying, and do not see the use of it, and even almost wish you were not a Christian. Is it not so? Older Christians than you sometimes feel so, but such thoughts are very ungrateful and wicked. The devil puts them into our hearts, and if we let them stay there they will drive away all our religion. . . . . There is only one way in which you can get rid of such feelings. You must go right to Jesus, just as you went the first time, when you felt you were a sinner, and tell Him all about it, and beg Him to have mercy upon you.

"Don't be afraid of your playmates. You profess to be a Christian, and they will think all the more of you for acting like one. Remember you are like a soldier, who has enlisted. You must fight for the Lord, and never desert, for you have *enlisted for life*.

"Your friend," &c.

TO HIS FRIEND BROWN.

"—— I have thought, Theron, how aimless, and hence how useless would be our lives, were it not for the glorious gospel of our Lord Jesus Christ. I bless God that He has given me something worth living for; and particularly that He has been pleased by the foolishness of my preaching to save some. Why, just think of such a weak vagabond as myself being made the means of saving an immortal soul! Sometimes when I think of it, I am lost in wonder, love, and praise. Oh, what exalted, pure delight! I know of no satisfaction that will compare with that arising from the consciousness that God has blessed and honored me thus." . . .

At the end of the summer term of this year, K. hastened to his father's, expecting to obtain a school for two or three months in the neighborhood of K–port. This plan was unsuccessful, and, unable to occupy the vacation with recreation and visiting, he immediately turned his face towards Rochester again, and the fine villages surrounding; resolved, if still compelled to be an alien from home, that he would cling at least to the skirts of his adopted city. After some negotiation, he engaged to teach the *Union School in Pittsford, N. Y.*, six miles from Rochester, for three months.

This introduces us to the third year.

CHAPTER XIV.

THIRD YEAR—NEW YORK—PITTSFORD, ETC.

IN the course of the journey back to Rochester and Pittsford, Kingman made his first visit, of any account, to the city of New York. In company with a college friend from Brooklyn he gave three days to the exploration of the great metropolis, wandering where the whim led him, delighted with the novelties that met his eyes, and far from suspecting that these sights were soon to become as ordinary to him as the view of the bare rocks in the pastures about Kennebunkport. In the streets that he walked, the very stones were soon to become familiar with his frequent tread; and many of the houses that he passed carelessly by, were inhabited by those who were destined to be among his dearest friends. Perhaps he brushed by strangers, whom, under the controlling providence of God, he was to influence for ever.

Of what vast import are our lives, at every instant of their passing! How intimate and eternal may be the relations which bind us secretly to objects and persons that we are looking upon with the most unthinking indifference.

Remaining in New York one Sabbath, he was in possession of an "opportunity which he had long wished for, of hearing some of the distinguished preachers of the city." He sallied out, therefore, "with anticipations of a rich treat." His comments on the three sermons to which he listened, in different churches, are interesting as specimens of his criticism at that age. It is evident that he had a distinct standard of some sort, both of style and of orthodoxy.

"In the forenoon," he says, "I listened to the great Dr. ———. A long introduction, general and hackneyed, consumed half the time; the rest was filled up by common-place, loosely-jointed remarks, with considerable cant and many lazy attempts at eloquence. He made himself entirely at home, easy and careless. I should judge it was not one of his great efforts. In fact, one of the people informed me that the Dr. was not quite himself that morning, as he had the dyspepsia."

Kingman would have judged more leniently a few years later; though he continued always liable to be warped from true candor, by his unwarrantable deficiency of sympathy with dyspeptics.

"In the afternoon," he continues, "I mustered courage to go to the ——— Street Church, where I heard Dr. M——. This was a sound, close, forcible sermon, and pleased me much. The Dr. is called eccentric; he is peculiar, but certainly very earnest, simple, and often striking. His text was 'Whom we preach;' (1) All Christ; (2) To all; (3) In all places."

"In the evening I went to ——, and heard a very

young sermon from a very young man, which displeased me exceedingly. I did not learn his name; of course it was not the pastor. The professed object of the discourse was to demonstrate the doctrine that infants are saved. Now I fully believe the fact, but not his exposition of its ground. The preacher demanded the salvation of the infant, not on account of Christ's atonement, but from the sinless purity of the being. Besides, as to *imputation*, he had never been able to ascertain with any preciseness what that meant. 'His opportunities of conversation had not been limited, yet he had never discovered any one who seemed to know what was meant by 'imputed.' Ah! thought I, if I could take you to some poor sinner who glories in the cross of Christ and that alone; whose cry is

> "'Vile and full of sin *I* am,
> *Thou* art full of truth and grace;'

he could tell you what is meant by the 'imputed' righteousness of Christ, if not the imputed sin of Adam."

In Pittsford, Kingman gave himself with due devotedness to his temporary calling. He succeeded with the school, and by his sociability and manifest interest in people, gained many warm friends in the village. He treated his scholars with great familiarity, as he could hardly avoid doing, with his ready sympathy for young hearts. They knew him to be their friend, and indeed half suspected him of a disposition to fraternize with them even in those frolics that were most untimely.

Yet he had a fund of resoluteness and an interest in their progress that sufficed to preserve his dignity and the discipline of the school.

He contracted special friendships with a few, chiefly the smallest. "Little Mary B——," he writes, "is my constant companion. Before and at the close of school, at rest and at recess, she is always by my side," etc.

Here is an incident of school-life that gives him occasion for moralizing :—

"*September* 13.

"Here I am imprisoned in my school-room this pleasant afternoon, although it is past four o'clock, and the school has been dismissed. Besides me there are three others : one boy sweeping, another studying a neglected lesson, and the third waiting to be punished for the crime, oft-repeated, of truancy. . . . N.B.! The boy who was waiting to be punished has just taken flight out of the back-door into the street! . . . . Well, if the fellow is so insanely forgetful of the inevitable final consequences of his audacity, why let him go!—Alas! such is poor human nature—thoughtful only of the present moment, regardless of the future! A little present pain must be avoided, though at the expense of vastly more hereafter. How do men deceive themselves in trying to persuade their restless fears that all will be well—the avenging rod will not overtake *them*—some unseen way will be opened for their escape. What delusion!"

After the commencement of the college term he maintained a close connexion with Rochester—visiting the city at least once a week, generally on foot one way, performing his regular parts in the literary society, and keeping well along with his class in their studies.

The opportunities for religious labor were less abundant than in some of his places of sojourn; but he improved such as were offered.

"I have engaged in the Sabbath-school," he says, "assisting the superintendent, etc.; and I am going next Sabbath to take charge of a school three miles distant, held before morning service. It is at a place called Bushnell's Basin, where there are five or six hundred inhabitants and a good meeting-house, but no preaching. I have promised to preach there at five o'clock," etc.

He adds:—"I certainly enjoy more spiritual religion than I have at almost any other place or time. I take more delight in private communion with God through His word and by prayer than for a long time before. Sometimes I almost taste 'the blessedness I knew when first I saw the Lord.' . . . . I have made a vow: it is, that I will endeavor by the grace of God to be the means of converting at least *one soul* during my stay in Pittsford. The place needs, as much as Kennebunkport, a powerful work of grace. . . . . I strive to be watchful. I would not willingly be guilty of inconsistency, or hide my light."

"Last Sabbath," he writes again, "I preached at Bushnell's Basin. There is a sad waste there. There are no Christians at all in the village, so far as I can learn. There are a great many young persons, and an interesting Sabbath-school. This is sustained almost entirely by a family living at some distance, who are all active, benevolent, devoted, whole-souled Christians. It would do you good to see them come to church. Not content with his three-seated wagon, the man rigs up his hay cart with carpeted seats, and brings a load of twenty-five people. They call this honored vehicle 'The Baptist Church.' . . . . I had good attention, and promised to come again next Sabbath. They are surely sheep (or rather goats, I fear) without a shepherd, and if I can do a little good there I shall be glad indeed. They must have the word of life; and if no one else will give it them, and God grants me power and opportunity, I dare not withhold it."

He mentions an interesting excursion to Albion:—

" *Oct.* 1.

. . . . "After closing my school for the week, I could not resist the temptation to make a hurried trip to Albion, to see the brethren 'how they did.' It was a good and genuine work which God wrought there. Their meetings are continued with great interest, even the young converts' meeting being still sustained. Returning Saturday evening I met on the cars a young man whose face I recollected, though I did not know his name. He recognised me, and we immediately engaged in conversation. His heart was full of the great theme, and as he told me what he had been, and *now was*, my own heart overflowed with gratitude to God. . . . . As he closed his history he added: 'If it had not been for *you*, I might now be what I then was!' O how I bless God for that moment! one of the happiest in my life! Let me live to preach that glorious gospel which can work such wonders! Thank God for the privilege. What a wonder that He should entrust this treasure to earthen vessels." . . . .

To his friend Brown he writes from Pittsford:

"Now I suppose you have reached the goal, or rather one of the way-marks. You are an inmate of Yale. Let me be the first to shower down upon you from the full cup of friendship congratulations and the best wishes for your—success, shall I say?—your *preservation* suits me better. May Heaven preserve you from following the course of so many who enter college as pious students! God forbid that the evil influences that fill the atmosphere of Yale, should eat out your piety! How different a place it will be from Suffield." . . .

The following letter to his eldest sister on the occasion of her marriage, belongs here:

"Joy, joy to thee, dear C., Heaven's choicest blessings rest on you and yours!

"God knows how I love you, and how I ought to love you. No being, next to my dear parents, has had so much to do with moulding my mind and character, and forming my principles. When our dear mother died, I was left a wayward boy—most needing a mother's fostering care. What cruel, wicked deceptions I then practised upon my father! How many were the bad habits I gathered from bad companions, and how strong the influences to keep me from God and bring me under the sway of the evil one.

"Do you know what it was that *kept* me from many a sin, and made more moral and religious impressions upon my mind than any other cause—impressions which were never effaced? It was those *letters*, full of sisterly love and concern, that perseveringly followed one another till God was pleased to bless them. . . . . Would that I could repay the debt! But you labored for no earthly reward; and if we are ever so happy as to meet in Heaven as ransomed souls, surely you will ask no other joy, ... More than one hint of yours has been the means of implanting in my mind a settled principle. For instance, do you remember coming into my room once when I was writing a letter—a religious letter, on the Sabbath? . . . .

"We talked the matter over, and the result was that I put away the unfinished sheet. That was *one* result: another is this—that I have *never* since, in a single instance, written a letter of any kind upon that sacred day.

"O, when I sit down to think, as I have been forced to do for a few days, of you and your love; how the past rushes upon my mind, and such scenes as I have just described make me weep for sorrow and for joy. I remember when you fell into father's arms, with the exclamation, that you had found peace in Jesus; and from that time I remember nothing but devotion to the cause you then espoused. . . . . I remember all of the several greetings and partings which have marked the past few years, and in *all* bless God from my heart of hearts that He ever gave me such a sister. . . .

"Farewell—God bless you! I know that amid all the festivities, poor, humble absent *I* am not forgotten. —God orders all things right for us.—A brother's love to C.: may a Saviour's accompany it.

"Your loving, deeply loving,

"KINGMAN."

Returning to the University, about the first of Nov., he expresses the usual hopes and longings.

"I am much gratified to find a better state of religious feeling among the students. The prayer-meetings are well attended, and conducted with uncommon heartiness. There is some desire for a revival. O that we might be willing and fit to receive it!—I want to strive for more consistency and devotion." . . .

The last letter of '53 has the regretfulness that must commonly belong to reflections upon any considerable past period of our lives.

"*Dec.* 26, 1853.

"DEAR MOTHER:

. . . . "The term has ended, and in some respects it has been an unsatisfactory one. I have studied more severely than sometimes—yet not enough; and I fear that in religious feeling I have lost. The quiet of Pittsford was good for me. When I returned, I soon became so much engrossed in secular duties that I allowed my religious fervor partially to decay. How soon will love for prayer and pleasure in reading the Scriptures decline, when not regularly and frequently indulged! I sometimes tremble as I look forward to the world which I am so soon to enter, and think how poorly—very poorly I am preparing to accomplish any good in it.—The last week of another year is fast speeding away, and I am—I scarcely know what. By God's help I will strive to accomplish more." . . .

Such regrets, accompanied by longings and strivings, are among the surest indications of progress in grace: for there must be the pulling down of the old, in order to the upbuilding of the new. In another figure, hungering and thirsting are the conditions of our being satisfied; but we cannot hunger and thirst by willing it, but only from the sense of real inanition. We languish, we die, then we pant for the living God, and live. The depths of our natures deepen as their cravings are filled—and so we hunger again.

An extract of a similar nature with the preceding follows:

"*Jan.* 26.

"I feel bound to record my cause for gratitude to God, for the increased satisfaction I take in religion. Christ seems nearer to me, the Scriptures a blessed book, and prayer a sweet privilege.

"I have been asking myself the question, to what extent may a Christian study, or allow of conformity to the world? To some degree conformity seems to be demanded, for the sake of maintaining influence over worldly people. But alas! how much there is of accursed pride in my heart, prompting to too watchful an observance of the fashions and maxims of the world!

14

Persons talk of the greatness of the sacrifices which a missionary makes, in abandoning home and country; and I have endeavored to weigh them, and form some conception of them. But it seems to me that, with the mountain duty before me of leading a *true* Christian life—a life such as Christ led—a life of entire subjection of pride and renouncement of what the world calls good—I might fly to heathen soil as a *refuge.* There it would be comparatively easy, among a strange people, and unshackled by the miserable conventionalisms of our society, and with the direct object of one's mission constantly forced upon him, to know none save Jesus Christ and Him crucified. Oh, I do not know but we have reason to cry out with Doddridge, as we read the commands of our Saviour, 'Blessed Jesus! either these are not thy words, or we are not Christians!'"

This concerning the college:

"*Jan.* 31.

"While there is an apparently good state of religion among us, yet I find—as I become more closely acquainted with the feelings of individuals—that there is much to lament and to be alarmed at. There is impenetrable indifference and painful trifling on the part of some—such *trifling* as only students know how to be guilty of. Some professors of religion are very far away, and even losing the evidences of their conversion: and these serve as stumbling-blocks to others. Individual responsibility is merged in the general; and the poor, irreligious young men are lost sight of, and left to perish in the very midst of their appointed guardians. Of the one hundred and seventy-one students catalogued as belonging to the Seminary and University, about one hundred and fifty are professors of religion. What a moral power we ought to exert!"

"*Trifling*," of the character referred to—that is, levity in the treatment of religious subjects—that 'foolish jesting' which, beyond all other styles, is 'not convenient'—Kingman always regarded as a high crime, and never, through any inadvertence, even in his most frivolous moods, indulged. He felt that this, at least, would be to give the lie to his professions of belief in some things sacred, and of anxiety for the souls of sinners exposed to a real hell.

On a similar topic:

"*Feb.* 8.

"There is to me something mysterious in the present condition of our churches—their habitual worldliness and occasional 'revivals.' It is exceedingly painful to reflect that so many persons are 'added to the church,' only to bring misery upon themselves and reproach upon the name and cause of Christ. I cease to wonder so much as formerly at your" [his father's] "strict conservatism upon this point. . . . . .

"But there are churches that are in earnest. The 'Brick Church' of this city recently appointed a day of fasting and prayer. . . . . . All their business men—some of them our principal merchants—closed their stores, and flocked together till their room was filled to overflowing. An unconverted man, walking the street, says, 'Why, what are these stores closed for? What does it mean?' 'They're having a day of fasting and prayer.' 'Well, they seem to be in earnest about it. I guess they *mean to do something*.' This, which was overheard in the streets, seems to me to indicate what the world want. Of course, God blessed that church. They now hold meetings every afternoon and evening, with much interest.

"Three weeks from to-morrow," he adds, "comes the annual day of prayer for colleges. I hope the church at home will observe it, and offer prayer for this University, and especially for one of themselves who is here—six hundred miles from home and church—struggling with temptations strong and many. I believe that if all the churches that have representatives in this college, would unite with us in strong prayer on that day, we could not help receiving an overwhelming blessing."

These earnest desires for a revival in the college were fully answered, though not now. The sequel will show.

Here is more "regretting" and more "hungering":—

"*April* 17.

"My Dear Father:

"The short vacation is fast passing away, and I shall doubt whether to be glad or sorry to see the beginning of my last term in the junior year. I feel now just prepared to enter college, no more. . . . My thoughts are very busy of late; they often lead me in paths that I never before knew. . . . . O! that my first consecration had been lasting! How sad that I should ever have allowed Satan to get near, and silently weave about me chains from which it is so difficult to become free! The Holy Spirit is in my heart. I am conscious of His influence. I feel His constraining power. He leads me as far as I will go, and invites me farther. It is not hard, comparatively, to break off known *acts* of sin; nor do I think that pleasure, or ambition, or covetousness enslaves me. *But*, to have *all* subdued to the will of God, so that I shall do perfectly His will, as made known to me through the Spirit—it is *high*—I cannot attain unto it! . . . What is required of me? Clearly, to tell the tidings of salvation. . . . Then comes the practical question: What can I do *now*, while yet a student—this term—this vacation—to-day? . . . Ah! nothing else will suffice than an entire giving up of everything for Christ! This must come, or I shall never be a whole Christian. . . . 'Are there few that be saved?' O, pray that my will may be swallowed up in the will of God!"

This during the present year especially was the great burden of his desire—the attainment of conformity of his own will to God's.

Thus he says:—

"I possess now something of that pure enjoyment that springs from a consciousness of duty performed. How sweet it is! May I have more of it! Sometimes I think I am the very happiest man in the world. Of course it is not always so. But the future causes me little anxiety. I think and plan about it less than formerly. Could I but attain a state in which I should have no plans, no will of my own, then pride and selfishness should be so subdued that God could use me easily as He pleased; then I should have reached, I think, the height of my ambition. But what a height!"

Then follows an agreeable example of his lighter manner of writing:

"*April* 22.

"DEAR C——:

"Our delightful spring weather has been renewed with three-fold beauty. These mornings are glorious. When I wake up, I can with difficulty believe that I am in the midst of a populous city. The air is fresh and pure, the birds twitter and sing, and a thousand inspiring *cock-a-doodle-doos* fill the air with life and exulting praise. Of the latter sort of melody, there is every variety; from the chant of the old-fashioned, puritanic 'rooster,' to the shrill 'fantasia' of the 'Premium Shanghai' or new-fangled 'Brahma Pootra' of yesterday's importation; now some youthful adventurer makes his hesitating debut; and now ring out the clarion tones of an old hero, coming up like the shout of a victorious army, and filling you with sympathetic exultation. . . . And then to walk out, as I often do, along secluded and shady streets, before city life has awaked, and note the hush and whisperings.

"'There's not a spring or leaf but has its morning hymn,
Each bush and oak doth know the great I AM.'"

The long summer vacation was again at hand, in which money must again be earned. Although disappointed once, he still believed in the possibility of obtaining a school at home. Upon inquiry, he received encouragement that a remunerative class of private pupils might be gathered, and in order to give this plan a fair trial by attempting it early enough in the season, he left Rochester several weeks before the close of the term.

He received a painful mortification just before his departure. He made the first and only failure of his life in a public address. The occasion was the public meeting of a Literary Society. His part was an oration, and he had prepared himself with more than ordinary care. The theme selected was thus entitled—"Something more Wonderful than 'Progress;'" with a satirical reference to the common semi-philosophical cant among popular lecturers and others about "Progress." The "something more wonderful" was: First, that so small a portion of the race has at any one time—or at *any* time, attained a great height. Second, that the backward step has so often been taken; and third, that the highest attainments fall so far short of true ideals. It was handled with considerable originality, and much beauty of illustration. But when the oration came to be spoken, midway—when the attention of the audience was closely fixed—his memory inexcusably betrayed her trust to him, and absolutely refused to deliver up from her archives another sentence or word of the important address. Nothing was left for him but to retire prematurely from the platform, carrying the sympathies instead of the applause of the spectators. Unused to failure, he felt the shame belonging to the consciousness of crime; and heartily did he rejoice that his arrangements had already been perfected for leaving the city that night. He bade farewell to few, but morning found him far out of the reach of the roar of ridicule that his excited imagination conceived to be pursuing him. This incident impressed upon him permanently the value of *thorough preparation* for any performance. He never approximated to failure again, in any formal public address. But his mortification for a time was excessive. "Think of it!" he says in a letter, "stammering, blushing, looking this way and that, and at last disgracefully retreating! I can scarcely credit it now. I could not possibly have looked the faculty and students in the face next morning. But see what friends I have! A faithful few will maintain that it was only a rhetorical artifice, slightly overdone!"

At home he speedily discovered that there was nothing to do. To his notices that "school would be commenced so and so," a truly select number of pupils responded. The maximum was attained when fourteen one morning darkened the door. The same day he dismissed the fourteen, and closed his doors finally.

"Here I am now, at safe anchorage in this 'port,'" he says, "but wind-bound. I shall set sail with first fair breeze, but whither is all uncertainty. I am carrying on my studies, that is, Greek and Geology, and am enjoying an excellent opportunity, if I would but improve it, of searching my heart and growing in grace. I have been reading some books; Mrs. Mowatt's Autobiography, Potiphar Papers, Humboldt's Cosmos, Dr. Judson's Life, etc., with occasional Milton and Young. *That Life of Dr. J.* has brought the tears to my eyes again and again. It gives new and loftier ideas of life and its responsibilities, and fires the soul with a holy ambition, when it exhibits how much *one man* can suffer and do for the glory of our dear Saviour."

Restless in his comparative inactivity, and feeling the importance of obtaining some remunerative employment, he finally made arrangements to serve the Sunday School Union a second time, but in a new field, the region, namely, of Lewiston Falls, Maine.

CHAPTER XV.

SECOND MISSION TOUR—LEWISTON FALLS.

LEWISTON FALLS, or Lewiston, is a flourishing young manufacturing city in the heart of the western portion of the State of Maine. The country surrounding, though populous, was not at this time, it appears, whatever it is now, above the need of religious culture; as indeed what most Christianized district of our whole land is above such need?

This second S. S. expedition, if less adventurous and novel than the first, was even more laborious. The distances to be traversed were great, the heat excessive, and the people, at any time sufficiently indifferent, at that season were specially occupied with their farming operations.

Kingman established his head-quarters at the house of Rev. George Knox, the respected pastor of the Baptist Church at Lewiston Falls. From this place his letters are dated.

"L. F., *July* 8.

"Here I am at last, in fine spirits and with good prospects, enjoying the hospitalities of Bro. Knox, to whom I already feel dearly attached. I feel already acquainted in the town, and most pleasantly too. . . . . . Last evening occurred the weekly prayer-meeting. How fortunate that I came in time for it! We were knit together in love, and our hearts burned within us as we talked of our Saviour and the glory to be revealed.

"This morning I awoke after a sweet sleep, full of zeal for my work. Here I am, Lord, send me! Brother Knox took me this morning to B——, a Universalist neighborhood, and a considerable village. Until lately it was said, that here for two miles there was not a house where family prayer was offered! What a field for doing good! I should like to live there a few months. My district is of vast extent, larger than I shall pass over in my allotted time. I am full of sanguine hope. I have a little zeal. I am quite happy and willing to work. May it be for the Lord!"

Immediately he begins his journeyings, from hamlet to hamlet, and house to house, and soon finds discouragements enough.

"The most disagreeable thing," he says, "is, that I am compelled to beg my daily food, no place to lay my head; being constantly among strangers and uncertain whether I am welcome or not. It is a horrible life—as those who have not experienced anything of it cannot understand. But this dependence to which I am forced may certainly give exercise and growth to humility."

"Wednesday, July 12.—I went through the 'Thorn District' and scoured it pretty thoroughly; calling on twelve or fifteen families. I felt homesick among strangers, and longed for a cordial smile or friendly word. I found now and then a blessed old lady, whose pious talk cheered me, and made me thank God for this glorious religion.

"I became quite encouraged respecting a Sabbath-school. I visited the day-school, and talked to the scholars. At recess I sat down on the ground, and gathering them around me, showed them my books, and urged them to come to Sabbath School.

"Thursday I visited a district in Webster. Here are the remains of an old Baptist Church. It is nearly dead, alas! but has seen its days of prosperity and of glory. They sustain no meetings, and have had no preaching for a long time. I worked here, but found it very dismal. I do not see how it is possible to stir a stone. It is a hard, hard field."

He is astonished to find the region "overrun with Universalism," and especially that "Baptist Churches have joined hand in hand with it."

"I have already found *three* meeting houses owned in partnership by Baptists and Universalists. Of course, the houses are about all that is left of such Baptist Churches. They are dead—twice dead, plucked up by the roots.

"This labor," he adds, "is not of a kind to satisfy me. It is not sufficiently *direct*. It is a round-about way to convert people. I would rather go *right at them*. I love the Sunday School, but love *preaching* best. . . . I would like to live out here in W—— a year, as a *missionary*. There is only now and then a family in the whole town that pretends to go to meeting."

In a supplement to this letter, he rebukes his own want of faith.

"I take my pen to add a little. But before I *add* anything, I want to take back part of what I have already written. Pardon what I have said about my labors, inconveniences, and discouragements. I wrote it after a week of hard toil, and before I had waited to see the fruit; and I must admit, with some feeling of rebelliousness. I am in a different mood now. Yesterday's (the Sabbath's) labors and blessings wrought a change. I wish you could have followed me through the day, or that I had time to picture it. . . . I travelled a circuit of twenty miles, taking Brother W—— with me; attended one Sabbath School and taught a class; heard two sermons; held two meetings in school-houses; attended a Sunday School concert, and, altogether, spoke five times to different congregations. I never had a better day! I think some part of my discouragement last week was *animal*. I got so *tired* as to make me disheartened. I am willing now to labor right here, in this cause, and do all I can. Lord, what wilt thou have me to do, is *now*, I think, my sincere inquiry; and may He forgive my unbelief and rebelliousness."

August 14, he writes:

"Lewiston has been a melancholy place for a week or two. Cholera has been raging fearfully, having already swept away twenty or thirty from this little town. Its ravages are chiefly confined among the Irish, who are settled here in large numbers. But several

15

Americans have died. Yesterday the principal physician of the place fell a victim. Many have perished from sheer neglect; some all alone. Sickness was regarded as sure and speedy death, until Mr. Knox and some others organized a plan for taking the sick in charge, and discovered that many cases, viewed as desperate, were susceptible of cure by careful treatment. I have been exposed considerably, watching, etc. The suffering is painful to witness. Such work as this, added to my Sunday-school labors, has worn on me," etc.

The following final resumé of the summer's labors occurs:

"*Sept.* 14.

——"I completed, altogether, seven weeks' services. I walked nearly three hundred miles, delivered thirty or forty addresses; established five new schools; sold $150 worth of books, and earned nearly $60. I find, on looking back, that I enjoyed the vacation better than I had anticipated, and far more than I realized at the time. Lewiston has been a good home to me, and I shall always love its people. . . . Since closing my Sunday-school engagement, I have supplied Mr. Knox's pulpit two Sabbaths, and the Free St. Church in Portland the same number."

From Mr. Souther (agent of S. S. U.) to A. K. Nott.

"FRYEBURG, *Sept.* 15, '54.

"DEAR CHRISTIAN BROTHER:

"The very full and interesting report you were pleased to send me, of your Sunday-school missionary labors in our State, gives me great pleasure.

"I trust the impulse communicated to the good cause will be lasting, and most beneficial in all that region.

"And now, dear brother, allow me to hope that you will still and ever be a Sunday School missionary, and that you may, by your influence among the young brethren at Rochester, be able to stir many of them to engage in this blessed work.

"May I not hope to meet you another season, and with you and others like-minded, ready to aid in building up the waste places of our Zion in this noble Eastern State?

"Yours truly," etc.

Mr. Knox writes, Oct. 28, 1854:

"Those Sabbath Schools in which you were concerned in this vicinity, have all been prosperous, are well attended, and doing good."

Mr. Knox furnishes also this interesting account.

"In the month of July, 1854, answering the bell-call, I found at my door a youth apparently about sixteen years of age. His dress was neat but simple, and adapted to the season of the year. With a pleasant smile, which is still visible in my memory, he introduced himself as Bro. Nott—Kingman Nott; had been directed by Rev. Mr. S. to my house—had come to labor in this vicinity, in behalf of the American Sunday School Union. Thus commenced one of the most pleasant acquaintanceships I ever formed. It was Friday. In the evening he attended our prayer-meeting, and participated in its exercises.

"Such was the intelligence and manly character of his remarks, that I said to myself the boy is abundantly able to preach. But his extremely youthful appearance, made me doubt the propriety of suggesting this idea to him. A little further intercourse, however, so confirmed my good opinion of his intelligence, piety, and modesty, that I could hesitate no longer. And when, to my question, if he had ever preached, he modestly replied that "he had sometimes tried to talk a little in the pulpit," I was fully prepared to say he must preach for me the next Sabbath morning. Without embarrassment, or hesitation, or apology, he modestly assented. He had not sought to preach—he did not decline the opportunity.

"Sabbath morning came. He appeared in the pulpit, and announced as his text, the words of David to Solomon, 'Show thyself a man.'

"So deeply were we all interested, that we wished to hear words of wisdom again from those youthful lips. One venerable man 'could but think of the boy David with his shepherd's sling.' In the afternoon he preached again. My people remember that Sabbath as a day of special interest. He entered on his labors at once—organizing Sabbath Schools at important points in the rural districts of this, and adjacent towns; preaching frequently, and raising funds for Sunday School libraries. He sometimes met with opposition, and was assailed with coarse and abusive language. Some told him "He had better go home and go to school;" some told him "he was an idler, and ought to go to work," and others cursed him and his Sabbath Schools together.

"But in every such instance, he disarmed these people of their prejudice, and won their good will and their co-operation. Men, who had never before favored a Sunday School, or contributed a cent for a library, and who when first approached were hostile, now became favorable, and gave such assistance as was needful to procure suitable books. In some of these rural districts, the few Christian people residing there were greatly surprised at the success attending his efforts.

"It is not you," said one good woman, as tears of joy fell from her eyes, "it is not you, it is the Lord; no other power could make these people willing." And so it was the Lord, for the Lord was with our dear young brother. The work in which he was engaged, was *work* indeed; but every morning found him ready for labor. In those hot days of July and August, when our roads were deep with dust, he usually walked ten or twelve, and sometimes twenty miles. While pursuing his work, he would usually be invited into the farmers' houses to take his meals or to spend the night, and they always found him an agreeable guest.

"But, sometimes noon overtook him among an inhospitable people; and after the protracted toils of the day, he would return to my house in the dusk of the evening, having taken no refreshment since early morning. No hardships, however, daunted his courage, or soured his disposition. He retained always the same manly, Christian heart, and the same earnest, cheerful zeal to be about his Master's work.

"During his sojourn here, the cholera broke out in this town (Lewiston), and raged fatally among the Irish population. Some benevolent persons, convinced that the disease was so fatal among this people mainly from a want of proper nursing, especially by night, arranged a committee of relief, to take care of the sick;—a sort of night-guard, to be relieved at regular intervals. The disease itself, the people, and their habitations, presented no attractions. There was no romance in these nightly watchings. Your brother Kingman, learning of this arrangement, volunteered his assistance. Frequently after his long walks through the day, he took his position in the *shanties* of the Irish, and cheerfully performed whatever was in human power to do for the relief and comfort of the unfortunate sufferers. He also found opportunity to visit them in the daytime.

" 'Who is this young man?' said the chairman of our Board of Selectmen, to me one day. 'He is very unobtrusive; but there is scarcely one of our own townsmen who manifests more interest, or labors more efficiently for these sufferers, than this young stranger.' It was a true testimony. Indeed, he was always finding opportunities to do good, and availed himself of these opportunities without hesitation. Whatever his hand found to do, he did it with his might. There was never any ostentatious display on his part, but whatever he took hold of you saw at once that he thought it *worth* attending to, and should not be deferred till to-morrow. He spent eight or nine weeks in this vicinity that season, during which time he organized and superintended Sunday Schools in the towns of Lewiston, Auburn, and Webster;—preaching, also, in all these towns with great acceptance, and, we trust, with lasting good results.

"Geo. Knox."

CHAPTER XVI.

FOURTH YEAR—LETTERS.

THIS year is barren of incident, but rich in the illustrations of a growing religious experience.

Thursday, Nov. 29th, he writes:

"My thoughts have been directed heavenward of late in a special manner, by some sermons from Dr. Robinson. His discourse last Sabbath evening, on the 'inheritance incorruptible and undefiled,' especially made a deep impression on my mind. The bare thought that I may soon be in Heaven, a few years more and all the glories of the upper world may be mine! How it lifts one up! how mean do all earthly things appear! How good, too, do all the providences of God seem even though afflictive, when I remember that He lays upon me no more than is absolutely necessary to make Heaven secure! What earthly blessings do I possess, that I would have God spare at the expense of my Heaven? What do I desire that I would purchase with my hope of heaven? These thoughts have been with me this week, strengthening me to the resistance of temptation, and making me willing to run in obedience to the voice of the Spirit in my heart. These holy thoughts—how precious! *One* of them can shed more rapture on the soul than all the world's attractions. Thanks for such messengers from Heaven!"

He continues :—

"Your heart, I presume, with mine, has been made glad by the good news from dear ——. What a boon! how good, how faithful is the Lord our God! 'Of them that thou gavest me, not one is lost!' I feel that I have a new impetus in my Christian course. Holiness and Heaven! Let these be my watchwords, and the goal of my wishes and my efforts. All else is vanity.

"So Samuel C—— is gone! another warning. Cut down just at the threshold of usefulness and happiness, his flock shepherdless, his bride a widow—his account for ever sealed. I saw him last August all health and cheerfulness. Surely I *must* be weaned from earth!"

EXTRACTS.

"There is so much work to be done, that the days, weeks, and months slip by while I am collecting my thoughts and *intending*. I see already work for a dozen lifetimes. Would that I might fill *one* profitably! This term half gone—college almost done—life done soon at the farthest—and *nothing* done!"

"I had a pleasant school yesterday at our Lower Falls Mission Station—which *was*—but has now grown to the dignity of the 'North State St. Church.'

"The new house is neat, pretty, and convenient.

"I have an interesting Bible-class there, most of the members of which have become converted since our labors began. I do not know but the school could live without aid from the University, but I have become so much attached to the field that I cannot easily abandon it."

"I do think there is *not a mortal on earth more favored than I!* God give me grace! Do not pray, dear father, that I may have more blessings. I have already more than I dare account for. Pray that I may have a heart to improve God's gracious gifts," etc.

"If there is anything which father's example and instruction have taught me, for which I am truly thankful, it is these two doctrines—*the Holy Spirit and Providence.*"

"S—— has the right of it. I believe if we are only willing to try, we can walk just as well by faith as by sight. There is a saying of Dr. R——'s, which will always stick by me: 'The man who walks by faith, feels that he is treading always on something solid as a pavement.'"

The following letter was written to a friend who had just been recovered from a state of alarming religious declension:

"UNIVERSITY OF R., *Nov.* 18.

"MY DEAR ——:

"I feel that the bond of union between us is stronger than ever. I confess—what you must have been conscious of—that although we have been drawing together for two or three years, as we became more intimately acquainted, yet there has been a certain indefinable *something* that has kept our hearts from flowing entirely into *one*. While my own inconsistencies of character have cut me off from exerting the influence I should, still I have felt that you were not what you knew you ought to be, and what I hoped you would be. Alas! we have not been of much aid to each other in cultivating religious feeling! I say it for myself as much as for you. . . . .

"You say that you had been growing *harder* all the while, etc. I thought otherwise. I do not think this is an entirely new, *fresh* movement on your part. . . . . I have been hoping for, longing for, and expecting this happy day. Though your letter made my heart swell with affection to you, and gratitude to our dear Lord, yet I was not startled nor surprised. I thought it must come. I knew you could not rest—that you must ere long take some decisive step; and I could not believe that in spite of your dear parents' prayers, and all the holy influences affecting you, you *could* plunge into deeper sin, or take refuge in skepticism. God is gracious, and He will yet do greater things for us. Let us have faith to come boldly to the throne. . . . .

"I do not allow myself to plan much for the future; but I have long thought, and especially of late, how happy you and I could be in studying theology together. Oh, could we, side by side, enter the ranks, and fight and fall together! If it is not hoping too much—if it is wise and best—I do pray that God may grant me this boon. . . . .

"Yours," etc.

They came to be "in the ranks" together; but he fell first!

TO R———.

"*Nov.* 1854.

"How much we owe to our home influences, and especially to the faultless Christian example and instructions of our revered father! I have felt of late that I have never *begun* to appreciate his excellence, nor the gratitude due to him and to the God who gave him to us, and has so long spared him. Ah—has *spared* him? and how much longer will this be? I have tried of late to look forward to his death—for it must come sooner or later—and if possible familiarize myself with the terrible loss, that I may be strengthened to bear it, when it shall come. I believe we ought never to allow ourselves to be *taken by surprise* by any of the dispensations of Providence.—Yet it may be that I shall be summoned *first*. For *that* event, too, I would live in constant readiness."

In the short holiday vacation this year he visited his brother, then teaching in a town fifty miles east of Rochester. One day, in the early part of this visit, his brother, returning from school about sundown, found him standing in a pensive attitude, and with the traces of tears upon his face, by a window which overlooked a large portion of the little town. "R——," said he, turning to his brother, and pointing to the little huddle of houses in sight, "this is a small village: I have been thinking how easily we might go to every house and carry Christ. I do not know but I must; will you?"

The next morning the impression of duty had deepened into a conviction. It was Saturday—there was a half holiday—and the two engaged to attempt in the afternoon a visitation of the whole village. R—— visited one house, drew a long breath, and went home. Kingman went through with the whole of his allotted portion, and talked faithfully with every man, woman, and child whose attention he could secure. It was no easy task; it cost a struggle; he was a stranger, and in appearance a mere lad, and his reception at some houses, while civil, was cool enough to show that the errand was thought an impertinence. This is a fair instance of the certainty with which persuasions of duty prevailed over selfish inclinations, in the regulation of his conduct.

The entry made on this occasion in his little pocket memorandum book is significant:—

"*Dec.* 29, 1854.

. . . "*The Spirit—do this!*—I tried to get rid of it, but couldn't. Made several calls, left tracts, and prayed. Talked with young C——."

He preached, at this and a subsequent visit, several times in this village. One sermon, in which he was entirely carried beyond himself by the force of his emotions, was long remembered for its great power. It was known as the "Jonah Sermon"—from Jonah i. 6: "The World's Appeal to the Sleeping Church."

LETTER WRITTEN AFTER HIS RETURN.

"UNIVERSITY OF ROCHESTER, *Jan.* 6, 1855.

"DEAR R——:

"I can never forget that visit. What a happy season it was! I never loved you so dearly before, as then when our hearts glowed with love of a common Saviour.

"Well, we are of one heart and one mind, and have everything to spur us on. And we are assured that we shall come off conquerors and more than conquerors. Death itself shall yield at last, and lo, when this corruptible—oh, how corruptible! shall have put on incorruption, and this mortal, immortality, then shall be brought to pass the saying, etc. What a splendid passage! Let us live for Heaven! Pray, pray, pray, and daily remember me.

"I have been wishing I might pray without ceasing. I think I at least begin to see what it means. How good it is to feel that you *love* to pray; where prayer is a delight, and you are unwilling to stop, and when you have stopped, you wish to pray again; when your desires come flocking in too fast to find expression, and instead of straining to make out a prayer, you feel that you cannot begin to tell your praise or enumerate your wants! etc., etc.

"Yours," etc.

At this time his desires for *immediate usefulness* became absorbing.

"Everything seems to turn with me now," he says, "to the point of *personal labor* with the unconverted." "Yet," he adds, "I do not obey without a struggle, I often hold long debates with conscience."

He continues:

"*Pride* and Christ are contending for the mastery in my soul. Yes, I am ashamed to say, I am too proud to do my duty. I am willing to toil, but afraid to be abased. Satan holds me with bands of iron. Last week I thought I had broken from them; but though I did get one hand free, I find myself again a slave. Still, I have had a *taste of liberty*. I have found there is a stronger than the strong man armed. O that I had such a state of heart, as always to obey instantly the voice of the Spirit! As it is, I shuffle, I argue, I plead to be excused, get almost angry, and when the point is pressed, *rebel*. It frightens me to think of it! I see plainly that I must triumph over this, or give up my religion. O how happy, could I be always passive in my Father's hand; if, rather, I always hastened actively like a little child, to do His will. Souls would be converted, I am sure."

A letter a few days later shows in how far he has triumphed.

"*February* 4.

"DEAR R——:

"I have just called on two classmates, a duty I have had before me for some time. I had an interesting conversation with them, though not half so earnest and faithful as it should have been. One I have great hopes of. I have talked with him before, and always found him theoretically sound, free from cavil, and apparently interested. He is of a godly family, and you and I ought to have faith in the prayers of godly parents. . . . I have talked with a few other students. . . . But this is all! I am ashamed of my negligence, rather of my rebellion. Still God has not forsaken me, and I am firm in my purposes. *I am resolved to converse this term upon personal religion with every unconverted student in college,* if my life is spared. It is surely high time for me to awake out of sleep. But what is this? There are only twenty or twenty-five irreligious students; I ought to have talked with most of them a score of times already. The occasional, reluctant performance of a duty, to turn aside the goadings of conscience. O how far is it from the consistent and constant labor of a Christian life! Yet how good is a single duty—performed! What satisfaction—what assurance it yields! 'If ye love me, keep my commandments.' '*Lord, I have obeyed Thee, and therefore I know that I love Thee.*' When I wish to nerve myself for any duty, I love to read that seventeenth chapter of John. There could be nothing more inspiriting.

"Yours," etc.

"*February* 24.

"DEAR L——:

"Just one week ago to-night was set apart for the delightful task of answering your excellent letter, and just one week ago to-night there came upon your unfortunate brother that mingled cold and fever, sickness and stupidity, which has blotted out just one week of his whole existence. By the way, have you had, the family 'influenza?' I am curious to know; for if not, you are an alien, and alone destitute of the genuine family sympathy which characterizes our stock. I took the sickness filially, forthwith upon the reception of a letter from mother. R—— the same; and it remains to be known whether or not you are awake to the true nature of your filial and sisterly obligations. . . . We had a good day upon the occasion of our annual Fast for Colleges. An excellent sermon, and a large and animated social meeting. . . . I have been endeavoring this term to make my religion more constant and all pervading. Daily study of the Scriptures and daily secret prayer have been especially precious to me. I have taken more pains than ever before to remember my friends in prayer. At the twilight hour I love to go over, one by one, the names of those I am especially bound to remember, and invoke for them immediate blessings. I have been surprised to find how each day brings with it some new claimant for my petitions.

"O L——, consecration to God is the all-essential thing. We may despair of satisfying ourselves with learning, but we may thirst for righteousness and be filled. Let us strive to help each other, etc.

"Yours," etc.

"*February* 28.

"I have not enjoyed so much as usual of spiritual zeal and comfort for a week or two, plainly traceable to neglect of duty, and consequent grieving of the Holy Spirit. It surprises me to find how dependent I am, physically and spiritually, on perfect *regularity.* A single departure from the routine often sets the whole machinery out of gear," etc.

CHAPTER XVII.

Fourth Year—Ideas of Preaching.

"*March 7th*, 1855.

"Dear Father:

—— "I have been listening to (X). Most of his sentiments, I think, are noble, but he ridicules the ministry in a way calculated, one would think, to do more harm than good! Is our age, indeed, tending to too great reverence for the ambassadors of God? What I have seen seems to show the contrary, to an alarming extent: and such churches as (X).'s, backed up by practice, will soon destroy the few remains of respect for the clergy, that yet lurk, perchance, in the breasts of a few New England bred men!

"Is it so, that one man.'*happens*' to take on him the cure of souls, another of bodies, another of laws, etc., and that there is no real difference in these callings? So says (X), and so say young men, who in a few months will have assumed all the duties of the—*profession!* (I may not say 'sacred') and with such exalted ideas of the peculiar and holy nature of their calling.

"Well, ambition has been making some loud calls. After witnessing such an admiring tribute paid to a man (as was paid to X.), pride says, 'I can do it—I know I can—I feel conscious of the power.' But grace tells me, 'Not by might, nor by power, but by my Spirit.' Earthly honors, wealth, and pleasures, fade, of course, before the glory of my mission; but more than this: I have come to the conclusion that I had rather be the means, in God's hand, of *converting one soul*, than of rectifying the politics of a nation, reforming scores of drunkards, and liberating hundreds of slaves—if this were all—and correcting any or all of the 'abuses of the day.' I would rather have the power of prevailing with God, than the strength of the mightiest logician, or the sway of the most eloquent orator. Such, I am confident, are the honest feelings of my heart. So much, therefore, for my ambition. It has never run away with me yet. Ah! but I am still afraid of it." . . . .

His strong conception of the sacredness of the holy calling is well evinced by the following account which he in one place gives of a certain occasional sermon, to which he happened to be a listener.

TO HIS FATHER.

—— "Well, I went to church—the house crowded full—a military company present in full uniform. The preacher, taking one of those highly poetical passages in the Song of Solomon, descriptive of Christ, treated us first to an elaborate justification of war; then discussed the excellence of variety, e. g. in a Thanksgiving dinner; and finished by dilating upon the importance of a sound platform politically, but with not a word about one morally or religiously. Not a single allusion—the remotest—was made to Christ, or indeed to religion in any way. Is this a church of God, I asked myself. Is this man a minister of Christ, an ambassador from the court of Heaven? Am I hearing the *gospel*—a *sermon?* One could not avoid the conviction, for it was thrust upon all, that the chief object of thought to the speaker was—his dinner! Repeated allusions were made to it—allusions which caused most to smile, but some to hang their heads for shame.

"It had been but a few moments, I had waited in vain for any gospel or any *point*, and as, at the close, I bowed my head in prayer, I had no faith that God would hear, for I felt that His house had been desecrated, and his word profaned. The splendid cornets of the military band led hundreds of voices in the glorious doxology, but I fear there was little breathing of heartfelt praise. I have said more than I intended, perhaps more than I ought; but I felt disturbed, grieved, and indignant. . . . . .

"Well, I cry out to my God, spare me, spare *me!* Suppose I become a minister—say of 'high standing,' what does it mean? To preach, week after week, to a fashionable congregation, who shall admire, and go away 'pleased,' making flippant remarks about the 'eloquent sermon?' I could not endure it! I would rather lift up my voice like a trumpet, and sound an *alarm.* Or, I would rather be a monk. Yet, think of it! I, your son, may degenerate to all this! Nothing but the great grace of God can prevent. This *cursed love of applause*, what shall overcome it? One thing I am determined upon: I *will not* try to preach to please men. I believe men *like* preaching altogether too well. One would think it no longer true that the carnal mind is enmity against God. Or else the bitter medicine is so sugared, that men do not taste it. Here am I, with I know not what great commission from my Father, with the footsteps of my Master before me, and the crown of glory in full view, loitering, plucking earthly flowers, living at this dying rate, as if this earth were heaven, and the present moment eternity! Pray that I may be raised up, have new grace, be made holy, and used as an instrument for great good. . . . .

"Your affectionate son," etc.

At another time he writes that he has been holding a discussion with some friends "on the subject of preaching for money," and in connexion gives the following incident and reflections:

TO HIS FATHER.

"*April* 24.

"I went away on Sunday to preach. Somebody, who knew I was terribly pinched, says, 'I'm glad you're going, Nott; you'll get ten dollars at that place.' I said nothing, cared little. Result—one dollar and twenty-five cents out of pocket!

"You would laugh heartily to hear the experiences of some of us among the benevolent churches. One student, who has been through college, and partly through theology, on his private property, told me yesterday that he had come within nine dollars of the end of it, and feared he must leave. 'Why don't you preach your way along?' I said. 'I tried that most of last term,' he replied, 'and the total results were two dollars out of pocket, and an upset in the stage-coach!'

"Well, well, I don't know what I am saying. I laugh to see them take it so seriously. The worst of it is, that a mercenary spirit is liable to be generated. Even the Gospel comes to be a matter of barter. A levity in the treatment of religious themes is encouraged, so extravagant, that it would be ludicrous if it were not shocking."

It seems this was not altogether understood; and in the next he explains more emphatically.

"*May* 1*st.*

"I am a little afraid that my last letter gave you a wrong impression. I certainly agree most heartily with what you say. I hate and despise the spirit which makes the Gospel a mere matter of trade. They will *sell* it for so much! I have always said here, and have tried to carry out the principle, that I would not allow any connexion whatever to be established between my preaching and *money*.

"I am the Lord's; I will preach when and where my master sends me, and look to him for the reward. Sorrows, cares, disappointments may be the fruits; even I myself may be a castaway. But no! I thank God for His great and precious *promises!*"

This is one side of the question, the side personal to the minister. Kingman held sound views. He would have reproved covetousness in a people, in as severe terms as a mercenary spirit in a preacher. "Take neither scrip nor staff," but "The laborer is worthy of his hire."

How it happened that correct conceptions of the nature, design, responsibility, and worth of preaching lay so clear and immutable in Kingman's mind, may be comprehended once for all from the perusal of the following letter from his father. Kingman had enquired respecting his future course, whether it were better to commence theological studies immediately after graduating, or after the lapse of a year or two. The reply is of wider scope than the question.

"KENNEBUNKPORT, *May 14th*, 1855.

"MY DEAR SON:

"With regard to your future course, after leaving college, I have but one thing to say. With the ministry in view—by all means, if it is at all possible, keep yourself right down to close study for it. This rather than school-teaching. Few, after teaching, go back to theological studies. This I say, on the supposition that pecuniary affairs can be arranged.

"It is true, God calls variously into the ministry. He is not tied to a Theological Seminary. Yet, in an ordinary way, and especially when the young are called to the work, the completest education and training are indicated as wisest. What you have up to this time gained are mere shreds of varied knowledge, that will be blown away when you are tasked to effort. You want now to dig for hid treasures. You may remember that Dr. Payson, when seriously contemplating the ministry, shutting himself up for some time to meditation, prayer, and the Bible—the only book. In theological training, you want, first of all, this deep spirituality of mind attained. You want to get filled up with God's truth, spiritually discerned. Study Theology in this way. Be thorough in this way. Thus you will prepare yourself to do more than please the people—to build up Zion. The want of this very thing is the occasion of the barrenness,—the *newspaper* standard of some of the modern ministry. Don't go out a dressed young man, to make a show in the ministry; don't ever preach else than the marrow of the Gospel, with the Holy Ghost sent from Heaven. But you cannot rise higher than *what you are.* A pint will be a pint. A butterfly will disport itself as such. A vain young man, and superficial, with a mere spattering upon him of secular knowledge, can only exhibit himself as he is. People are discerning, common people especially. And if not so, God knows the heart, and will only bless in a way whereby He may be glorified.

"With this substratum of preparation, you then want Hebrew, Sacred Logic, Sacred History, Study of Doctrines, Exegesis, etc.

"I cannot help you with money . . . What can you do for yourself? Can you arrange to preach some? Can you be aided through charity in part? Can you live on a loan in part? Would all or any of such ways be practicable? I do not know how to advise you at all, until I hear again, etc., etc.

"Home well, as usual.

"With much love,

"H. G. NOTT."

We add, at the risk, perhaps, of tediousness, a letter from Kingman to Theron Brown, in which he urges that friend to devote himself to the work of preaching. It is inserted here in the hope that its arguments may be availing in still other quarters than the original.

"U. of R., *May 29th*, 1855.

"My Dear Brown:

. . . . "I think if we could but remember to what we are destined, we should not stoop to join in the vanities of worldlings. We should consent to be in the world only as *missionaries.* Our aims would be entirely apart from theirs. We are of heavenly birth, and ought to move in a higher, purer ether than this polluted atmosphere. But we seem to catch the poisonous breath, and are intoxicated by it.

"I feel it, so do you. It stunts every plant of grace. We become all on fire with worldly and selfish—think of that!—*selfish* ambition! We labor intensely for *our own glory*, and, alas, for our *Master's shame.* Do you know anything about *self-denial?* That is the question I have asked myself of late. I do not mean the denial of one passion for the gratification of a stronger, but of *all* for love to Christ. . . . .

"I hope that God has designed not only to place you among the redeemed in glory, but to make you shine as a *star* in the firmament, as one having turned many to righteousness. Of course you are making and *will* make it the object of your life *to save souls*—your own and those of other men. Doubtless you have often asked yourself the question, how with your gifts and circumstances, you may best accomplish this object. Perhaps, also, as you are now nearing the close of your college course, and must soon choose your profession, you sometimes feel that the question ought to be settled.

" When I have thought over the alarming deficiency of ministers, and the urgent cry for help, that comes up from every quarter, and then remember that you, my earliest friend, with your Christian profession, your talents and opportunities, are not yet consecrated to the special work, I cannot rest until I have at least unburdened my own heart. Think of 4000 Baptist churches in the United States alone without pastors; think of the sad state of our present mission fields, and of the new fields that are *waiting* for occupants; and then remember that the supply coming from our seminaries, etc., is not even sufficient to fill the places of those who are annually removed by death!

" I do not know but you are already fully persuaded to preach the gospel. Of course it is a matter between your own soul and God alone, with which your friends have little to do. *I* will say no more, then, for fear of saying too much; but oh, how I should delight to welcome you as a fellow-workman by my side! There is no side work, no *indirect* way of promulgating the truth, which can compare with the direct *preaching* of it. This is a *luxury*. I have never enjoyed anything else in the world so much as this. The truth seems more precious as one proclaims it to others," etc.

CHAPTER XVIII.

FOURTH YEAR CONTINUED—GRADUAATION.

EXTRACTS.

"*February* 28.

"I SHALL rejoice when the time comes for me to devote myself entirely to the study of religious truth. Yet the qualifications for such an occupation, I am well aware, are Spiritual rather than intellectual. How great the danger of departing from the simplicity of Christ, and the teachings of the Spirit, to be led away by the wisdom of men!

"For some reason I find my own tendencies decidedly conservative with respect to doctrine. I have a love for the old-fashioned truths, which in many quarters are so fast becoming ridiculous. Providence, Election, and similar doctrines, I incline to accept in their fullest sense, and cling to with jealous love. Still, I feel cautious, on account of my ignorance."

"*March 7th.*

"*Prevailing with God!* that has been occupying my attention for a few weeks past. It flashed upon me from some remark thrown out on our Fast Day, and I saw at once that it was something of which I was almost wholly ignorant. O if I but had that power! what could I not do? Without it, utterly vain my acquirements, futile my labors. There's something worthy the ambition of a man, yes, of a Christian."

"*March* 21.

"DEAR MOTHER:

"My eyes have been filled with tears to-night, and my heart with wonder and gratitude. 'The Lord will *perfect* that which concerneth me.' Why, mother, I shall rival Dr. Stillwell, or even the raven-fed Elijah. Your letter brought with it one from L. B. S., inclosing five dollars, which had been sent me by Miss ——, the lady who, as you will recollect, gave me the same amount last summer. This evening's mail brings a letter from my good, kind friend, Mrs. Ilsley, inclosing six dollars, 'from a few sisters in their little church, to purchase any books, or pay any little bill that may be troubling you.' So to-night I have paid ten dollars, on my term and board-bill, and I feel quite lightened.

"And so it is, notwithstanding all my unworthiness. I neglect God, but he does not neglect me. He is teaching me lessons of trust and faith every day. Pray that I may have full grace to be humble. One of our students prayed in meeting a few evenings since, 'Lord, if we need to be humbled, make us willing to do things that will humble us.' I find enough of these.

"Well, mother, one more event. This is Wednesday night, March 21, 1855. To-morrow makes me twenty-one! May I put off the old man with his deeds, and put on the new man Christ Jesus. To-morrow must be a day of reflection, resolution, and prayer. Good night."

"*April* 5.

"DEAR C——:

"It is vacation; what is that to me but aggravation? Most of the students have departed; a few cadaverous beings assist me in maintaining the honor of our Alma Mater, in this her hour of desolation.

"I began this day with a walk, at five o'clock. These mild, sunny spring days, how delightful! All nature seemed rejoicing. The golden sun was just lifting his head, still half muffled in a nightcap of clouds, to listen to the salutatory of the robins—yes, real, live, singing robins! Then I spent an hour or two in the reading and study of the Scriptures;—the history of the Prodigal Son. I felt, I thought, willing like him to return to my Father's house, and acknowledge all my sins."

"After breakfast my room-mate and I played ball for an hour, between ourselves for exercise: then I sat on the stoop, in the sunshine, reading Aristotle till dinner. This afternoon we have been in the President's library, and have borne away a huge pile of volumes for our vacation reading. So go the days, and so they will go for the next fortnight. Do pity me in my loneliness, and send me letters."

The end of the college course was now at hand. The last recitation was had:

"*June* 9.

"There, dear mother, it is all over! I have attended my last recitation and my last lecture, and Dr. Anderson has spoken his few parting words. . . . I would like to be at home this afternoon and upon the holy morrow; and yet I find myself instinctively clinging to this dear place as though I never could leave it. I dread the time when I shall finally say good-bye to Rochester. The associations of every student here, and especially of one constituted like me, must always be peculiar, because they are not confined to the college, but extend to the city and its society. I may leave R. and not return for a generation, and yet even then, I shall not have to search the College Records for mementoes of my life here. I shall be remembered and known by some at least of its warm-hearted people and in a few of its hospitable homes.

"My course has been peculiarly happy. From the ordinary jealousies and petty strifes of college life I have been mercifully kept free. I have not had an enemy, that I know of.

"If I had money I would now go home, where I might stop and think a little; and write my oration, with your inspiration, and under father's eye, and declaim it to the roaring sea. But this, of course, is not to be thought of. . . .

"Yours," etc.

"*June* 15.

"My Dear R——:

"No sense of honor, in particular, requires me to write to-day. Nothing prompts me but the pure brotherly affection with which,

"I subscribe myself,

"Yours, till death,

"Kingman."

———"What a splendid chance that was for a signature! I could not lose it, though I am not ready to stop. . . .

———"Well, I am through college! I feel profound

gratitude to the wonderful providence that has led me blindfold through all the way, and brought me safely to the close. I am *through*, and by God's grace my character and my religion are still preserved. . . . We had our last recitation. Dr. A—— made a few feeling remarks. . . . . I got out of the room, ran down cellar—and cried. Came home and wrote to mother—and cried. Pshaw!

"Yours,

"K."

His graduation was not without honors. "I cannot become satisfied with a subject for my Commencement oration," he wrote a little before. "I am at a hard, dry one now. 'The Impossibility of Atheism,' *i.e.*, to prove that an atheist is a philosophical impossibility—never did, never can exist." This was his theme, and it was handled in anything but a hard and dry manner. Many literary gentlemen who were strangers to him, were greatly impressed with the indications of power, both in the matter of the oration, its style, and the eloquent delivery, made interested inquiries concerning the speaker, and freely predicted his future eminence. Many of these sought him out, and heartily tendered their congratulations. "You must have given great pains to the study of elocution," said a distinguished professor of Rhetoric. "Hardly ever an hour, sir," was the reply. His excellence in these respects was the gift of nature.

of prizes for the "Senior Essay." Kingman had not intended to compete. He had, however, given the subject ("The Ancient and the Modern Idea of a State"), careful examination, defined his own views, and gathered some rough material, which he had then flung aside. A day or two before the time fixed for the presentation of the essays, Nott was summoned before the President.

"I posted off to his room—he shut the door and began. 'I have just incidentally learned that you have not written on the essay,' —'I have not, sir.' He seemed to feel much disappointed, if not hurt. Cannot you go home and write something this afternoon? I would not promise—but went straight home, and *at it.* Before breakfast next morning I had the essay written and copied, and handed it in—the first one. Of course I do not expect anything in the matter of a prize. This was only for the President's personal gratification. I feared he might fancy I did not feel well towards him."

The feat itself would have been nothing, if the work had not been well done; but it was performed in a style to win the admiration of the Committee of Award, and when the circumstances of the composition became known to them, to move their astonishment. Only one prize had been offered. This was properly awarded to a more elaborate composition by another writer. But, to Kingman's complete surprise, he heard on Commencement Day the announcement that a second prize had been assigned to him.

CHAPTER XIX.

Dover.

It had been arranged that Kingman should enter upon his theological studies without delay, and there now intervened only the usual summer vacation of eight weeks. This was occupied with preaching and pastoral duty with the Baptist church in Dover, N. H.

That church was then without a pastor, and in a languishing condition. Kingman had, at first, to contend with an additional disadvantage. He was young, and wore an unprofessional garb. Appearing on the scene in a light coat and broad-brimmed straw hat, and with a remarkably fresh cheek and innocent eye, with none of the pale hues of study, of that peculiar solemnity of look that might be deemed appropriate to the ministerial profession, it is not surprising that high anticipations were not at once entertained by the people who saw him for the first time. His first sermon, indeed, set anxiety at rest; his voice and manner carried their own persuasion in the very reading of the hymns.

But even then, his objects were not immediately comprehended. He had come with the understanding that he was to *labor with the church* for a certain space.

His conception of the operations to be included under this general head, was essentially a different one from theirs. They expected in him a "supply;" by-and-by they hoped for a pastor, and, finally, a better state of things in the church. He intended *work*, by himself and by the church, and a better state of things *now*.

These explanations are introduced to make way for the letters that follow, which read like the unfolding scenes of a drama.

"DOVER, N. H., *Aug. 6th*, 1855.

"MY DEAR MOTHER,

"I should have written to you this morning, had I not then been determined to return home. I have had some curious experience since I came here. Luckily for me I am so constituted as to look on the bright side of life, otherwise, instead of writing this letter, I should be bringing water for your tea.

"But to begin at the beginning, I had a very pleasant ride. . . . . . . I found my way to Mr. ——'s house. He had been to the depot to meet me, but did not find me. How strange that he should not have *known* that I was his minister! He is a very pleasing, social, and intelligent man, and I have a very agreeable home in his family. . . . .

"Sunday came, a beautiful airy day. I was quite dispirited to find a very small congregation sprinkled over a neat, comfortable church. My words seemed to me to fall heavily on cold auditors. In the afternoon, there was a large increase in the audience. At six o'clock, a very good missionary concert. . . . . . On the whole, I felt quite encouraged by the day's exercises, and by what I learned of the state of things.

"I really began to feel quite enthusiastic for my work, and eager to *move* in some direction. I began to revolve various plans, and concluded to begin with the Sunday School, to preach at once upon the subject, and get them to increase their library and the number of scholars. Then I was going to establish an evening service for the Sabbath, and try to get in the *unconverted young*, of whom there are so many here. This, I thought, would be *one* step in advance. Still, I felt the necessity of moving very cautiously, and yet what I did *must be done quickly*. But these fine plans were quite disconcerted by the cool inquiries, 'When do you leave?' 'Do you go to-morrow?" 'Are you going to spend the week with us?' etc. I did not know what to say. I did make bold to tell them that I thought I might spend the week in Dover. Of course I could not form any plans for *advance*, unless they expected me to be with them. So the conclusion that I come to is, that in Dover '*laboring*' means preaching twice Sundays. My vacation will be frittered away, with no good to myself or others. I prayed again and again for wisdom, for direction, and for grace. Oh, such a field as there is here! There is nothing in the way for this church to move forward and do a great work! No other church is doing anything. I shall not come home at present, if I can help it. To-morrow, I am going to sermon-writing, and in the afternoon to making calls. Pray for me" . . . .

"DOVER, N. H., *Aug.* 13, 1855.

"DEAR FATHER:

"I really did not know I had written so discouragingly; I am sorry I did so. I now see that my trouble was the result of inexperience and impatience. None of the people here, I suppose, expected me to become a fixture among them for six weeks; but now that they see there is no remedy, they are rapidly becoming reconciled to the idea.—True, the church is in a low state, but the only distressing circumstance to me was, that I could see no way to get at work among them, as I wanted to do, right off.

"But I assure you matters now wear a different face. My only question now is to improve the means I have at hand. The Lord has opened door after door in His good time. . . . . I have called this week on a dozen or more families, talking and praying with them. Our Wednesday evening meeting was highly encouraging. . . . . Sabbath evening I had the privilege of preaching to an audience by far the largest yet, and though consisting mostly of young persons, with a fair sprinkling of rowdies, yet very attentive. I have not enjoyed preaching so much for a long time. It was a true Albion season. . . . I have begun a series of improvements in the Sabbath School—which is now very small. . . . . I have planned a busy week, yet there is not one of these duties which I do not anticipate with pleasure; and the pressure of the whole makes me elastic and happy. I never enjoy myself so much as when brim full of business. . . . . I have been making calls again. This experience is valuable, I assure you. I am acquiring quite a bold face and ready tongue in talking with all sorts of persons face to face upon the salvation of their souls. It was hard at first, but I am learning to love it. . . . I believe if the church would pray we might see the conversion of sinners. I cannot bear to stay without seeing an advance here. There is an advance already.

"So if I was *down* last week, you see I am as far *up* now. I know you will charge me to keep *humble*, and I need that you should. Yet every time I preach I feel more strongly my own utter weakness, and the weakness of every *human* instrumentality, except as attended by God's power. I feel the need of great wisdom. I have been led to pray for it, and God seems, thus far, to have conducted me in just the best way.—Continue to pray for

"Your affct. Son," etc.

The next news that came, was the tidings of his sickness. He was overworked, and down with fever. One of his friends from home hastened to him, in some trepidation. But determination brought him up, and the very next Sabbath he preached all day. This served as a tonic.

"I grew better and stronger all day long," he writes. "I could have preached half the night, in fact I did—to myself. It seemed almost miraculous, as if in direct answer to prayer." This was always his grand panacea—to preach!

"How delightful a Sabbath it was," he continues: "my cup was running over. Such nearness in prayer, such views of Christ, such sweet dependence on Him, such tenderness of heart and anxiety for sinners! When in the morning I read the first hymn,—these beautiful lines

"'I would not sigh for worldly joy,
Or to increase my worldly good,
Nor future days nor powers employ
To spread a sounding name abroad.

"''Tis to my Saviour I would live,
To him who for my ransom died;
Nor could all worldly honor give
Such bliss as crowns me at his side.'

"I could not conceal my emotion; for the words seemed transferred from the page to my own heart; they became my own thoughts." He continues: "I have appointed an inquiry meeting. Three persons came to see me the first evening. Others, I am confident, would converse if I went to them. How can I keep still? Yet the doctor tells me I must have perfect rest; and I am compelled to give up the week."

Finally:

"DOVER, *Sept.* 5, 1855.

"DEAR FATHER:

"A field white to the harvest, and no one to reap it! The thought has continually distressed me for many days, as I have beheld with wonder and anxiety the workings of God among us. The Holy Spirit waits for us to receive Him in a bountiful blessing."

Then an account of many inquirers; and then he continues:

"I never so understood my weakness. If one would know how weak is man, let him undertake the work of a God! Let him try to open blind eyes, and enlighten understandings darkened by sin. . . . Yet I have had such a dawning of faith as I experienced in my conversion, and never since. I plead the sacrifice of Christ; I trust the promise of God; I place *these souls* where I have rested my own. A holy calm fills my soul. . . .

"Thus has a day of temptation and anxiety been succeeded by the firmest faith and glorying in God. This experience of a few hours I would not give for worlds. It repays all my labors in Dover. It is enough —my vacation is well spent. . . . And now I renounce my wicked unbelief, which has been my curse. Now, as I leave this field, I repose this Church, this little band of inquirers—these unconverted souls, all in the hands of Infinite Love, with a sweet assurance that God will care for them, and as well without me as with me. . . . I understand some things now better than before. I have the key to your sleepless nights; your constant care; your agonizing prayers. I wonder that ministers live so long as they do. It has seemed to me that five years would suffice for this spark of life to exhaust itself, in such a sphere as this. How it may be in the future, I know not. I may get hardened to it; but I cannot see how I could spend a long life in Dover except by miracle. And yet the reason why I could not; the reason why ministers have suffered so much, and killed themselves so soon, seems to me to be *unbelief*. Unbelief is the disease; and their epitaph might be, 'Died of unbelief.' This is the secret of corroding care. If we had faith constantly in living exercise, could we not labor without *care?* Pray that God may consecrate me to His glory. Hoping to see you to-morrow.

"Yours," etc.

CHAPTER XX.

THEOLOGICAL SEMINARY.

NOTT returned to Rochester well prepared for the peculiar studies in which he was now to engage. The "substratum of preparation," spoken of so earnestly by his father, the spiritual apprehension and experience of truths, had been already acquired in a far more than ordinary degree. He came to the investigation of theological problems with the solutions already written in his own experience, and requiring only to be adequately expressed in formulas. "Know ye not this parable? how then will ye know all parables?" The spiritual insight which interprets one, may solve all mysteries. But this is not "innate"—except in the "new man," by spiritual birth.

The two years in the Seminary were of incalculable advantage to Kingman. He grew in grace, in manly traits, and in intellectual grasp, with astonishing rapidity. Each year had its peculiar array of providential means of culture, both in grace and knowledge.

Kingman failed to discover that disastrous incompatibility, of which students are so frequently in the habit of complaining, between the constant application of the mind to *thought*, even on topics of religion, and the maintenance of a good spiritual frame. "The most gratifying thing," he says, in one of his early letters, "is this, that the nature of these studies and the manner of conducting our daily exercises are such as to have an immediate bearing on my future work, and *directly tend to keep the mind in a devotional frame.* When all my studies are of the Bible and the Church, and when at the close of the day's labors we all meet together, classes and instructors, and read, sing, and pray, each day seems a Sabbath; work is sacred, and drudgery is elevated to devotion." Yet how many lament a steady declining of spiritual power, as an unavoidable concomitant of growth in mental.

He was more industrious now than ever before. He was in exuberant health, "perfectly overflowing with vim," he declares, and constantly in high spirits. He more easily now, than when he was younger, diverted his energies into the channel of mental labor. He strove to become systematic and regular, always a difficult feat for him. "I am making myself the most regular methodical individual to be found," he says. "I rise every morning at five, jump into a tub, attend morning prayer meeting, and study the Bible till breakfast, attend to my theological studies till eleven," etc., etc. He gave much time to the careful study of the Scriptures, comparing the Hebrew, or Greek, with German, French, and Latin, in the manner described by President Anderson. It was in his first year in theology, too, that he reviewed his mathematics and read Plato. Besides this, he instructed a private pupil in Greek and Latin, bestowing upon him regularly an hour or two each day. He professed great interest in the Hebrew. Yet, he declares, giving a true account of his disposition, " I shall never be able to metamorphose myself into a book-worm. My nature cries out rebelliously at the gentlest insinuation of the thought. I never shall know much, and what I do acquire will mostly be gathered by experience and mingling with nature and with men." He had always an eye to the practical. He prized facts, as he did money, as means of power over men to their good.

The first year in the seminary was especially favored with tokens of God's graciousness to him and around him, in revivals of His work. Kingman had "three great prayers;" he often speaks of them. They were for a revival in Rochester, a revival in Kennebunkport, and a revival in Dover. On this theme he dwells unintermittingly. Each of these prayers was this year answered, beyond the full extent of the request, and in a manner extremely significant and encouraging to a spirit of prayer.

As to Rochester, he was oftentimes in an agony of desire. He had come through college and no revival! In the senior year he had visited every unconverted student, many more than once, and there was no fruit! He was hastening to the time when he should bid farewell to each loved scene in R., and yet no outpourings of God's spirit to sanctify his recollections! He could not endure the thought. He craved it as a great boon from his Heavenly Father, that he might be permitted, in his day, to see a revival of religion in the University.

Not only his prayers, but his *practical efforts* were redoubled.

He endeavored to preserve unimpared his influence in the college. He kept up old acquaintanceships and sought new. He made a point of attending the meetings of the Literary Society, of which he had been a member, took part in their debates, and for a considerable time was a regular contributor to the society paper. The popularity thus maintained he endeavored to turn to holy account. He was the moving spirit in establishing circles of prayer, in which undergraduates chiefly were gathered. He sought out students in their rooms, and conversed and prayed with them. And it was remarkable that he expressed the most confident assurance of a coming work of God: "It will come—it *will* come," repeated he again and again. "I well remember this," was the recent remark of one who was in college at that time,—"not only his activity and hopefulness, but his extraordinary positiveness." This, which would have been presumption without a corresponding inclination to work, was simply inspired faith.

In order to show, in the present instance, how "faith wrought with his works," and was thus "made perfect," a series of extracts is subjoined, taken from several successive letters. It will be seen that they advance to a climax.

"*Sept.* 19.

"Our dearly beloved institution has never yet been blessed with a revival. How sad it would be for me to leave Rochester as it now is! I do not believe I shall be compelled to do so."

"*Sept.* 26.

"A little band meets at my room at half-past six every morning to pray. We have had delightful seasons of prayer. We are going to pray for a revival. Do you think we shall see it? There are more than 'two or three'—there are *five* of us. *Prepare yourself for good news.*"

"*Oct.* 8.

"There is a better state of things with us spiritually. We are all very low, it is true; stiff, cold, and hard; but there is a little lighting up, I think. I am not without strong hopes of a revival. How delightful! how it would endear to me each scene of each companion! how it would bless the world by consecrating the talent here collected! We have now, besides our regular Sunday and Wednesday meetings, six daily circles of prayer, in different rooms, at the same hour—from six o'clock to half-past six in the morning. We commenced with one and it has spread to these. It is wonderful what a blessing this praying gives to the day!"

"*Oct.* 10.

"I am still clinging to my belief in a revival about to come. There is, there must be a blessing in store for us, and I think we shall pray it down. I already rejoice—exult. It will come—it *will.* God save me from flinging away my faith. . . . . I still feel my rich experience in Dover. I am a different man for it. I know something of faith, and prevalence in prayer."

"*Oct.* 15.

"Our number of daily praying-circles has increased to *eight*—developing a power of prayer which *must* prove effective. God will bless us, despite our coldness, and give us a revival, in spite of ten thousand opposing influences."

"*Oct.* 17.

"We still pray. But most of us are either too indolent or too engrossed in worldly affairs to attend properly to the care of our own souls or to the rescue of others. And the devil does not sleep meanwhile, and already he has in preparation a host of active, evil influences. The more of life I have to look back upon, the more narrow seems my escape from utter ruin, and the greater my indebtedness to sovereign grace.

"I have seldom taken more delight in the ordinances of worship than I do now. I live in hope, and try to live in faith. Soon, soon enough, the full work of God will be upon me. God spur me on to the hottest of the fight, and when I fall, take me to receive the crown."

"*Nov.* 8*th.*

"My dear Father:

"It has come—*It has come!* The blessing is upon us, just as we were giving ourselves over to discouragement and unbelief. Last Monday night saw the admission of a soul into the Kingdom of God! It was a solemn hour: we two were alone with God, and in the dark. The struggle was intense. It seemed as though an evil spirit were wreaking its last vengeance before being cast out. It ended:—all was surrendered to the conquering Jesus, and he vouchsafed such peace as he alone can give. It was a very clear case; the transformation was complete, and the very point of transition was plain. I felt most deeply that here was the omnipotence of God, working in its own wondrous way.—O what a night that was! I found him a sinner, and left him a brother in Christ. . . . .

"Last evening, after meeting I was called to see and pray for a young man of the Sophomore Class, whom I found in great disturbance of mind. Others, too, are thoughtful; and unless Christians *determined* to do *nothing*, and by unbelief or presumption drive away the Spirit, I do believe God will work greater things for us. . . . .

"God has come to the help of my faith just in time. I had begun to be almost frightened at having said so much here, and in my letters, about a revival, while all around were ready to say, 'Where are the signs of his appearing?' Then I was becoming so distracted by my studies and daily work, that I began almost to excuse myself from going to labor among my fellow students, and now feel that wherever my master most requires my services, there I shall be found.

"Yours," etc.

So much for the beginning of the work. Other conversions soon took place, and in the winter the interest in college received fresh impetus from a powerful revival that sprang up in the city.

Still another answer to his prayers is immediately recorded.

"God is cheering my heart with good tidings from my dear people in *Dover*. The spirit is among them, so that they are greatly encouraged. Now if I could only hear of a revival in Kennebunkport," he adds, "then my *three great prayers* would all be answered. I can *almost* believe that it will be so. I believe much the more, now that you hold meetings to pray for that special object."

This third prayer was to be answered later. He continues, encouraging his faith by recalling his still fresh experience.

"I told you of my experience relative to *prevailing prayer* during the summer. I came here, fully possessed with the thought, and I ventured to talk it out. We began to pray—as feeble in numbers as you are, at first—resolved that we would *continue* to pray until the answer came. *Now* what a lesson God has taught me! It was not presumption! While we were praying and doubting in our rooms here, how little we knew what was going on around us. In another room a party of young men, all irreligious, were together, talking—and about what?—about Religion. One of them, moved by an unaccountable but irresistible impulse, started to his feet, stood before them and said, 'Well boys, for my part, I wish I were a Christian!'

"I hope you count me among your number at your Monday evening meetings in Kennebunkport. If my prayers can avail aught, by faith in Christ, be sure they are with you.

"'Though sundered far, by faith we meet
Around one common mercy-seat.'"

A little later:—"Good news still from *Dover*. They are about settling a pastor. Their meetings are increasing in interest, and awakenings and conversions occur. I wait to hear great things.—We are holding on here as well as we can. We pray still," etc.

While the history pauses, there is time for a few miscellaneous letters and extracts.

TO C——D.

"I was especially gratified by the religious tone of your letter. My conscience has made me commit more than one epistle to the stove instead of the post-office, because there was no religion in it."

"Beware of being cheated out of present usefulness by fancying what you would do if God had placed you thus and thus, or by dreaming of exploits in the future. I believe that God places every child of His just where he can render the most effective service. May He give you grace," etc.

TO R——.

"I believe we are alike in one particular. Each is remarkably dependent on constant contact and association with the means of grace and with Christian labor, to enable us to keep up spiritual life. Hence I doubt very much whether I could hope to preserve much religious activity in a secular calling. The ministry is, in some sense, essential for me. I should like to know whether your unwillingness to think of the ministry has not risen with the decline and fallen with the increase of your religious vitality? I can but fancy that you will find no solid, satisfactory, and permanent enjoyment of religion, without laboring directly in spiritual things—directly and exclusively, I may say. If you do not think yourself to be depended upon as a public speaker to a constant audience, why, go into the woods and the jungle, or preach with your pen. *I* hardly dare to look forward to a pastorate at home. But what the leadings of Providence may be, of course I do not know. I want to take my stand between the altar and the plough, and say, 'Lord, ready for either.'"

In a letter to his friend Brown, he says:

. . . . . . "I am a different man from what I was even a few months ago. My happiest days are past, in one sense. There is a *higher* happiness more soul-filling, found in laboring for Christ, which I hope yet to experience far more largely. Here is an exhaustless fountain of joy, from which I have as yet taken the merest taste. But for this, I would with my whole heart second you and Montgomery and Muhlenberg in sighing to sleep in death. As it is, I feel that I have a work to do which should engage my highest powers, strained to the utmost of cultivation and of activity. Life is none too long for my work. I want to make my own calling and election sure, and then I want to be one of the wise to win souls, shining as a star for ever in the firmament of God. Nothing less than this glory is my ambition. Let me rather say, then, that my days of folly are past, while the happiest are yet in store for me.

"I am unwilling, my dear brother, that our friendship should abate a tithe of its ardor. It already begins to claim the sacredness of age. . . . . . The more we are our Saviour's, the more we shall be each other's. Had it not been for your coming into my room one night, an inquirer after Christ, and afterwards finding that Saviour, we should not be such friends to-day. Our paths would have diverged, and the constantly widening and deepening breadth of separation might at last have become an impassable gulf!

"But I would not preach to you. I hope the tide is not banging you against the rocks, nor sweeping your head beneath the waters. A Senior in Yale! You must exult in your position and prospects. O, I hope you will come out with a heart all burning with a Saviour's love, and fresh for the work of our Master....

"Yours," etc.

"*November* 14.

"DEAR MOTHER:

"There are no new developments among us, but our prayer-meetings are increasing in frequency and in interest, and I think there is a deeper piety settling down on the hearts of many. I do hope I am growing in grace. Gently the Lord is leading me to Himself, despite all my rebelliousness. It is with tears of gratitude that I acknowledge it. This has been a blessed day. I have enjoyed prayer, enjoyed study, and all my duties. . . . I get a great deal of new light for every hour I study the Scriptures. Old difficulties vanish, and new meanings come home to my soul with a delightful force.

"One thought to-day has especially impressed me, and is with me yet. It is, that Christ, in no instance used his miraculous power for display, nor to gratify curiosity, nor yet in his own behalf alone. It was always for the direct good of others. He could not be tempted to cast himself down from the temple pinnacle. That would have done no good: it would have been simply for display. . . . With all his powers, Christ never 'showed off!' Yet I, his follower, have made that how often my effort, all my life!

"I am pondering this resolution: when I have sufficiently prayed for grace to keep it, I will try to adopt it for the practical rule of my life. Never to write a sentence, nor speak a word, nor do an act, but what shall tend, directly or indirectly, to the good of some of my fellow-men. Then, and not till then, shall I be consecrated to my work."

"*November* 14.

"Dear R——:

. . . "I have a fault to find with your last three or four letters. I allude to it, because it is uppermost in my mind. You do not give me enough of your Christian experience. While I am praying for you, several times a day, and constantly thinking of you, and wishing for you, I long to know whether my prayers for you are answered, and to receive the assurance that yours are ascending for me. I confess to a feeling of disappointment, when I read entirely through your letter, and find almost all I want, or have a right to expect,—all but just what I most want, and most have a right to expect. O, I do hope you are not freezing spiritually. You cannot afford to lose the vantage ground acquired in the last year. And I suppose a very short period would suffice to throw you back into that dreadful state of inactivity, wretchedness, and almost despair, which you knew for so long. . . .

"Yours," etc.

"*November* 28.

"I have received and have accepted an invitation from my friends in Williamson, to spend to-morrow with them, and preach a Thanksgiving-sermon in the Baptist church.

. . . "I discover, on thinking of it, that a Thanksgiving-sermon is, or ought to be, a peculiar thing. I really hardly know what to do. I hate political harangues, as desecrations of the day, the place, and the ministerial office; and yet I never preached or thought of any sermon that would be at all fitting. I have pitched, however, upon this text—see what you can make of it: 'The Sabbath was made for man, not man for the Sabbath.'"

CHAPTER XXI.

Lecturing—Revivals in Rochester and in Kennebunkport.

The vacation at the Holidays was occupied with a lecturing tour in the far East. The Lyceum Committee of Dover, N. H., had extended an invitation to him to lecture before their association. Great Falls, N. H., and Calais, Maine, sent similar requests. The article on "The Ancient and the Modern Idea of a State," was accordingly re-written, expanded to the proper proportions, and made to serve the purpose of a lecture.

It was first spoken in Calais, a town more than two hundred miles east of Portland (which forms the boundary to the conception of the East to most persons), and accessible only by a long and hazardous sea-voyage. "At Eastport," says Kingman, "we doubled the North Pole, and advanced, clear of ice, into Dr. Kane's Open Sea." This was really the St. Croix River, distinguished for the remarkable beauty of its scenery. Calais, a young city, deserves to be as celebrated for the intelligence and thrift of its inhabitants, as it already is for the enormous production of good lumber.

Kingman's lecture, in this and in other places, was received with warm approbation. It was spoken without notes.

Writing from Dover, he says, "I have no reason to complain of the verdicts brought to me. . . . . But I will tell you what I enjoyed most—the prayer-meeting last evening. The vestry was nearly full, and the Lord was with us. There was much free conference on the theme of the cross of Christ."

Returning to Rochester, he found himself recruited in health, and with a fair pecuniary equivalent for his pains.

The winter of '56 was remarkable in Rochester for a powerful and general revival of religion. Already, as we have seen, in the college there had been more than ordinary interest. In the city the work began and continued in connexion with the preaching of that well-known evangelist, Mr. Finney. For months the churches were thronged daily, both to hear preaching, and for conference, inquiry, and prayer. The converts were numbered by hundreds. It was the precursor, in the State of New York, of that great religious awakening, which, in 1858, extended over the whole North, and introduced a new era in religious operations.

At first Kingman was fearful and cautious. The excitement might not be genuine. "I trust the Spirit is in all this," he writes. "I think He is. It *must* be the Spirit; certain I am it is not the effect of eloquence, it is not a fanciful excitement." As the work advanced, the hand of God was clearly exhibited.

Kingman found the difficulty at first which many

have experienced, in estimating Mr. Finney—who as a well-known, public character, concerning whom public discussion has been had, may freely be spoken of by name. "I do not know what to make of Mr. F.," he says. "Certainly he is far enough from any approach to a 'popular preacher:'—as dry as an old bone—but fearfully personal and close. It benefits me to hear him in many respects."

Later he sees more clearly: "I have been trying all the term to comprehend Mr. Finney. I have been as much at a loss to see where his power lay, as the Philistines were with reference to Samson. I have styled him the man whom nobody likes, and everybody goes to hear. And so it has been. But last evening he struck a new vein, and I *felt the Finney*. It was a stupendous sermon. I was half beside myself. The subject was, 'Conscience: its Nature, Authority, and Revelations.' It was a mass of bold, compact, solid logic, poured out in the most forcible manner, and perfectly irresistible in its power. It was not rhetoric, not passion; yet *Gough* did not affect me more. Oh, well, what a poor, little, weak, superficial mortal am I, intellectually and spiritually!"

Feb. 25, more about the work itself.

"God is doing a wonderful work in this city. It seems miraculous that so thorough a change in popular sentiment should have been wrought in so short a time. It is said that there has been no period since 1830, when the minds of the community have been so generally awake to the subject of religion. No church in the city can contain the throngs that press to hear Mr. Finney, and scarcely a lecture-room the numbers that attend the daily prayer-meetings. Inquirers show themselves by hundreds.

"I magnify the Lord and bless Him for His wonderful works to the children of men. . . . To-morrow is *our* great day" [the day of Prayer for Colleges], "the day to which we have long been looking forward, hoping for and expecting God's rich blessing in answer to prayer. I know you will remember me and us all in an especial manner. Dead and unworthy as we now are, God deigns to bless us, and four of our fellow-students have recently indulged hope.

"I enjoy Mr. F.'s preaching more, the better I understand the man. There is a severe holiness about him, that makes me revere him, while he manifests the utmost humility and homely sincerity. I sometimes feel a weak point in his theology, but he does not seem to make it his mission to proclaim his peculiar views. He is manifestly in search of *souls*, and is winning, I think, the increased confidence of Christians. . . . He is very cool, cautious—and deals with conscience. There is no machinery—no noise, but a wide and deep feeling that is amazing. The work takes hold mostly on men. . . . There is a great spirit of prayer—intelligent prayer."

TO A SISTER.

"*February* 29, 1856.

"DEAR L——:

. . . "It rejoices and strengthens my heart to have you breathe such desires for me. You must be willing to *pray* much for me also, for I assure you that, if I ever become what you wish, I must greatly change.

"My Christian experience is very *shallow*. It does not lie deep enough in my soul. Truths float about on the surface of my mind, but do not pervade my nature. I often think of a remark which Dr. Anderson once quoted to me from father, 'After all, a man can preach effectively only so much truth as he has experienced in his own soul.' That is what I want, and must have—*more experience*. All else is unavailing. This is just where I am weak, utterly weak," etc.

The letter then proceeds to describe the celebration of the Day of Fasting and Prayer in the College. One paragraph gives an illustration of his remarkable susceptibility to powerful impressions from good oratory. It was the same with magnificent scenery, or music of peculiar grandeur. Their effect was sometimes exciting even to a sort of painful extacy.

"We had a solemn day. In the morning there was preaching. I do not know what to say of the sermon. I have not got over trembling under it yet. It made me shut myself up, fling myself on my bed, and cry for an hour. It gave me new ideas of the heart and power of the preacher—and I may say of *man*, for I never before felt the power of any human being so. For that hour —— was Massillon. The text was from Ps. xc. 'Who knoweth the power of thine anger! According to thy fear, so is thy wrath.' I hope the good effects of this blessed day will go with us," etc.

It was now the set time when the third great prayer of this young Jacob, who had learned to prevail with God, was to be answered. For many years the little church at Kennebunkport had known no refreshing from on high. But the ground had been sown, and watered with tears, and suddenly over the field that seemed all barren, a harvest stood visible, and ready for reaping. A vacation in the Seminary was at hand. Word came to Kingman, "Home—and help us thrust in the sickle." He hastened away, grateful to the Hearer of Prayer.

In the course of the journey, incidents occurred, which are thus dramatically narrated.

"Dear B——:

. . . . "I received my father's letter Friday, and took the cars the same night. Reaching Springfield Saturday night, I dropped down to Hartford for the Sabbath. Oh! how that portion of the journey filled me with remembrances of old Suffield! We came to 'The Locks.' I got out and looked about in the dimness. I remembered the first time I came there, the greeting I received from my old teacher, the kindness he showed to me for my own and my father's sake. I burned to fall down and tell him, that, for what I was, I felt myself indebted to him more than to any man, save my own father. When should I see him again! Certainly next summer. Meanwhile I would write him a long letter.—'Anybody going to Suffield?' cried 'Old Prout,' or somebody else. I almost said 'Yes!' but no—it was impossible. So I hurried on, busy with thoughts of past days.

"I arrived at Hartford—sought the same hotel where H. and I companied one night long ago. In the morning I went to church. After I was seated, a lady swept in, proceeding up the aisle. I looked again, I could not be mistaken—no, it was my old schoolmate, ——! At the close of the service, as she passed out, I stood before her. 'Mr. Nott!' exclaimed she, wondering. Then there was an introduction to various friends. We talked of Suffield, and of Mr. Woodbury. I lauded him from my heart. 'Yes,' said Mrs. ——, 'we all feel his death very much!'

. . . . "I cannot tell you how I felt. Dead—dead?—'Yes, we buried him yesterday.' And I might have been there! My visit was spoiled, my journey was saddened, and I passed Suffield Monday morning, feeling that all was gone now. There is no one in Suffield for whom I care, or who cares for me. Some time—not now—I shall like to go and kneel at his grave, and offer a thanksgiving for his life—a tear for his death.

"You knew him—loved him. You have doubtless heard the particulars of his triumphant departure. He passed away with the words on his lips, 'Half in earth and half in Heaven!'"

Kingman remained in Kennebunkport nearly one month, preaching almost daily, and giving assistance to his father in the necessary visiting and conversing.

He thus describes the scenes transpiring.

"KENNEBUNK, *April* 17, 1856.

"DEAR R——:

.... "I hope you appreciate the paternal affection that has dragged me out of bed half an hour earlier than usual this morning of blue Monday, for the express purpose of despatching a letter to you by the early mail.

"The work here has been advancing, in spite of rain, mud, and unbelief. The last week has been tedious—all rain, drizzle, and fog; there are no walks, other than gutters between great snowbanks. I preached Tuesday and Wednesday evenings; since then we have met in the vestry, and have had delightful meetings. Eight persons have been added to the church, all of whom are heads of families. They appeared very happy in their baptism, and shouted aloud when coming out of the water. It was long since I had seen a river baptism. To see it here made my heart full of rejoicing. Friday and Saturday evenings we had the most heavenly seasons of Christian communion. The brethren seemed almost transported. Father preached on Baptism yesterday; what it is—what it symbolizes—what its obligation; an elaborate and irresistible argument—enthusiastic too. I spoke afternoon and evening. Five members received the right hand of fellowship, among them the woman whom father baptized a month ago on his own responsibility, the church refusing to receive her. We had a solemn evening, and one poor sinner was so pricked in the heart as to rise, overcome completely, and only able to say, 'I want you to pray for me!'

"The brethren are frightened, and wanting to retreat. But the Spirit is not yet grieved, and we shall push on the meetings as fast and as far as we can.

"Dear Lizzie [the youngest sister] is fully brought out now, so as to give undoubted evidence of an intelligent and thorough conversion. It is a practical thing with her, and she talks like a Christian of years' standing. Bless God! thus is brought in the last of our dear mother's offspring. Do you not suppose she looks with joy on this event, and takes infinite satisfaction in knowing that all her children are safe—three in heaven with her, the rest in the bosom of the church? Prayer is answered.

"Letters from Rochester are encouraging; others are converted, among them F., whom I have loved so much as a classmate.

"My own heart is full; sometimes I seem to live in heaven by the hour. Last evening these thoughts so filled me, as to drive away the sermon I had prepared, and I was forced to preach on 'Heaven.' But, I cannot tell you all. Father seems to renew his youth. He is full of fire. He talks all the while of the 'All Power' and the 'worth of a soul;' he laughs, tells stories, and seems supremely happy. Good bye.

"K."

At no time, probably, in his whole ministerial career,

not in Albion or Dover, nor in New York, did Kingman continuously, for so long a time, preach with so much *power* as during these three weeks at Kennebunkport. The discourses were, altogether, perhaps fifteen in number. Most of them had been delivered several times before, and so were weapons more accurately fitted to the hand than untried productions often can be, while yet, from his living earnestness, they were kept sharp, and launched with the same vigor and directness as when they were new. These sermons, as often fondly spoken of by his father (and judged in a literary way), were chiefly remarkable for their perfectly *artistic arrangement* and *finish*—the more singular since they were unwritten. An exact logical order reigned throughout, controlling even the sentences and words; so that on any point neither too much nor too little was said, nor anything irrelevant admitted. The method was *constructive*, not *aggregative*. Thoughts, whether the principal or the subordinate, stood not side by side, but in line. As there was no verbiage, so also there was no independency of parts or phrases. No straggling fancies were allowed to go ambitiously foraging for the beautiful and elegant; all were kept in rank, and the ranks in column—marching straight forward on to the final issue. The easily besetting disposition to wander was effectually forbidden, and the inclination to impertinent ornament relentlessly crucified. Words, giving up their individuality, aimed only to contribute to that perfect unity in which dwells power. Thus, there was a steady surging onwards from the beginning —the wave gathering head as it proceeded, until, at the instant of its greatest mass and momentum, it broke with the aggregate force of all its atoms. Yet, the style was by no means barren. The theory of construction demanded perfect accuracy of language; consistent however, with ease, glow, and a pruned luxuriance. Such, at this time, was Kingman's ideal of a sermon—his model. Afterwards, when a settled minister, he adopted much of the time a somewhat different method—at least allowed himself the liberty of methods. He was more frequently picturesque and discursive; and sometimes chose the guerilla plan of warfare—stopping anywhere in the course of the sermon to skirmish, and shooting vigorously whenever he was able to take aim. And he frequently preferred an effective grouping to a logical procession.

His style had also this excellence which is beyond price—absolute transparency. The language was purely the medium of the thought, and no one was ever at a loss for an instant to comprehend his meaning. But the discussion of the general features of his composition belongs later.

His customary ardor was, of course, augmented here at home, preaching under his father's eye, and for the salvation of his own townsmen and friends. He aimed to declare the most solemn and pungent truths, and to drive them home to men's consciences.

Two sermons are held in special remembrance, one from the text, "Who told thee thou wast naked?" the other, that on "Heaven," in which he seemed to be, indeed, "living in heaven" for that hour. In the pulpit he appeared never otherwise than as having the accomplishment of a great result in view, and eagerly longing for it. Hours of leisure he occupied much with prayer, since he hungered for the Spirit's aid. He was more than once heard weeping and pleading; in fine, from all representations, words could hardly describe his yearning and earnestness. The "All Power" was with him, and many were converted unto the Lord.

CHAPTER XXII.

Letters—Vacation—Tremont Temple—White Mountains.

On his return to Rochester he finds the religious interest not cooled.

April 24.

". . . . But now for the wonders. I have been to the prayer-meeting this morning. They have adjourned to the churches. The church was almost full—six or eight hundred persons. Finney is here, preaching with unabated vigor. The meetings are more powerful than at any time yet. A band of young men, who had formed an association for their better growth in vice, have all been converted. It has been agreed to continue the prayer-meetings during the year. . . . . I feel overawed at God's power :—'*Stand still*, and see the salvation of God.'"

A reference to his late visit occurs :

To his Father :—

. . . . "Perhaps I did wrong in leaving you as I did. But the time of my preparation seems so short at the longest, and so strong is the pressure to push me off my course, that I am perhaps in some cases over-jealous. . . . . To know that I have in any way been a means of personal gratification to yourself, is the highest joy I know on earth, next to gaining God's approval. My visit home was to me the most satisfactory I ever made. It will prove of lasting advantage to me."

A lively letter of vigorous good advice to a young sister, who was, for the time, ambitious, self-reproachful, and doleful:—

"*May* 10.

"My Dearest C——

. . . . "What a pity it is, indeed, that the vast sum total of all human knowledge cannot be condensed and crammed into your little head in one summer term's work! How strange, indeed, how sad, that C——, like the rest of us, should be doomed to be a plodder, learn little by little, and leave the great bulk of knowledge untouched after all! Yes, it is very sad, C.; and you are homesick and disconsolate, and you meditate and mourn and cry, and grow very solemn and very white and very pensive, and thus fulfil the requisitions of a young ladies' boarding-school. In all of which, allow me to suggest you are the opposite of *wise*. Your father would rather you should be a romp than a nun. Your brother would certainly prefer it. Don't tumble into reveries and repinings and aerial aspirations, and mope and sigh because you cannot make yourself perfect in a day.

"You confound father's ideal of what he would have you do and be, with what he actually expects of you as a limited, imperfect, and depraved being, and under circumstances in many respects unfavorable. . . . . . Your complainings remind me of the scene of poor Willie's distress, when, with a good dinner before him, he stopped and literally cried because he could not be more than five years old! Of all human follies, *the blues* are the most reprehensible and foolish. It is a waste of time to indulge them. I would fight them, I'd laugh at them, sing them away, or whistle them away, or shout them away, or *scream* them out of sight. I'd drown them with joy. I'd shoot them and bayonet them with compulsory wit.

"'Hence! to the realms of night, dire demon, hence!
Thy chains of adamant can bind
That little world—the human mind,
And chain its noblest power to impotence!'

"And then to think—

"'O how many a glorious record,
Had the Angels of me kept,
Had I done instead of doubted,
Had I *warred* instead of *wept*!'

"Well, you have my opinions. I hope you will profit, and in your aspirations after endless knowledge and immaculate perfection, not forget the Christian duty of wearing a cheerful face. Bless the world with smiles, C. Let your words and tones be silvery with pure joy. You have a right, bless God, to be happy. The world—without God and without hope—have not. God have mercy on them!

"If I did not make it a matter of *principle* to be happy, I should not always be so happy as I am.

All is well here, I am busy again, next time I will give you more news; this is one of my *lectures*. Good night.

"Your good-for-nothing brother,

"A. K. N."

"*May* 28.

"I am still conscious largely of the strivings of the Spirit, sometimes, too, of a conquering Spirit in my heart. I think I hear God's voice. Great questions begin already to be pressing upon me, and I am made to feel the utter vanity of all worldly prudence, and to look only for the wisdom that cometh from above. . . . .

"The summer vacation—how shall I best apply to it the principles which I take for the regulation of my life? The great future—in what direction will it open? I am driven to my God. . . . . Ah, I sometimes have thoughts, too sacred to be uttered, of a work—a great work—yet dim and dark—which I shall be suffered to enter into. I wait patiently on the Lord."

The question of the employment of the summer vacation was not easily settled. Several churches sent in requests to him to supply them.

"I have something of a fever to go West," he says. "It would certainly be a great satisfaction to my roving propensity, and might be of use to me in one day choosing my field of life-labor. But I do not find anything very *holy* in *this* desire."

An invitation to supply the desk, or rather platform, at Tremont Temple, Boston, during some weeks, in the absence of the pastor, Rev. J. L. Kalloch, who was his former schoolmate and friend, was finally accepted. The decision was made in deference to his father's wish to have him near home.

The place was important, and for many reasons difficult to be occupied by a young student.

"I am afraid some of my friends will think me foolhardy," he says, "and perhaps vain; but I have not sought the place, and do not propose to go in my own strength. . . . . . If I fail, it will very likely do me as much good as success, and perhaps a great deal more! So I am sure of benefit in any case.

"Help me to pray that I may go in the fear of God, and deliver His messages, supported by His power. . . . My responsibility and my risk I feel. I have no trust except in God."

Nott preached at Tremont Temple six or seven successive Sabbaths, with great acceptance, and not without result. The congregation was maintained at its full ordinary number, notwithstanding the inevitable exodus of people into the country at that season of the year. The strangers and stragglers that were drawn in more than made up the losses. The Temple has an audience room of capacity for seating, at the maximum, three thousand persons. This room, in good weather, was comfortably filled, and sometimes packed. Public attention was more and more attracted to the young preacher. The highest encomiums were passed upon his sermons by men best capable of forming a critical judgment, while the favorable suffrages of the mass were secured at once by his grace, simplicity, and earnestness. He preached with great boldness, "speaking the truth in love," not dizzied by applause, nor swerved by any "policy" proposed by the weak or the jealous. As formerly, the "All-Power" was with him; the church felt the influence, and was quickened; and there were a few conversions. Here also he followed his habit of making religious visits, and pleading with individuals.

. . . .

"MONDAY, *Aug.* 11, 1856.

"MY DEAR FATHER,

"My fourth Sabbath has passed, completing one half of my allotted time in Boston. What a beautiful Sabbath God gave us yesterday! . . . .

"In the morning, I had not that fulness of soul and access in prayer which I have known at times when I have preached best, *i.e.* most effectively. But I wish you could have been with us in the afternoon. I changed my subject during intermission, as by the voice of the Spirit, taking a sermon that I preached a long time ago, and had almost forgotten. The congregation was the largest I ever saw, and furnished a splendid sight. I was granted the closest attention, and enjoyed speaking. Our evening meeting was by far the largest and most encouraging known yet. *Christ* seemed to pervade our hearts in a remarkable manner. He was the soul of every prayer, and of all that was said. The brethren seemed to have faith. It really appeared revival-like. . . . . . . I am becoming more interested in my work. . . . .

" . . . .

"*Aug.* 13.

"'We are encouraged:'—so say all the church members who speak of the state of things. The congregation is contantly increasing. Better than this, the vestry is filling up, and life is infused into the meetings. Numbers come in, who I find are strangers to all of us. Some of them have appeared very serious. O, if I could only get hold of them! We see their faces, and they are off! But God seems ready to bless us. . . . . By the grace of God I hope I may be able some time to preach better than I *can* now. Give me, O Lord, a work to do, a life to do it in, and grace to do it!"

"*Aug.* 18.

"Yesterday I exchanged half the day. . . . . I can hardly describe to you the relief and childish delight I felt in getting back, in the afternoon, to my good old Temple. I fairly laughed for joy. As I sat down on a free platform, having no excrescence of a pulpit upon it; with my glorious chair behind me, and the front rank of my hearers so near that I could almost touch them, while the solid mass extended to the distant doors,—why I felt so inspired that I could not have *helped* speaking. . . . . There was more feeling than I had seen before. . . . . A gay girl met me on coming out, and at once spoke of the sermon. 'It brought the tears and the *prayer*,' she said. Another I saw in the evening, and said to her, 'You have serious thoughts sometimes; have you had any to-day?' She immediately answered, with deep feeling, 'I do not see how any one could help it!' . . . . Think—six weeks ago there were thirty at our evening meeting; last evening there were more than a hundred. I believe the Spirit is working among us." . . . .

The only drawback to his felicity was his loneliness. He lodged and studied in the empty house of Mr. Kalloch, and discovered something of the miseries of solitary imprisonment. "I must confess," he says—"this fine house, amply furnished, of which I have the range from garret to cellar, but without so much as a cat or a canary to share possession, is becoming a prison. I wander through it—peep into every attic and open every closet, to see if I cannot find—something or somebody. If the bell would only ring! Twice I have run down stairs to the front door, but alas! it was my neighbor's bell," etc. . . . .

The writer was present at the Temple on one of these Sabbaths. The afternoon discourse was from the text, "The wages of sin is death." It was an argument, to show the nature of the "death." The preacher's voice, expression, gesture, were evidently controlled solely by the absorbing solemnity of the theme. The chief characteristic of the discourse, as respects its composition, was the steady, rapid, straight-onward, fearful march of the argument. The heart responded at each step, "*true*," "*true*." But—awful! the premises involved a conclusion:—to that you were relentlessly forced:—there is a judgment—a second death—a Pit of Woe! I sat where the whole audience, silent as the grave, were before me. I thought a pallor overspread the faces of many, and I said to myself, this *is* a Judgment Day, men's hearts failing them for fear! Yet there was a pathos, as of restrained tears, in the speaker's voice, that awoke the tenderest emotions, and excited the slumbering longings of the soul for peace with God.

At the close of his engagement at the Temple, Nott seized a week for a rapid excursion to the White Mountains. The party consisted of four, of whom the writer was one. Kingman was in the gayest spirits; he shouted, sang, hurrahed, and kept us all in continual exhilaration. His power of physical endurance was astonishing. It was impossible thoroughly to weary him, or quench his ardor. After a long and exhausting ride, he insisted on making a push to the "Flume" by moonlight. From "Crawford's" he took an evening run to the top of the nearest mountain (that to which a carriage road conducts), while the rest of the party were glad enough of beds. In the course of the ascent of Mount Washington, which was pedestrian, two of the party had lingered behind, overcome with fatigue. Resuming their upward toil, and approaching the noted

"Lake of the Clouds,"—a considerable basin of pure water a mile above the level of the sea, and as impregnable by the sun's heat as an Arctic glacier—they were surprised to hear a vigorous splashing in the almost icy waves, and running to look, beheld this wild contemner of the threats of Nature luxuriously swimming in the precious bath, with perspiration effectually checked, but loudly applauding his superior comfort and refreshment. Few have bathed in the Lake of the Clouds. Most would hesitate which to choose, that, or the bath of Empedocles in the crater of Etna.

Returning from this excursion, K. had still time to give a Sabbath to Kennebunkport, and another to Boston, preaching this time for a new church at the South End, now known as the Thirteenth Baptist Church, of which Philip S. Evans, Kingman's classmate and friend, was the first pastor.

A distinguished gentleman, who heard him on this occasion, remarked this in effect: "I had heard of this young preacher, and of the 'sensation' that he produced, but imagined he might be the possessor simply of certain showy and superficial gifts, sufficient only to gain a transient popularity. I listened, therefore, with critical ears, and I was obliged to confess, at the close of the day, that I had not for years heard more powerful sermons."

Thus everywhere the impression grew, that K. was destined to some important service for the Redeemer.

CHAPTER XXIII.

Second Year—Letters—Visit to the Broome St. Church, etc.

This year was occupied with the study of *theology proper*, and was peculiarly delightful and profitable to Kingman.

It is also the year that closed his preparatory course and introduced him to the final stage of his too brief but happy and useful life.

Much has already been indicated respecting Kingman's conception of the solemn responsibility belonging to the work of preaching. Two or three letters setting this in a still more impressive light, could not justly be omitted.

It has been stated that after his return from the White Mountains, one Sabbath was spent at Kennebunkport. His sermons on that day, though not wanting in the usual rhetorical power or fluency, or in animation, yet were pervaded with a manner that was unusual, a certain *flippancy* and apparent indifference to results. "There is no *power* in K.'s sermons to-day," remarked his father to a member of the family. "His *heart* is not enlisted. K. can do nothing unless his *heart* is right. I must write him a letter about keeping his heart.

The letter was written, and this was the reply—showing his humility and right aims :—

" *Sep.* 26, 1856.

" DEAR FATHER :

. . . . " I am greatly ashamed and distressed over the wholesome rebuke contained in your letter. Perhaps it is better that I suffer in silence, and endeavor to make my heart right with God. I feel the truth of what you say. I did feel it at the time, and I knew the causes of it. Yet I was disposed, while conscious of not having fully discharged my duty, to pass it over as a trivial matter. But now I am alarmed to see that I have committed a great sin, and I beg you to pray the Lord with me that I may be forgiven. Some foolish *liftings-up* in Boston, and more than all, a week of most thorough dissipation in pleasure-travelling, with the excitement of expecting an immediate return to Rochester, had wholly unfitted me for preaching for you," etc., etc.

He adds :—" I am now as thoroughly in the midst of study as ever in my life ; yet the most of it is of a nature exciting rather than dissipating to religious thought. Besides this, I have determined to devote some time each day to purely devotional reading ; I find it as profitable as any study. Arthur's 'Tongue of Fire' has done me much good in enlarging my faith in the practical power of the Holy Spirit. A Kempis' 'Imitation of Christ' affords me delightful daily food. I am finding great satisfaction in a more critical study of the Scriptures in private. Some new light dawns upon me every day. I have taken Paul's Epistles to

Timothy as especially appropriate to me at this time," etc.

A little later he laments a fault similar to that above confessed.

TO HIS FATHER.

" *Nov.* 30, 1856.

"I have been for two Sabbaths past at B——. This is the first preaching I have performed for some time. My heart was not prepared for the work, and I am afraid I preached somewhat as I did at home, when last I was there. *I look now on such sermons as among the greatest crimes of my life.* I hope God has given me grace to weep over them and repent," etc. . . . .

" Among the greatest crimes of my life!" Such is not always the feeling of ministers when their sermons are faultless, except for the trifling defect of heartlessness!

At another time K. is refusing a certain tempting proposal :—

" It would not be right," says he, "and so I will not; because it is not well to do what is not right, and because I have found that when I am to *preach*, I am beset with some special temptation. When I yield to it I am shorn of my strength. I can talk, rant, make an oration, but I cannot preach. I have come to the conclusion, that if I am to preach, I must *keep my heart.* I pray the good Lord to teach me entirely His will."

Miscellaneous letters follow.

R. T. S., *October* 1, 1856.

"DEAR MOTHER:

"My religion daily becomes more precious to me, and I think that the grace of God is bringing me to that point where I shall be able either to endure affliction or practise self-denial for Christ's sake. Of neither have I known anything as yet. My life's work, I doubt not, will be abundantly fraught with both; but what that is to be remains as yet a mystery. I fear of mistaking here; I fear that I may choose for myself and not for Christ. I cannot thrust the subject from my thoughts, though it assumes as yet so undefined a shape. I gladly commit its future shaping into the hands of Infinite Wisdom.

"We have had another of our most delightful college meetings. These differ from any other meetings I have ever known. We are so exactly on a level, and in such thorough sympathy, that all restraint seems broken down. Men do not seem to talk or pray for the sake of performing an exercise, but for the simple expression of feeling. The morning meetings of the city continue increasing now in interest and numbers. They are a great delight to me.

"I had a pleasant Sabbath at Auburn. The day was fine, and some of my very pleasant friends there seemed glad to see me. I preached a new sermon from Luke iii. 16, on the Baptism of the Holy Spirit. Some of the thoughts were newly presented to my own mind, and have done me good. It is sad to see a large church in a fine city, with its membership scattering, its congregation falling off, its prayer-meetings declining, and its spirituality dying out, for the want *of a pastor*.

"Well, we shall have fourteen ready—the Lord willing—in some months; but, like the five loaves for the five thousand, what are they among so many. One thing the churches may be assured of—if these-to-be pastors all imbibe the spirit, and catch the zeal, and obey the teachings of our instructors in Theology, they will certainly be at least pure and faithful men.

"Yours," etc.

The next letter suggests the first hint of what was in reality, though unsuspectedly to him, the advancement of destiny; the shadow of the future beginning to assume definiteness, at least to our eye, who have seen that whole future unfold, and move backward into the past.

"ROCHESTER, *October* 9, 1856.

"DEAR FATHER:

"A matter has come up, which you will naturally expect me to mention to you. I wish to refer it to you for confidential advice. It is an invitation from the First Church, New York, to supply them one Sabbath. What do you think of it? Of course it is only as a supply; they have had fifty such. I do not like to answer until I hear from you. ....

"*October* 17

"DEAR MOTHER:

... "I have decided to go down to N. Y. next week, in answer to the invitation of the First Church.

You will probably mark it as one of those special favors which an almost over-indulgent Providence seems to delight in bestowing upon me, that I should have this opportunity of attending without expense the meetings of the American Board. The Anniversary is at Newark," etc.

In the following letter he describes his first visit to the Broome Street people and his impressions.

"ROCHESTER, *Nov.* 4, 1856.

"DEAR FATHER:

"Well, I have been to New York. . . . . I have now seen various fields of labor, and am ready in conclusion to *go* wherever the Lord shall choose to send me. I think there is very little choice of places—except to go where the Lord designs. . . . .

"I preached twice on Sunday, to about eight hundred people, and attended prayer-meeting. I could not quite drive out from the pulpit the ghost of Dr. Cone, so that I got along only tolerably.

"They are a good people—a 'lovely church'—strong, united, social, old-fashioned, and stiff. They are 100 years old, preserve the old forms of doctrine, which I like, and have had in that time four pastors and three church clerks.

"They use 'Watts and Rippon' yet, have no musical instruments whatever, sing quite generally over the house, and at the close of each service rise and join unanimously in a doxology—always selecting one that has not 'Ghost' in it. Tuesday evening, I attended the weekly 'lecture,' and Friday the prayer-meeting again. They pray *well* and sing good old-style songs, such as 'How tedious and tasteless the hour,' 'The Lord into his garden comes.'

"I spent Tuesday and Wednesday at the Newark meetings, enjoying them very much. It was a great satisfaction to hear and see men, whose names had always been household words to me. The views developed by the discussions were very instructive to me, and the whole spirit manifested was one of concord, love, and missionary zeal. . . . .

"Well—the expected preacher for the following Sunday failed to come—so I was stoutly besieged to stay another Sabbath; and, as it seemed providential, I could not well refuse. Sunday was a beautiful day, we had 1000 people present, to whom I preached with more freedom, though upon less thorough preparation than the previous week. In the afternoon I sat down to communion with a much larger number, than ever before in my life. It was a refreshing season. Our evening prayer-meeting was delightful. I was introduced to scores of persons, who almost shook my hands off, and loaded me with good wishes. Monday morning I took an early start, and was here at evening. So I have had, you see, quite an episode, and am laden again with extra bounties.

"I do not think there is any creature, whom the Lord seems to favor more than me. It is a constant wonder to me. May he also vouchsafe to me all grace!

"Your affectionate son," etc.

Several following extracts show how, as the sense of coming responsibilities increased, there were mental strifes and forebodings :

"ROCHESTER, *Nov.* 12.

"DEAR C.:

"How soon I shall be compelled to say, Farewell to the life of a recluse, farewell to light-heartedness; welcome busy strife, welcome heavy care! If I could have my own way, I would give another year to study; and it may yet appear to be the Lord's way, but it looks differently now.

"'Ready for either.' I rejoice in what you say of *your* desires respecting the future ministry in which the Lord may permit me to engage. I trust they are my own heart's wishes, and I am thankful that I am not surrounded by false friends to nourish my worldly ambition. Providence seems to have led me through a considerable range of different fields of labor—the large and the small—to *peep*, at least, at each. My conclusion is that the fascinations, in most cases, lie in the enchantment of distance and of name. The Law of Compensation works, and makes most essentially alike.

"My visit to New York was pleasant in every possible particular, and the recollections of it afford me the greatest satisfaction. Since returning, I have kept very quietly at home. To-morrow I address the students of the M—— Collegiate Institute, at their closing exercises. I just begin to be troubled about it; I have done scarcely anything in preparation. Positively I am, for the time, thoroughly *theologized*. I think of nothing, morning, day, and night, but doctrines, preaching, etc. I cannot succeed in turning my thoughts to anything that is *literary* alone," etc.

"*November* 30.

"DEAR FATHER,

"My heart and mind have been occupied to find out what it is to preach. I do not feel that I have ever yet fully known. The Lord is leading me. Last Saturday He gave me a little light. I was able to humble myself in part, just a *little;* and on the Sabbath, the Lord blessed me as he has not for a long time. The holy influence is with me yet. My heart, for many months callous and cold, and that increasingly, has at length been touched by the finger of the Lord. Now, I can feel a little. My tongue has been loosed in prayer. I could weep as I prayed, and as I preached; but it is only a little. Pray that the Lord will humble me *entirely;* I want to be *broken up* completely. Oh! how utterly unfit for my work!—Of its magnitude, of its nature, and of my responsibility, I have had not an *idea.* It is looming up. I just begin to get a glimpse, and am overwhelmed. O, may the Lord lead me farther into his secret counsels! I have some dim ideas; O Lord, enlarge and clarify them! My heart is touched; O break it with thy love! Let self melt away, O Lord, and Christ possess me! O, this is a great problem which I have to work out. Lord, Lord, open it before me, and lead me to its solution! I almost shrink from the future, which is pressing upon me. May your prayers, in your son's behalf, be answered." . . . .

"*December 24th*, 1856.

"My Dearest C——:

. . . . . "I have been trying to pray. I feel myself a helpless, worthless sinner. I thank God, through Jesus Christ, I am not in hell. I never can sufficiently praise His sovereign grace which redeemed me. Why He saw fit to have pity upon me, I cannot tell. Life is crowding upon me like a Juggernaut. A few years of crushing and all will be over. It seems very short and very vain. Were it not for the hope of being purified by trial, and thus made more meet for the inheritance of the saints in light, and the hope of winning souls to Christ, I would like to lay me down this night and awake in heaven. But I would rather wait and toil, and then go with a crown studded thick with jewels, which God has given me.

"Well, I am changing; I feel it every day. I shall never be what I have been; and, for the most part, it is well. I wish I could change entirely; I sometimes get a glimpse of what I would like to be.

"Yours," etc.

Thus, every man, who is to be fitted for great labors of love, must pass through his Gethsemane.

CHAPTER XXIV.

Call to First Church—Letters.

The consultations, on the part of members of the Broome Street Church among themselves, were now in progress that resulted in the calling of Kingman Nott to the vacant pastorship of that church. The post had been unoccupied for more than a year. Many causes made it a difficult place to fill. The last incumbent had been Cone. When he died, he left interests that still seemed bound indissolubly to his hand, and a people who, if they had been Papists, would have canonized him. The affections that had flowed so long in one channel refused to be suddenly diverted. Besides, Dr. Cone had been a man of such force and intellectual height, as to have constituted himself, to some degree, a standard of judging and thinking among his people: he was the measure by which they measured opinions and men. The first thought concerning every new candidate, thus was, Is he like Cone? Preacher after preacher had stood in Dr. Cone's pulpit, but not one, to the people's eye, stood up to the dimensions of the man—or rather, *was* the man, for not equality alone, but identity of gifts was sought. More than fifty, including some of the brightest lights of the land, had gleamed from the desk, and still the people were unmoved.

Meanwhile the church began to suffer. The congregation, though remarkably steadfast, began to decrease, and the Sunday School to decline. Numbers of irreligious youth, children of converted parents, were becoming confirmed as well in the habit of wandering from the venerable mother-church, as in impenitence. A pastor was indispensable. Yet the question had come to be asked despairingly all through the denomination, "Who can be the standard-bearer of the Old First?" But the church had faith and works, and so were sure in the end of God's blessing. They sustained all their meetings with energy, and established besides an extraordinary weekly meeting, for the express purpose of praying for a pastor.

Another cause limited the number from which a selection could be made. They were lovers of truth, and of truth as they understood it. They knew with precision what they believed, and they, of course, and very justly, tested every preacher by their religious sooner than by their literary creed. Literary blemishes they might endure; a heretical taint, never. They braced themselves with all their might against the fatal proclivity of the age to laxity in doctrine, and would not be mocked with sentimentalisms in place of sharp truth, or bewildered by any dazzling pyrotechnics of rhetoric: they would be unmoved even by the heavy boom of logic, if the ammunition was not plainly taken from the armory of truth. Their preacher must be first good, then *sound*—then simple, clear, and earnest—then a man alive and energetic—then, please God, eloquent and able to be "popular." This was their scale, not so much in theory as in practice. Primness of garb, a melodious voice, an imposing manner—even the gifts of fluent and fervid rhetoric, that are so often the secret or open demand of congregations, were not so much as thought of by this people, as positive desiderata.

It was now clearly perceived, by the wise of the church, that to fix upon any man of such age and acknowledged standing as to occupy a position at once marked and independent, and to have a right to challenge a comparison on his own merits with their late lamented leader, was simply impossible. Agreement on such a person was out of the question, while for a minister to accept a muttered call, given with a look askance, and a scowl contending with the smile, was suicidal. Pushed by the exigency, they turned and saw light in another direction. A young man, if one of the right qualities could be found, might come in and do them good. As nobody would think of elevating him to Cone's pedestal, so he would enjoy the advantage of standing on a pedestal of his own; he would be independent, untrammelled, and have ample scope to do his own, peculiar work. If he should prove deficient in the gift of *management*, there were wise deacons. If he should not be the ideal preacher, he might still have excellences, and "save our young people." With these thoughts, they had first sent for the young Kingman Nott to supply them.

His preaching had, in every essential respect, secured their unanimous approval. He was sound, he was earnest and simple, he had fluency, he spoke without notes, and besides, had a thousand nameless and unartificial fascinations of manner that caught the indifferent and the young, and fixed their attention to the truth that was illumined, and not disguised, by these graces. His social qualities also gained their liking—his free, cordial, unembarrassed, and manly manners. They felt, almost unreasoningly, that he had also the traits of a *leader*, and was capable of inspiring heroism in his followers. His devotion to Christ they were sure was genuine. In the course of this first visit he had one day stepped into the counting-room of a merchant, a member of the church, but whose partner was unconverted. Receiving an introduction to the latter, and passing the ordinary compliments, he did not bow himself out of the store without first inquiring of the gentleman respecting the safety of his soul. "Who is that young man?" said the unconverted partner after he had gone out; "did you say he was supplying your pulpit? *That's* the pastor I want; obtain him; he *believes* his religion." This was universally the impression.

One day, about the first of December, two gentlemen rode in a close carriage up to the door of Professor R., in Rochester. "They came as if they were detectives in search of a convict!" They were ushered into the library. Prof. R. entered. "We must see nobody but yourself and Mr. Nott. First, we wish to confer with you. As a question of policy, what do you think of our inviting that young man to be the pastor of the First Church? Would he succeed?" "I think there would be no risk." "Has he the requisite talents, in variety as well as in degree?" "In my opinion he has." "But could he bear the labor? Would it not strain his powers and speedily exhaust him?" "No, he is like an india-rubber ball; throw him down and he'll rebound; bend him, and he'll spring back like a hickory sapling; his energy is inexhaustible."

They went in search of Mr. Nott, and were closeted with him. The interview was productive of nothing important. Mr. Nott had an engagement in Boston. He had promised to preach a Sunday or two at the Canton Street Church at Christmas, and meant to go there untrammelled.

To Christmas time we now pass.

"Boston, *December* 22*d*, 1856.

"Dear Father:

"I arrived here Saturday evening, after a comfortable ride. We had a pleasant day at Canton Street, yesterday, though I went feeling quite oppressed by distracting cares and the perplexities of the week. Some of my former Temple people were with us. Among them, right before me, were the shining eyes of the new convert that the Lord gave us just before my leaving, as a seal of his special favor........The people would press me to a decision this week. If I get through with this matter without sinning, and am guided to a decision on which I shall rest with an assurance of God's approval, I shall be grateful all my life. I do not know when I have felt so helpless. I never, since I became a Christian, needed your prayers and those of all who love me, and love Christ's cause, as I do now. The responsibility is crushing. Did it regard myself alone, it would be of less importance. But the cause of Christ—that I love—is concerned. May the Lord show me His will. I wish almost every hour of the day that you were here. This is indeed a great field. I feel above all human advice. I painfully realize that the case is beyond their judgment," etc., etc.

TO HIS FATHER.

"ROCHESTER, *Dec.* 30, 1856.

...."With the surroundings I had in Boston, I stood, of course, in need of a degree of watchfulness that I had never before known. I think it was a means of grace to me, for as I never more completely felt my dependence on heavenly wisdom, so now, in looking back, I am sure that I am guided and aided by a power above. My mind, for a time distracted by the very novelty of responsibility, soon rested in God, and at the last of the week I could praise the Lord, who had brought me out of my perplexity into a *large* place and a *clear*. I have many dear friends in B. I could be happy in spending my life with them. But my course was made perfectly clear to me, and the result I am willing to leave with God. I am *sure* to be satisfied. The good brethren and sisters in Boston love me, and I love them. But I have been perfectly frank with them, they have admitted the justice of my position, and I rejoice in being confident that, whatever the result, there will be no reflections cast and they will love me none the less." . . . .

The First Church in New York, at a meeting held on the 29th of December, 1856, unanimously voted a call to Mr. Nott. The letter of the church was conveyed to him on the 1st of January, 1857, and elicited the following reply—implying an acceptance.

TO DR. DEVAN, OF NEW YORK.

ROCHESTER, THEOL. SEM., *January* 2, 1857.

"MY DEAR DR. DEVAN:

"I need not tell you that I have soberly reflected on the subject left with me for consideration. I feel this evening prepared, after seeking divine guidance, to decide for your people all that may now be necessary.

"The Lord willing, I shall be glad to come and preach to your young people their annual sermon.

"I shall at that time be able to convey to your people my decision, and what I trust may be the Lord's decision upon this solemn call. Meanwhile I will hint to you one or two thoughts that have occurred to me.

"I have considered most the judgment which you gave as the judgment of the church, that, in case of acceptance, I could best serve them by supplying them occasionally between this and the time of actual settlement. I have now time only to say that my thoughts so lead me back to my first impression, that I am now *firmly* convinced that such a course would be not only without special advantage, but an aggravation and essentially disastrous to both parties. My reasons I can unfold more fully when I see you. Meanwhile this, so that no false anticipations may be raised. I know eight months is long to ask your church to wait. I do not *dare* to ask it. Yet I cannot be ready for such duties sooner if I must assume them," etc.

"ROCHESTER, *Jan.* 10, 1857.

"MY DEAR DR. DEVAN,

"Many thanks for your kind note of the 5th inst. The preaching service for the third Lord's Day of the month seems satisfactorily arranged. I am much obliged to you for the additional week.

"I think you do not quite understand my feeling with regard to the matter of the *vacation*. In fact, it was strongly against my own feelings that I made any allusion to the subject; when I did, my attention was fixed, not so much on the *amount* as on the necessity of a vacation of *some* length. I suggested the matter, I will confess, not of my own idea, but as urged upon me by my friends. I blushed to do it at all. . . . . . . A '*demand*' my dear Dr., I should *never* make. Such stipulations I should never think of incorporating into a call, or the acceptance of a call. They argue and promote a mutual want of confidence.

"Perhaps you do not fully know me yet. I sometimes think that your church are taking more upon *trust*, in their late action, than most would be willing to do. But this very fact makes me love them more. Whether I shall possess 'less interest in their welfare,' or betray less 'anxiety to labor,' than any one else, remains yet to be manifested. At present, I can only speak of a full heart and earnest purposes, with a reliance on God's grace.

"I have not forgotten that it is your custom to offer special prayer for the Spirit's blessing on the Annual Sermon to the Young. May God, for this time, give you a special unction, and enable you to prevail in prayer," * * * * *

"ROCHESTER, *Jan.* 14, 1857.

"MY DEAR FATHER:

"I was very glad to hear from you this morning by your kind letter. Your counsel and sympathy do me great good; and I am always relieved by being assured of your continued life and health.

"There is something about the *form* of that call to New York, which to me is striking and solemn. The same godly spirit has pervaded all their intercourse with me, and made me feel that God was in the whole. Sometimes I tremble at what I have already done, and start back as if I were about to make a fatal plunge.

Were I conscious that I had deliberately done anything to bring about the present juncture of affairs, I should not dare to take this step. But, feeling as I do, that it has all been beyond my control, I will trust the hand that has thus far unerringly guided me, and follow where it points.

"Of course, I have thought of little else for the month past, and now conjectures and half-formed plans for the future are busying my brain. Still, I have felt inclined to *say* very little about the subject. Both the excellences of the position and its difficulties are, I know, not comprehended by me at present. I am surprised at my own coolness.

"Yet, while I shall love to *think* of my future home and vineyard and work, I am resolved not to be in the least degree distracted from my present preparatory pursuits. Under the reflected light of opening life, my heart and mind are revealing their glaring deficiencies to me, as I have never seen them before. The thought that I must be *reconciled* to these, as now past cure, is insupportable to me: I pray for grace to rise once more in desperate and victorious conflict with them. O, how I ought to, how I MUST grow in acquirements, in discipline, and more than all in GRACE, before I shall be fit to enter on my work! How *specially devoted* ought such an one to be!

"The church and I are to come into severe, though I trust not serious, collision on one point. They wish me to supply their pulpit once in two or three, or, at the very farthest, four weeks; so that they may feel that they have a pastor, and that we may prosecute a mutual acquaintance. I have become so convinced of the folly of this, that I shall be forced to decline doing so, and, if necessary, even make it a condition (and the only condition) of acceptance, that I am not to be called upon for any service till the 1st of September.

"I go down to New York to-morrow night, to visit my beloved people; preach the Annual Sermon to the Young, and give my answer to their solemn call. Monday or Tuesday, I shall try to go to Boston for one day, returning directly from there on Wednesday or Thursday to Rochester. Is not this best?

"So soon as I know more about my good church, I will write you of it. Meanwhile, I send her Articles of Faith. . . . Much love." . .

"NEW YORK, *Jan.* 19, 1857.

"MY DEAR FATHER:

"We are having what I call a 'splendid,' what New-Yorkers call a 'terrific' snow-storm. The great city is blockaded, and all who can be are housed. I have accomplished three calls, and made my way down town. Now I am writing in my host's store.

"I had a hard journey from Rochester, and found myself in poor condition for Sunday. It was a bad day, but the house was filled *full*. I had some difficulties. I had discovered that my unlucky coat-linings were torn, so I tore them out. I lifted up my arm and found the *white* showing. So I stuffed one of the coat-linings (being black) under the coat-arm. That was very good, and so I went to church. I was flanked by a minister on either side. I went on pretty well, when I suddenly discovered that the wretched 'coat-lining' had both escaped from its service and was running out at the wrist. I tucked it up, but thenceforward my right arm was imprisoned. Just then, for the first time, my eye fell on a rogue of a reporter just beneath me, who was scratching away, just as though I was saying something. So pretty soon I stopped, said 'failure' to myself, and sat down.

"So my prayer 'to be humbled' has been answered, and I remember Dr. L—— and bless God. I sought His face and found him, and preached in the afternoon with a delightful calmness and trust in God, and felt greatly blessed. We were obliged to dispense with the evening meeting on account of the storm. I shall get away as soon as the snow will allow. I wish I could write more. God is with me. Good bye.

"Your affectionate Son,

"A. K. N."

"ROCHESTER, *Jan.* 29, 1857.

"MY DEAR DR. DEVAN:

"Since I got successfully back from N. Y., I am daily convinced of the wisdom of our decision, that my visits to you should be like angels', so far as regards frequency. Really, I find myself pining, like an absent lover (i. e. as I suppose an absent lover would pine), for *my church*. It is the first thing by morning and the last by night. It follows me into my dreams, and pursues me through the day. So you see it is well that the snow-blockade did not longer imprison me, and well that I do not look upon you until April. On the one hand shrinking by reason of conscious unfitness, and on the other hand burning with desire to enter the lists at once, I am in a continual contest with myself. But I must try to forget you, and yet remember you. . . . . It is painful to me that I cannot let the church know how greatly I love them, and how much I am willing to do for them. But if God will, the time will come," . . . .

"*Jan.* 30.

"MY DEAR R——:

"I called on Mrs. —— in Brooklyn the other day. She talked of my prospects in New York, and said: 'Ah! how your mother must feel at this time!' It struck me strangely. I forgot for the moment present blessings, and could think only of the mother of our infancy and birth. Mr. —— is a strange man. He talked with me two hours or more the other day, then suddenly exclaiming, 'Nott, I feel like praying with you!'—dropped on his knees. He rose, walked to the window, looked out, and said—'Nott, our mothers were remarkable women!'" . . . .

TO S. T. HILLMAN, OF N. Y.

"ROCHESTER, *Feb.* 21, 1857.

"MY DEAR BRO. HILLMAN:

"I suspect that you business men acquire a habit of more promptness in correspondence than some of us are apt to possess. But however destitute I may seem myself to be of this quality, I assure you I have no dulness in appreciating it.

"During the weeks passed since your kind letter, I have been very often reminded of you, even by the very duties that have hindered me from writing; for the topic of our class lectures and discussions has *providentially* been that same blessed doctrine of *Providence*, which struck the key-note to your epistle. We concluded that the Christian was the object of God's special care, and that every event, whether in the life of nations or of individuals, whether vast or apparently insignificant, was directed by Him and made subservient to His purposes of grace. But I rejoice that I have not been dependent for the learning of this doctrine on a theological course. My own life, wonderful probably to no one but myself, has been a constant commentary upon it, and has enforced and illustrated it to me as no human teacher could ever do. Where, without it, were the perseverance of the saints? Where our comfort in the midst of adversity? Where the final and glorious triumph of Christ's kingdom? . . .

"I need not say that I think of you all every day, and remember you in all my prayers. I hope that the church may be preserved from the sin of deferring earnest activity in saving souls, and growing in grace to a future time and more favorable circumstances. I trust that great advance may yet be made, before you have a settled pastor. I ardently desire that both parties may be fully prepared to enter at once into the hottest of the fight, when we join hands. To do this, *I* need a very great advance in spiritual knowledge and zeal, and in every grace. For this I am trying to pray. And you, too, pray for me. In this I rejoice. On Friday evenings, too! That is just the evening on which those of us here who are looking forward to the ministry, meet to pray that the Master will fit us for our work. So you see that you do not pray alone, for

> " 'Though sundered far, by faith we meet
> Around one common mercy seat.' "

" *February* 23.

"The conduct of the church has surprised and delighted me. Their absolute confidence in me is almost preposterous. Moreover, you will, I am sure, be pleased to know that it is their desire that I keep clear from *all* public societies, and give myself exclusively to the church. Indeed, who cannot see that any other course would be suicidal? Dear R——, I hope you will pray much for me, that I may be fitted for my mission to the young people of that congregation. 'We are dropping off, and we want some one to come and save our *children!*' say the good *old* people to me." . . .

TO DR. DEVAN.

" *February* 23.

"On the foreign mission subject I am becoming interested, though I do not feel competent to express an opinion. *Amended* the Miss. Union may be; but could you think of seeing it *abandoned?* I do hope that the May Anniversary may unite the divided hearts of our brethren, and we go about the better business of saving men from perdition. This is what *I* want to see—men *saved.* I am glad that you cast your influence against precipitate measures. It would seem that Baptist history for the last six years should have taught to all of us *that* lesson. Do you not think it is wrong to withhold funds from the Union on account of its troubles or even its faults? It seems to me unwise, not to say ungenerous. Let us stand by the Union till our *debts* are paid off.

"To leave it in the lurch at such a crisis has a suspicious look about it. Even if we were to abandon it, it seems to me that we ought *first* to do our share towards relieving its pecuniary embarrassments.

"I should greatly enjoy being present next Lord's Day to see you baptize those new converts. Especially do I rejoice with you and Mrs. D. in this mercy of God to one of our own kindred. I shall be glad if you may find opportunity to assure these lambs of our flock, of my deep interest and earnest prayers in their behalf. May God keep them!" . . . .

"ROCHESTER, *Feb.* 28.

"DEAR MOTHER:

. . . "Now you must not blame me altogether if I was dumb on the question that most interested you, during the two short days of utter bewilderment, which constituted my last visit home. Beyond a few words to father, my lips were sealed against the utterance of '*First Baptist Church, New York,*' both while wandering about at home and during all that painful week in Boston, even until the whole matter was irrevocably settled, some days after my return to Rochester. It may be I was wrong. But I felt as I did during that silent week in January, seven years ago, when I wandered about from attic to sitting-room, and from sitting-room to attic, transacting business with Jehovah, and settling my eternal destiny.

"My room-mate, who is free and confiding, accuses me of living within myself, and having some talent for keeping my own 'counsel.' Is it so? Has the tattling boy comè to this? I should be rather disposed to congratulate myself if I believed him, for it is some satisfaction even to change one fault for another.

"Your letter of three weeks ago came in good company. The first one that I opened that morning was in a strange hand, and called my attention to a Sabbath spent by me in B——, some weeks ago; expressing earnest anxiety for salvation, and saying, 'If I am ever saved, it will be through your instrumentality.'... Well, thought I, 'In the morning sow thy seed, in the evening withhold not thy hand, for thou knowest not whether shall prosper, this or that.'

"And so I opened the second letter, which was in the hand of a dear old friend of Suffield days, now a Yale student. I had not heard from him for a long time. 'Do you remember,' he began, 'writing to a certain friend a year ago, and in that letter saying, "*Flee to Christ?*" That friend has done it! And you asked too, "Are you a pardoned sinner?" I answer, *Yes.*' So it went on with the rejoicings of a new convert for six pages. Well, thought I,—and I began to wonder and be humbled—'Cast thy bread upon the waters, and thou shalt find it after many days.'

"Well, mother, so you see the 'church that is in our house, is about to lose one of its members."

He was about removing his church relation from Kennebunkport to New York.

"It seems almost like going out of the church *quiescent* into the church militant. I do not know what is before me, nor do I care to know what *else* may be, so long as the cloud and pillar of fire are. There are, as you would easily suppose, a great many head-shakers, and not a few evil prophets. Were you to believe some of them, you would resign yourself at once to the prospect of seeing your son drop out of sight—before the 50's of this nineteenth century are done—either into insignificance—or the *grave.* Diligent newspaper correspondents assure the public that the young gentleman in question is 'young—very young'—'young and *wholly inexperienced*—and the field of labor *hard.*' Good! The Lord, I have noticed, likes to do 'hard' things, and even to do them by feeble, 'weak' things. I do not think any of us can be more sensible than one paper, which remarks that the question of the young brother's probable success or failure is very freely discussed, not only in New York city, but in the interior towns of the state, and many are ready at once to prophesy,' etc. etc. And then adds: 'And, indeed, it would not be strange if some of these prophecies should prove to be true,'——I think so!

"If I rain down upon you in April (April showers soon pass away—they do not stay even 'two days') I must bring you some of my good letters from New York. I am impatient for you to get acquainted with the dear brethren and sisters of this 'lovely church.' . .

"Your loving Son, "K."

"*March* 6.

"DEAREST C——:

"The other day I went to my desk to help myself to a fresh supply of my correspondence-paper, when lo! to my astonishment none was to be found. It was some time before I could realize that I had written over, in so short a time, a half ream of paper, employed only for letters, and scattered it by single sheets among my various friends. Many questions rushed upon me; some of them sober ones. Who have those sheets? Where are they? What thoughts have been conveyed? What emotions excited? What harm—what good has been effected? Now, C—, if you bring the powers of your mental and moral nature to bear upon this subject, you will see that the thread of moralizing might be spun out indefinitely. Do you then appreciate the self-denial and generosity with which I resign so fine an opportunity, and spare you the infliction? Then I will pass on. . . . .

"Have I told you that I have at last been forced into preaching in Rochester? . . . . By the way, in my last attempt at preaching the Lord was pleased to give me, without any effort or fitness on my part, one of those gracious experiences with which He sometimes (oh! that it were oftener!) vouchsafes to visit me. I do not know that I ever spoke with a more direct consciousness of His presence. Without, the night was stormy; within all was very still and solemn. I went to the church with a carefully prepared, general discourse, supposing that only (or principally) church members would be present. Looking about, I observed a majority of unconverted young people. My sermon seemed heavy and inappropriate, and I felt called by the Spirit to speak from another text, which I had recently employed. It was in this obedience and faith that I received the blessing. So you see I have a lesson learned.

"I usually preach each Sunday afternoon at one of our mission stations, of which we have several in and around the city.—We hear of revivals from the villages about us," etc.

ROCHESTER, *May* 12, 1857.

"MY DEAR R——:

"I think you will have to preach. Perhaps it may be with you as with me—for God, it seems to me, had a double purpose in bringing me into the ministry. One, to save the souls of men by me; the other to save *me*. Perhaps God sees that for some of us are needed the discipline and the constant demands of so sacred and responsible a profession, in order to *compel* us to consistent piety. Abhorrent is a professional piety—yet may not a profession aid piety? A *church* profession does. Do you not believe the ministry has made me a better Christian, poor as I am? Very likely without it my piety would have gone by the board. God designed just this as the means of grace to save me. The call was a gracious one—as to the world, so to *me*. Had I resisted it, I dare not think of the consequences to myself. Very likely I should have been a castaway. Is not the path of duty our only path to Heaven? In the practice of law, "Work or die." In the ministry it is, "Be pious or a hypocrite." I think you would prefer the former.

"I doubt whether you will ever attain your own standard of an active, faithful, honest Christian life, out of the ministry. If you cannot be a faithful *Christian* minister, much less (I believe) will you be a faithful Christian lawyer or teacher. I think I could saw wood, or manage a law-suit, with a cold heart [towards Christ]. But I *can't preach* with it—at least not extemporaneously. What then? give up preaching—and take the cold heart? It might possibly do—if that were the end of it!—But that cold heart must endure hell. No, better carry the heart to Christ and beg him to warm it with his love; then go and preach. See! if it had not been for the impulse to preach, you might not have known that the heart was cold—or have been content with it. I do not remember ever to have preached without getting a spiritual benefit. If I have grown in grace at all, preaching has been a *great means.*

"True enough, it will not do in the ministry to 'do good lazily, comfortably and spasmodically.' But the difficulty is, it will not do *out* of the ministry. Neither does one get rid of the obligation by declining to assume the responsibility. . . . . To be the Christian is the *all*—the minister is included. How would you talk to one who should urge your argument against his making a public profession of religion? If he could not live up to its vows by assuming them, could he, while refusing to do so? Would he not of all others *need* the stimulus of such a profession? Could you, without a profession of religion, have attained the standard of piety you have? By the profession of the ministry you would be enabled to attain a correspondingly higher standard. I find it *easier* to do good when people expect it of me.

"Besides, I think that the reason why you do not do better as a Christian now, is because you feel that you are leaving *the great* duty of your life undone, and consequently have less heart for other duties. So soon as you feel that you are precisely where God would have you, there will be some encouragement to work and to be pious.

"A minister has the advantage over every other man. The absorption of an *engrossing business* is added to all the other motives to faithfulness and impulses to zeal."

TO S. T. HILLMAN.

"*March* 19.

"I have been studying considerably on the picture you presented in your last letter of a New York Sunday to a Christian man. I should not hesitate to say that you have too much to do. As I presume there are many similar cases (I wish there were more!) it is worthy of some study to ascertain how and where retrenchment is to be made. Perhaps one Sunday-school is enough. If there are two sessions, there ought to be two sets of teachers. I do not know but one sermon is enough. One, with an afternoon to digest it (not to doze off the effects of a Sunday dinner), and an evening to talk and pray over it socially, would be better than *two* gulped down without thought or prayer. I would rather have my church attend my preaching once and my prayer-meeting, than preaching twice without the prayer-meeting. But I *would not* preach to a 'half-day congregation.'

"Against this I have a capital remedy to suggest.

If a man wants to stay at home in the afternoon, let him on one condition—that he always fill his place in his pew. Send his clerk, or coal-heaver, or hired girl, or find out some poor family and say, '*There*, you have a pew of your own, as good as the best, every Sunday afternoon, *go*, take it, and be at home. I would far rather have such a needy, hungry audience than undertake to stuff the overfed one of the morning."

After a visit in the spring vacation to New York.

ROCHESTER, *April* 22, 1857.

"MY DEAR BRO. HILLMAN,

"I found myself, immediately on coming here, plunged into business so deeply, that I have sent out no letters yet, save a hasty note home. Yet I have not forgotten my friends, least of all my beloved people of the First Church, now dearer to me than ever. . . . .

"Life in New York as a Christian preacher, and our mutual work, loom up before me now in more distinctness and vastness. As a church and pastor we have a mission to perform. The temptation to divert from it and the liability to misunderstand it seems to me fearfully strong. 'Not many noble, not many mighty,' etc. 'Go ye out into the highways and hedges and compel men to come in.'

"But all this in good time. I sometimes dare to expect that the Lord will do great things for us. Why not? I hope you will all get in a large stock of faith, stores of promises and prayers, for us to begin on next fall if God please. I do not mean in yourselves, and least of all in me. You know what faith is. Sometimes glorious visions pass before me of scenes in old Broome Street, which make the very walls shake. O, that God may send His almighty Spirit down! We lack the *power*. We preachers lack it—the churches lack it. We multiply the means but vainly till God make them efficacious.

"But it will not do to dwell much on the future. It often occurs to me that I may after all not live to be the pastor of the First Church. God give us grace to do our duty *to-day*.

"There are some among you for whom I am pressed with a constant anxiety, and for whom I daily pray; D—— B——, and others. Write me everything you can about them. I long to hear of other conversions, and already repent that I did not do more while with you.

. . . . "Love to all the little household. I hope A. and F. are very good girls every day, and I want them to learn to love Jesus." . . . .

TO S. T. HILLMAN.

"*May* 12.

"So you have been experimenting in Congregational singing. I wish I might have been there to hear, I saw a gentleman the other evening who had that privilege, and who gave a very favorable account of this first attempt. I feel considerably enthusiastic in the matter, and hope it will be earnestly pushed forward. I want to hear *God praised* in Broome St. 'Let the people praise thee, O God; let *all* the people praise thee.' I think when I come down I shall be quite tempted to preach on the subject.

"That Home Mission Society must honor itself by a more faithful attendance of the members, or I shall not be proud of being on its Board. You certainly need an active, practical head-officer upon the ground, and it seems to me that you had better rest satisfied with having tendered to me the compliment of election to the Presidency, and, accepting my resignation, proceed to elect the most driving man you can find among you, to push the society into maturity. You have made a beginning, and not a bad one; may the Lord enable us to do much greater things."

In May he attended the Anniversaries in Boston, and writes:

"*May 23d.*

"I would have written you earlier this week, but really I have made a business of attending the meetings, and have consequently found time for almost nothing else, not even for calling on my friends. Still I have met very many pleasant acquaintances, both old and new, the latter predominating.

"I have been compelled to feel sadly out of my place oftentimes while here, but I assure you I have been only a silent observer, keeping in the corner and eagerly listening to learn. And I have learned much. It has been a profitable school to me, and I cannot regret coming. It is a satisfaction to one who expects soon to enter the brotherhood, to see and hear and know his future confrères. But do not think I should ever be ambitious to appear conspicuous in the Baptist Societies. Less so than ever. I have seen small men and young men make themselves ridiculous enough to be a warning to all who come after. Of ability I have seen three worthy displays," etc.

"*July* 1*st*, 1857.

"DEAR BROTHER HILLMAN:

"I sit down to write what is likely to be my last letter to you as a theological student. I hardly know what I shall be for the next two months. Simply a *boy at home*, I think. I cannot tell you how much satisfaction the thoughts of the First Church and my correspondence with them have yielded me through this brief winter and spring. It has been half my life. And now I am *through*, I feel brought much nearer to the church. It will not now be unlawful for me to think of them as my own. Surely never was found so patient and considerate a people. I feel very grateful to them. I rejoice in the prospect of having soon an opportunity to manifest my devotion to them. You have been very kind to keep me so constantly informed of matters among you. I hope you will not withhold your epistles during the summer, but address me at my home in Maine.

"Cling to the *Congregational Singing!* If I can in any way give it an impulse when I come, I shall do it with all my might. I believe God demands it of us.

"But a few weeks and I shall be among you, to work and to love. May God prepare us for the union!

"You amuse me by wishing that I may bring a 'helpmeet,' so that nothing may 'distract' me! Have you so soon forgotten Brother Paul? 'He that is unmarried, careth for the things of the Lord, how he may please the Lord; but he that is married, careth for the things of the world, how he may please his wife,'" etc. etc.

"ROCHESTER, *July* 7.

"DEAR R——:

"Examinations all passed, and we are graduated. Only the final bow remains. Dr. R. held us yesterday for ten mortal hours, seven on theology and three on strawberries. We are going to have the greatest Commencement ever known yet. I shall probably leave here next Thursday, and hope to see you the week after.

"Have I told you my theme for the Anniversary? It is 'The Independence of the Pulpit.' Is that right? I am just going now to get it from the hands of the professor. Hope he will find it orthodox, for I don't want to write to-day. It is hot—the weather I mean—not the speech.

"I don't think it best to write much now. There is no Fourth of July in particular here. Your loving brother," etc.

"NYACK (ON THE HUDSON), *July* 11*th*, 1857.

"DEAREST C——:

"I am in a barn-chamber. This is the only sheet of paper in the region, this is the dregs of the ink, and the pen has seen hard service. Before me rows of 'yarbs,' hanging against the board wall, yield their musty fragrance. On my right is a great heap of new mown hay, and a window leads my eye in frequent wanderings down a slope of lawn to the broad expanse of the river, and across to the beautiful village scattered along the heights of Tarrytown. At my back, a joiner's bench and a window which overlooks a garden. There the chickens peep industriously, and little feet are pattering. Below the horse testifies his presence by sundry thumps upon the floor of his stall. From the house come the sounds of children.

"This forenoon I spent in the saddle. First, I went along a road lined with pretty cottages and gardens, and skirting the river bank. At the end of two miles the road stops short in front of a steep, rocky mountain, which overhangs the river in a bluff promontory. So I came back to a lighter ascent, which led around it. After a half mile's ascent I turned back to behold one of the most beautiful landscapes the eye ever looked upon. Down the steep hill was a succession of cultivated fields and cozy cottages. On the right was the bold promontory first spoken of, on the left the pretty village of Nyack, and farther down was Piermont, with its great pier a mile long. The Hudson stretched out its glassy surface for twenty in length and *three miles wide*, covered with river craft which had all their sails set to a fine breeze. The banks rose high on the other side, with smooth fields, neatly trimmed cedars, and handsome villas. Yonder is the town of Sing Sing, with the State prison, lying like a long white line close on the water's edge. Next is Peekskill. Directly opposite is Tarrytown, of Revolutionary fame. Below is sweet little Irvington, and the white cottage peak of Washington Irving's house, modestly peeping out from its bower of trees. Away I went over the hills, stopping occasionally to admire some funny Dutch old cottage, or to pick cherries from trees along the roadside, while my horse browsed upon the lower boughs. After a considerable circuit, I began to descend into a most *glorious* valley, great, fertile, and walled on every side. A turn to the right brought me to a large lake. Here we rode into the lake, where my pony snuffed up the water with great delight, and I stooped down and picked pond lilies.

"Last night a little company of us had a delightful sunset ride down the river road, in full view of the river and the opposite shore. Nyack is an old Dutch village, nestled in here for a century or more. Only lately have the rapacious New Yorkers ferreted it out, but though the city has set its marks upon it, it has not had time to spoil it yet, but only to add variety to its odd beauties. There are the most venerable and funny little old Dutch houses along the road, protected on one side by the river, and on the other by a great hill. These houses are built often with a lower story of brown stone, quarried out from the hill behind them, and the upper of wood, and almost always with a portico the whole length. They are indescribably quaint. Along this road the Yankees used to worry the British frigates by firing into them from behind the trees. O, the grand hills and rose-embowered cottages—this grand historic Hudson! I do think this is the most charming spot I have ever yet seen. . . . . . . But my sheet is full, after much tribulation with this wretched pen. Good bye.

"KINGMAN."

CHAPTER XXV

VACATION—FIRST YEAR IN NEW YORK—CAUSES OF SUCCESS, ETC.

THE time that elapsed between his graduation and ordination, was occupied with travelling and visiting. He preached every Sabbath, however, and even more frequently. His joyousness was never more remarkable than during this interval. In an excursion to St. Johns, he attracted the attention of the passengers by his overflow of spirits, and almost charmed away even the demon of sea-sickness. The sea was his friend: he was a congenial spirit; and whatever landsmen poetically dream might be exhilarating in riding on "the bounding billow," he enjoyed in fact. To the healthy all things are healthful. Spiritual life especially brings not only happiness of its own, but invites, sanctions, and sanctifies *all* gladness! What an advantage is it to have the natural gaiety of healthy childhood carried forward into mature life, consisting with and ministering to the purest thoughts and holiest pleasures! Sorrows are indeed the cost at which most mortals obtain appreciation and thence possession of the higher life; but this is because of sin. How blessed to have conquered the worst of sin through grace, before the susceptibilities to pure and elevated joy are corroded! In a worn-out heart, receiving Christ, slow and painful often is the advance of the new creation. The mind and desires are set right before the emotions; these do not respond readily to the appropriate incitements; and long is it often before the water of life wells up with facility and regularity through the fountains that have been accustomed to pour only poisoned streams. With Kingman it was different. The Spirit had taken possession of his being while yet the nice adjustments of the emotions to the intellect and will were undisturbed. The Christ in him was Lord also of the whole material world, and he rejoiced freely in all that was bright, and beautiful, and innocent, in nature and in social life. Thank God, would more than one heart, storm-beaten itself and incapable of mirth, say in looking upon this happy being, thank God for constituting one mortal, who, in this world of strife, can be both *glad* and *holy*. Perfect the specimen, exalt these rudiments in their present combination to fulness of development, and it is what the angels are—glad, holy.

He made an excursion also at this time to the Lakes in the north-eastern part of Maine, not far from Calais, travelling in a birch canoe, and making a lumbermen's camp his headquarters. Here trout and togue abound; through the wide forests the moose, inhabitant only of

Evening had come, the fishing tackle was put away, and the excursionists were housed. Merriment reigned in the loggers' camp. Stretched on their beds of boughs, the men smoked, laughed, and told stories. Nott was merry, too, and all day long he had been roving about the camp like a strong wind, fresh, bounding, and boisterous. But when it was time for sleep, and the men were turning prayerless to their hard pillows, he said, "*Can* we sleep without praying? I always pray—shall I pray aloud?" Obtaining silent consent, he knelt and poured out his soul to God, while all wondered, and were solemn and reverent. How it brought the remembrance of a present God home to each in that wilderness, where commonly in all thoughts God was not! It required some strength of principle to venture thus on probable ridicule—but with Kingman such principle was a habit.

He passed two delightful Sabbaths in Calais. On one, at noon—a still, calm noon—when the hot sunbeams were mellowed by a dreamy August haze, and the water rippled on the strand with a melodious sound, there was an impressive baptism at the river side. A multitude covered the high bank and the slopes that descended to the brink, and were silent as forest trees when only a solemn, quiet wind creeps over them, or joined with loud voices in the hymn,

> "'Tis done—the great transaction 's done—
> I am my Lord's, and he is mine!"

K. assisted in the services, and with such emotion that his voice was scarcely under command, and tears flowed freely down his cheeks. He referred ever to this occasion as one of singular enjoyment—the delightful introduction to an ordinance that he seldom could administer afterwards without tears of rapture.

We pass with him now to New York, the scene henceforth of his activity and toil.

Of his examination before the Ordaining Council, he writes:—

"Few questions were asked; not the least carping or criticism was apparent, but a delightful spirit pervaded the whole. I began my statement of doctrine by saying, first, that I knew no teacher but the Bible, accompanied by the Holy Spirit, and could only follow my own experience; then, that I was not prepared to give mature, much less *definitely expressed* views of doctrine—that I was just beginning the real study of theology, and applying the true test of my views by the preaching of them.

. . . . "I have this satisfaction: that in my statements of doctrine I tried to be honest to my present impressions, and that I committed myself to no man's phrase-*ology*." . . . .

The ordination services were of solemnity and interest adequate to so important an occasion. The sermon was preached by Rev. Dr. Robinson, of Rochester.

The hand of fellowship was given by Rev. Dr. Sarles, of Brooklyn.

The charge, given by the father of the candidate, was peculiarly earnest, touching, and appropriate. One passage was prominent for energy: "Be Christ's minister; in Christ's stead plead with dying sinners, and beware of adopting anything of theory or creed that would fetter your tongue from proclaiming a free gospel to all." How faithfully the solemn injunction was obeyed the sequel has revealed: "Only the sovereign grace of God can save you"—"Come, sinner, lost and helpless, to a Saviour's arms;" these, as the Bible does, he continually placed side by side, and urged, believing that the Spirit would save through this proclamation whom He would, and longing, with strong passion, for the salvation of all.

His first sermon after ordination was from Jonah:—"*Go unto Nineveh, that great city, and preach unto it the preaching that I bid thee.*" The discourse was not up to his standard in point of literary merit, but there was vigor of thought, and above all, earnestness that told with what spirit he began these duties. The congregation was immense, and he preached by an open baptistery. On every succeeding communion Sabbath till his death, the baptistery was open.

It so occurred that the duties of the first Sabbath furnished to the new pastor a complete synopsis of ministerial service. Besides preaching, baptism, and communion, he officiated at a marriage and a funeral.

We now quote letters :—

" PASTOR'S STUDY, SUNDAY MORNING, *Sep.* 14.

" DEAR FATHER :

" I suppose that by this time you are restored tc home, to regularity, and to labor. I hope you are not the worse for the trip ; for it would be unjust if, having imparted so much to others, you should not have received somewhat in return.

" I have passed through another week and another Lord's day, and have to praise the Lord for His goodness. He has blessed me in all things thus far, and enlarged my faith for the future. I have not spent so happy a week for years, nor enjoyed a Sabbath more. . . . .

" I prepared two sermons (without writing), and do not see why, with health and freedom from interruption, I cannot do the same every week. My texts were in the A.M., 'God forbid that I should glory,' etc. We cannot glory in *aught else* than the cross of Christ, because by the cross all things else are slain. We *do* glory in the *cross*, because—

" 1. In the cross is the fullest exhibition of God's glory.

" 2. In the cross all things truly glorious do centre.

" 3. (Personally to us) the cross is the instrument of our salvation.

" In the afternoon—'That ye may be able to comprehend with all saints what is the breadth and length and depth and height, and to know the love of Christ, which passeth knowledge.' The *dimensions* of the love of Christ; *broad* as the world; *long* as eternity; *deep* as hell; and, *high* as heaven; finally, immeasurable.

"These are different texts from those I have been most accustomed to preach upon. I find myself in entirely new circumstances. The cry is for *food—spiritual food*, and it comes from Christians of ripe growth and deep experience, whose demand is for strong meat. They know when they get it; nothing else will allure or satisfy them, however '*smart;*' and when they do get it, they go out of church saying, 'Ah, that is food! —solid food to-day!' So I have something to learn, and I know I shall find it richly repaying my own soul. . . . .

"The more I know of my church, the more I admire and love it; and I feel that to it as a body, or to individuals of it, I am forming stronger attachments than I have as yet known upon the earth, aside from my nearest kin. . . .

"Yours," etc.

To P. S. Evans, his late class-mate, then minister in Boston, he writes—

"*Sept.* 19.

. . . "Do you not enjoy the work? I was never so happy in my life. It is a continual feast to my soul. I feel that I have something tangible now to love and live for. I feel my life-work upon me, and it makes me another man. Yet I am grieved and humbled to find that spirituality does not come with the necessity for it, and that I am yet a creature of weakness, temptation, and sin. But I know my people pray. I *feel* their prayers. It is in the prayer-meetings that I have found the greatest encouragement. Our lecture-room is fast filling up. The Young People's Meeting had become much reduced. At the first only about a dozen were present. At the next I was astonished to find the room crowded full. The Female Prayer-Meeting had been dead for more than a year. To-day it is renewed, and I am anxiously waiting to hear from it. But I know it is successful." . . .

"*Sept.* 21.

"DEAR C——:

. . . . "I am surprised that I so seldom think of the great transformation! The '*Rev.*' on a letter—for even father employs the title now—brings me to my senses; but I am pretty much absorbed, nor do my thoughts often wander off beyond the bounds of my parish.

"I had a happy week last. Lectured on Tuesday evening to a houseful on Acts xviii. 11, 12. 'These were more noble,' etc., on the Importance of a Diligent *Study* of the Sacred Scriptures. This is designed to pave the way for a course of expository lectures. I made twenty or more calls during the week, etc. . . .

"Sunday was rainy, but our congregation good. Preached A.M. on John xx. 28: 'My Lord and my God!'—on the Divinity of Jesus Christ,—P.M., from Ex. xxii. 36, 'Who is on the Lord's side,' etc. I live more than ever in your prayers.

"Your loving

"K."

"*Oct.* 6.

"DEAR MOTHER,

. . . . . "I must report to you last week's events. Tuesday I came upon three inquirers in one house. In the evening I lectured on 'Lord, save me!'—Peter's walking on the sea. Our room was full of eager listeners. Wednesday I found two young converts, who gave me accounts of their conviction, long struggles, and final conversion, to which I listened in amazement. They had been converted that day. Thursday a lady came to beg me to see and talk with her husband, who was in great alarm. In the evening our Young People's Meeting was very solemn, and at its close several persons remained to talk and pray with me.

"Friday we had a meeting full of prayer—and Sunday was a day of days. I preached in the morning on 'One thing I know,' and baptized three precious converts. Each of these cases had a special point of interest, of which I spoke while standing with them in the water. The first was converted through Dr. Cone's death. The second through the loss of her child: for a long time she 'could not give it up; but now *praised God* for taking it.' The third—a dear child, illustrated my text. She is a timid little creature, and when before the church was too frightened to tell her story. At last she said, 'I felt I was a great sinner—I prayed God for Christ's sake to forgive me my sins—*and He did!*'—and burst into tears. 'One thing I know.' The house was full in every part, and a number standing.

"In the afternoon I preached on Christ our Sacrifice, and gave the bond of fellowship to twelve. . . .

I have appointed a meeting for inquiry, and last evening a few came. . . . .

"Yours," etc.

"*October* 16.

"Dear L——:

"An uncomfortably large pack of 'Unanswered Letters' is accumulating in my desk, but the days rush on, and few hours come which can conveniently be devoted to correspondence. The Lord is with us here, and we are kept busy. When men will hear, they *must* be talked to. When people are ready to pray, they must be prayed with. Inquirers must be directed to Jesus, that they may not be lost.

"I said the Lord was here. Week before last He came and brought two of my congregation from the kingdom of darkness into that of His dear Son. It was in one day. I went to the house one evening, not knowing what had befallen them, and was instantly greeted with, 'Well, sir, you are a welcome guest to this house, to-night,' etc.

"Last week He came again, and took two more. One was an intelligent man, whose wife I had baptized. He brought him to the very gates of hell, till, in his horrible distress, he cried unto the Lord, who heard him and had mercy, and filled his soul with glory. The other was a young woman, who begged the sisters who had come to attend *her mother's funeral*, to *pray* for her—such was her distress for sin. They knelt beside the corpse, and pleaded until the Lord was pleased to come to the house of death, with *life*, and brought joy for mourning.

"To-day, two others have given me their story, and are rejoicing in the Lord.

"Pray for us, L——. Why have you not written to Miss ——? If you do, you must try to draw her out upon religion, and faithfully warn her of her duty. I hope you are very happy, and entirely successful. What are you doing for Jesus? Whom are you bringing to Him? Laboring for Christ is all of life. May we be absorbed in it!

"There is a great deal of trouble in the city—'hard times!' which the Lord is turning to good account. A daily prayer-meeting down town is one of its fruits. I preached last Sabbath on 'What shall it profit a man if he gain the whole world and lose his own soul?' The Lord be with you.

"Doubly your brother," etc.

These suffice to exhibit what beginning was made. The question naturally occurs, what were the causes of this immediate prosperity and steady advance?

One was, that the church had for months been fervently praying, and had thus become prepared to expect and to receive a blessing. It could hardly take them by surprise; they were ready.

Another was that God had arranged circumstances in the city itself, calculated to turn men's minds from material interests to spiritual themes. The great financial revolutions of '57–8 were in progress, riches were taking to themselves wings, and the true wealth shone clearer An uncommon solemnity rested upon the whole city.

Another was, that the church continued to pray, and supported the pastor by their sympathy, and ready and active co-operation in "every good word and work." Monday morning they began praying for God's blessing on the sermons of the day before; on the same morning they began praying for blessing on the sermons of the Sabbath next to come; and so morning and evening through the week. Every Sunday the preacher entered a sanctuary that was consecrated with the incense of a week's prayers; every discourse was commissioned to its work by the anxious dedications of five hundred praying souls. Again, the ground was full of seed. The Gospel had been faithfully preached for a quarter of a century by the revered and devoted predecessor of the young pastor. The people had been well indoctrinated, and in the hearts of many of the unconverted, truth, though buried out of sight, possessed still a vital and a germinating principle. Kingman, obeying the impulses of youth and of a fervid nature, dealt much in persuasion and glowing appeal, urging the invitations of the Gospel, expressing upon the sinner the obligation of immediate repentance. This preaching God blessed.

Upon the church he constantly impressed the duty of implicit faith, and of laboring directly for the salvation of souls, with the expectation of continual blessing. If we pray enough and work enough, believing that the power is all of God, and yet we responsible, the power will never be withheld. As often as we shall smite the rock, waters will gush forth. Such was the style of his persuasions.

He gave an example himself of fidelity and endurance. Assuming immediately the full burden of the duties properly or possibly belonging to his office, he bore the load steadily and manfully. From pulpit labors he accepted no respite by exchanges or supplies for many uninterrupted months. Each sermon was studied on his knees, and aimed at a particular object. A weekly lecture was given on Tuesday evenings; to this also he permitted no exceptions. He was uniformly present at the prayer-meetings, taking the lead of them, and thus impressing his own valuation of their importance upon the hearts of the people.

With the pressure of these labors, he nevertheless found time for *pastoral visiting.* A memorandum in a diary, under date of Jan. 6, 1857, while he was a student, says:

> "Mr. —— talked to me an hour about New York. Says I must make everything bend to my *pulpit*—to make that *first*—so I shall, in ten years, stand among the *great men.* But if I *visit*, etc., in ten years I shall not be *known.* Pastor and preacher—one cannot be successfully. *I am going to try it, if it ruins me;* I WILL KNOW MY SHEEP."

This purpose he carried out resolutely. Beginning in September, '57, he had, before February, 1858, visited, personally, the whole church-membership of more than five hundred, and commenced a second circuit—this time more leisurely. He aimed to preserve an acquaintance with the phenomena of the religious life in the heart of every member, and to bring his personal influence most forcibly to bear on each, to induce religious activity. This was accomplished by energetic perseverance, aided by a tenacious memory,—for he never forgot a name, or a face, or a fact. Thus, he was the personal and esteemed friend, spiritual adviser, and, it might almost be said, "father confessor" of nearly all the individuals of his church, and of not a few of the outside congregation. Inquirers and converts he managed to meet frequently.

His sermons were not always models—sometimes far from it. With such a burthen of cares, how could they be? Yet, why did they keep the house thronged? By clap-trap, or florid, gaudy rhetoric? The Tuesday evening lecture, at first given in the basement, had to be transferred to the large audience-room above, which was often filled with eager listeners. It was because of the "*power and spirit*" with which he spake. True himself to one object, God was true to him and to His own cause. It was evident to men that he was *in earnest:* he did not assume, or lash himself into, the emotions that were proper; he felt them. On his method of preparation, and peculiar traits as a preacher, a few words hereafter.

We are now prepared for the succeeding letters, descriptive of the constantly advancing, spreading work of the Lord. These letters are simply a register of pastoral experience; they profess to be nothing more. We make selections from a large number.

A single paragraph touching his habits:

"I rise at six, ride horseback at half-past six, breakfast at seven, get to my study by eight, study till twelve, admit callers for an hour, dine at one, come to my study and map out the afternoon's round, and then go on it till tea. The evenings are all taken."

Only four regular hours of study; but in these much work was accomplished. His power of mental concentration, and of rapid analysis, enabled him to treat time economically. He studied in the streets, moreover; and studied the *streets*, and the people in them. Constantly on the watch for sermons—and the world was filled with them.

He was fond of the critical study of the Scriptures, for which the fine library of the Bible Union, close at hand, furnished him with implements beyond the reach of most pastors.

CHAPTER XXVI.

FIRST YEAR CONTINUED—LETTERS.

"PASTOR'S STUDY, *Oct.* 20, 1857.

"DEAREST C——D:

"It is evening after Lecture, a bitter cold evening seemingly, so sudden has been the change from our beautiful Indian summer days. I confess I was surprised to find our vestry full of people, and my heart was greatly moved for them. I just begin to yearn for the salvation of these souls. I have been so amazed to see God work here that I have looked on in wonderment, half petrified with surprise at his miracles of grace, when I ought to have been active and expectant.

"I look on these converts with a new and strange feeling of wonder and delight. I have seen converts before, but they were converted under other men's ministry, and were the fruit of *their* labors under God." [He forgets how many had owned him as the instrument.] "But these are *mine*—my own spiritual offspring given me of the Lord. It scarcely seemed possible that souls could be converted under *my* ministry. Conversions never before appeared so mysterious—incredible to me.

"I wrote in one of my letters of three inquirers found in one house. Salvation has come to that house, and two of the number met me yesterday with shining faces. Another dear child, who has long been mourning, is happy in Jesus.

"Sunday was a specimen of beautiful days. I preached on 'The Lord is *risen* indeed.' I think I have never so feasted on truth as I did on this. I do not know how much blessing was left for the people. I am afraid I stole it all for myself.

"In the afternoon the good old saints who come from afar to the First Church, saw a strange sight. Behold the front pews, six deep, and all the side pews, taken possession of by simple Sunday School children! When it came to the singing, the children sang; and when it came to the preaching the children were preached to. The house was full, even to the galleries, and all to hear children talked to! Humph! Never mind. I have since heard of one little boy who has been much troubled because Mr. Nott said that if they were not converted while young, they were less likely to be so ever. I read and expounded to them Eccl. xii., and gave them just so many reasons why they should seek God while young, as they had fingers on each hand.

"Last Sabbath was an *extra* day, because I went to a dedication and preached. 'Who is on the Lord's side?' was my text. There was some solemnity, but it was afterwards all coined into money. . . . .

"Good night. . . . . My heart is feeling heavy to-night for souls that are dying, and my eyes ache. I must get one of my solid night's rests, so as to be fresh for sermonizing to-morrow.

"O, we have started a daily morning prayer-meeting. Won't you all meet with us around a common mercy-seat? It is from eight to half past eight. . . . . I am well yet; everybody's well here, and I especially.

"Yours," etc.

"*Nov.* 2, 1857.

"DEAR FATHER:

"I should like to say very much to you in relation of God's dealings with me and my people, since I last wrote, but cannot enter upon the story, because I should not know where to leave off. . . . .

"Two or three weeks ago, I lectured on 'Behold I stand at the door and knock;' and disturbed some good minds a little, because I applied to sinners what the Spirit said to the *Church*. So the next week I lectured on the dry bones—'So they were very many, and behold they were very dry,' in which I stated my views very plainly, and my heart was greatly enlarged, and the Lord blessed us all. However, one person was converted by means, in part, of the poor, faulty 'knocking' sermon, so I do not feel very badly over it. I enjoy these Tuesday evening sermons. . . . .

"Well, we have had another of those incomparable church-meetings, and another blessed ordinance-day. That was the great day of the feast. The Lord permitted me to baptize four precious converts. I wish you could see these converts, and hear their old-fashioned deep experiences. . . . . Then one of our large communions, with the galleries nearly filled with serious, tender-hearted spectators!

"In the evening all was turned upside down in the old First Church. Old deacons exhorted, and told their experiences like young converts, and young converts like old deacons. It was a *praising* meeting. So we are very happy—almost too happy.

"Another new convert has come to me to-day. There is not a general melting yet, but I *hope* it may come. . . . . "Yours in love.

"K."

TO EVANS.

"*Nov.* 5.

"I stayed at home last evening for the first time. . . I have an amazing cold that I must shake off before another Sabbath. You know I am so unused to ills, that I have yet to learn patience under even the most trivial of them. It sometimes occurs to me that before I leave the world the Lord may give me abundant opportunity. Hitherto my danger has been that of receiving my good things in this life, and I have lately been praying that this may not be. . . . .

"I know I love the work! The mere thought of being interrupted in it, for even a brief space, fills me with distress. I feel that it has a stronger hold upon me each day. Last Sabbath was so precious! My tears will fall as I write of it. I preached on *Christ—the blessed and only Potentate—King of Kings, and Lord of Lords,*—and baptized a few precious converts into his glorious name. . . . . .

"On Tuesday I was present at the funeral of ——. The scene was to me very solemn and affecting. Bro. —— seemed divinely sustained. Dear man! My heart yearns for him in his sorrow, for I reverence and love him. The sermon was preached by ——, and the best I have heard for a long, long while. I could not help wishing that the First Church had him to preach to them. True, he is an indifferent speaker, but that is all lost in the richness of the *truth* which he lavishes upon you. . . . . I went to Greenwood, and saw the body laid in the grave. The ground was cold, and the leaves were yellow, and falling. The people stood about and sung

"'Unveil thy bosom, faithful tomb!'

"It was a sad, yet a delightful funeral, it was so *Christian*. . . . .

"We have 'Young Pastors' Meetings' in my study. There are several young Pastors that I like much. But I have yet no *companions*. Sometimes my heart yearns for the old friendships—especially when I come home at the close of Sunday's labors. But if I knew more of communion with *Jesus*, it would be less so. . . .

"Yours, etc.,

"K."

"*Nov.* 16.

"Dearest Mother:

. . . . "I have been talking with inquirers of every sort for two hours, as they have come into my study. . . . . May the Lord take them all! I never trust myself to this work alone, but always have one or two of my good deacons with me. We have now before us seventeen applicants for admission. . . . .

"Yesterday was good. I preached from Eph. v. 25, etc., a passage of which the Lord was pleased to give me a very precious view, though I could not express it all in preaching.

"Last week I commenced lecturing on Philippians in course. . . . .

"O, how weak I am! After all, city pastors do have annoyances and cares to which all others are comparatively strangers. Every defect of my character and heart is now brought out in bold relief. . . . .

"Good bye, "Your son,
"K."

TO EVANS.

Dec. 8.

"Well, my heart has been pretty full for these three days. Last Sunday *eleven* precious converts were baptized. I can hardly realize what the Lord is doing for us. My people and my work are becoming dearer to me every day; but nearest is our little band of converts, numbering now nineteen. . . . .

"I am still trying to preach *Jesus*, and do not find the theme exhausted yet. I get into the country to preach once or twice a week for a change, and find it does me good.

"Did I tell you of my temerity in attempting *exposition?* I have ventured to take up Philippians, for our Tuesday lectures, and have given three or four talks. It is a queer kind of expounding, as you may well imagine; but the people have been generally patient, and I am becoming fond of it. It gives me the pleasantest day's study of the week.

"Our daily meeting is one of the feeble conies, but we love it.

"I look for you at the holidays. I, for my part, cannot think of leaving New York at present—for a day. 'Back! back! It is impossible!' Pushing him back with his gun!"

(SAME DATE.)

TO C——.

"Yesterday was a jubilee with us. O! my heart is full and overflowing, and I want you here that some one may fully sympathize with me.

"I have just written down the names of *eight*, who, I feel assured, ought to be baptized another month, and I must begin at once to care and pray for them. Last night I found a convert and two tearful inquirers in one family. Such happy families as these are! ——, a dear child, stole aside to me the other evening, bowed her head and said, 'I have found the Savior.'" . . . .

"*December* 14.

"DEAR MOTHER:

. . . . "Yesterday was a perfect Sabbath. The fine weather gave us large congregations, and their deep and serious attention to the plainest truths showed that something more than sunshine had brought them there. I tried to preach in the morning on father's text, '*And he brought him to Jesus.*' It was not so good a sermon as his. In the afternoon I spoke from John iii. 8, on the Mystery of the New Birth—in which I fell back simply and alone on the sovereign, mysterious, omnipotent agency of the Holy Spirit, to be called down by prayer. It's hard working—tugging at dead men without *that*. The truth was a great relief to my own mind. We closed the day with a good prayer-meeting, in which the brethren were on their feet two at a time all the while.

"We seem to have reached a kind of status. The first flush is over, and now comes the real, hard work. Things are quite disposed now to *settle*, but I pray God they may not, and so far as I can help it by His grace they *shall* not settle yet. We are not ready for it.

"My sad deficiencies reveal themselves to me more alarmingly each week, and my greatest wonder is, how labors so faulty can be owned of God at all. But it strengthens, while it surprises me, to hear my sermons brought up by our new converts as having been used for their conviction or conversion. To the glory of God be it said, mother, that the *majority* of the sermons thus far preached, have already been made to appear as blessed each to the good of some one soul, while some, as 'Come unto me'—the 'Resurrection,' and 'Lord, save'—have been blessed each to two or three. This both humbles and encourages me.

"Last Saturday afternoon there was a scene, which, to me, it was worth a world to witness. Would that you and father could have looked upon it! I gathered together my little band of converts, and spent an hour and a half with them. As I first surveyed them together, the sight overcame me entirely. I could hardly credit my eyes. Well, I sat in a chair among them, and talked to them, urging on them the motives and the means to *eminent piety*. A strange theme for *me* to talk on, was it not? I felt it so, but I could not help speaking upon it. Then we all kneeled, and three of them led us in prayer. We have arranged to meet every week for '*Instruction in the Articles of Faith*,' etc.

"I cannot tell you how I love these precious lambs.

Their names are continually with me. I could not bear that they should sink back into the mass of the church membership, and my personal hold upon them be lost at once. I shall keep them near to me as long as I can.

"Yours," etc.

The interest of the young pastor in the young people of his charge was abundantly repaid. He saw them obtaining clear, practical, and experimental views of Christian doctrine, and early adopting those habits of Christian usefulness, which are the sure means of happiness and growth. They became trained like a phalanx—compact, united, steady, while yet each felt individually responsible for the battle. To him, their leader, they had an attachment that was well nigh enthusiastic. The degree of his personal influence over them was almost unexampled. He was the confidential adviser of scores, in their most minute affairs—so far as relating to their Christian progress. Questions of duty, mental struggles, practical difficulties, oppositions, temptations—all were opened to him with the same freedom and artlessness as to a dear parent. He had a charm to attract confidence and confidences. It happened more than once that strangers—a prodigal perhaps—hearing him preach, felt irresistibly impelled to open the heart to him, and seek sympathy and counsel.

"*Dec.* 21.

"MY DEAR FATHER:

"Yesterday was an encouraging day. I felt that my church and my friends must be praying for me. My heart, so long cold and well nigh dead, was melted a little while preaching in the morning on 'Lovest thou me?' I did get a glimpse of the love of Christ, more sweet than any I have for a long time had. It overcame me. Never shall I forget that refreshing season.

"I think my heart was softened for preaching by the events of Saturday, in part. That afternoon I was with my little band of converts for an hour or more. Then one or two came to talk with me about their troubles, the greatest of which was, a fear that they did not love God. This led me to the very sermon I was preparing, and we talked till my mind was greatly enlarged, and we were all bathed in tears together at the love of Christ. I could not regret this interruption, for it was the best 'study' I could have had.

"The same evening a young man came to talk with me, and before he left I felt that he had been guided to Jesus, and been able to believe on Him. This prepared me for my *afternoon's* sermon, which was to be on the Prodigal Son. In church the Lord seemed very near to me. The house was still and solemn as the grave. At the close of morning service I observed a lady waiting in the aisles, and conversing with one of the deacons. I found she was deeply convicted of sin. Afternoon came. I had announced that I should speak on the parable, and there was a great running of the people together. It was the first time I have seen the house so full. I could not preach much, but the Lord was in the place.

"At the evening meeting the old saint, Dea. C——, after two or three fervent prayers had been offered, rose and said, that a gloom and shivering which had been upon his mind, was that day lifted off; he could say, 'Thou knowest that I love thee,' and earnestly exhorted the young converts to trust in the Lord, who would never forsake them. We sang, 'How firm a foundation.' . . . . Here I tried to close the meeting, but another of our younger brethren was too quick for me. He gave an earnest exhortation, and then we sang a verse, and went home reluctantly. A good day in Zion, was the general pass-word—and I kept saying to myself, 'I wish father were here!'

"But I must say good-bye, with much love to all, and entreating a continued interest in your prayers.

"Your dear Son, K."

"*Dec.* 29.

"DEAR MOTHER:

"A long letter from you is an unusual treat. I have had a feast over your last, and hasten to thank you for it, though briefly.

"We had another solemn day, Sunday. The afternoon text—'*To-day, if you will hear his voice, harden not your hearts.*' I never preached a closer sermon. I knew some of my hearers would be sure I had *them* in mind. There was great tenderness. Poor Mrs. ——! She did not lift her handkerchief off her face from the beginning to the end of the sermon, and a number of others were in tears. God help me to plead for these souls. Do pray for Mrs. ——. The presence of the Lord is in our sanctuary. Strangers observe it, and no one appears to escape its influence. At times the solemnity has been *painfully* oppressive. I lately gave a running talk on the Prodigal Son. As a sermon it was indifferent, but a lady (whom I expect to baptize next Lord's day) since remarked to me, 'Do you know, Mr. Nott, that I could not realize that it was *you* who were speaking at all? I looked at you, and it seemed as though it must be some one else speaking through you. I could not think of you at all." Ah, it is the Lord! Would that I might ever be thus lost—both to others and to self, and Christ alone appear! . . . .

"Yours," etc.

"*Jan.* 18.

"We are blessed with an unusual succession of bright and beautiful Sabbaths, which enables the people to come together to hear the gospel. Lately I preached the Annual Sermon to the young from the text 'Deliver us from evil.' The people prayed more than usual, holding a special meeting on Saturday evening for the purpose—and the Lord was with us. The next day three new inquirers came to me. I think the feeling is gaining.

Yesterday I wonderfully enjoyed preaching on the jailer's conversion, and to-day I have been cheered by a number of new cases of inquiry. . . . .

"I find occasionally a little extra work for amusement. Last Wednesday I preached in Jersey City, and this week I go to Philadelphia." . . . .

"Last week I went to M——, where one of my classmates is just settled. They had a dedication in the morning, installation in the afternoon, and gospel in the evening—I being fortunately chosen for the last. There was a great crowd, and they listened with solemn attention while I spoke for more than an hour.

"With us the Lord still continues to own his truth in a surprising manner. It almost seems as though nothing could be lost. Sermons well nigh forgotten by me, are referred to from time to time by converts as having fixed the arrow in their hearts.

"Sunday was a day long to be remembered. After preaching to a large and solemn congregation on 'If the righteous scarcely be saved,' etc., I was permitted to baptize ten happy converts. One was an old lady of sixty years, who for twenty years had felt her soul blessed in attending on this church. A while ago I preached a sermon on *The Duty of Publicly Confessing Christ*, and she remained weeping in the house to tell me of her convictions. It was a great undertaking for one so old. Two others date back their convictions for ten years. One came from a Congregational church to us, another from a Methodist, etc.

. . . . "After attending a funeral of one of the old pilgrims, I returned to the church just in time for afternoon service, and enjoyed preaching again. The congregation was dismissed, but when I rose to administer the communion, a scene greeted me which I never before saw. Our large galleries were not sufficient to seat the *spectators*—many were standing. It was solemn to commune thus. Why should they remain through such a service? Do you not think this betokens a peculiar tenderness? Indeed many of them looked on in tears.

"This was the anniversary of Dea. H——'s baptism, which occurred forty-five years ago. For twenty-five years he was constantly at the side of Mr. Parkinson, and then walked with Dr. Cone during all his pastorate. . . . .

"The Lord is pleased to keep me in good health. Indeed you could not think it might be otherwise, to hear these people pray for me. I am now fresh for another month's campaign, and at its close hope to report yet greater doings of the Lord. Pray for me.

"Affectionately,

"K."

"*March 2d.*

"I had a strange experience about preaching Sunday, which convinced me afresh of God's care of His ministers. Last week the 'influenza,' or something else, took hold of me and shook me, made my bones ache, and ran my pulse up pretty high, leaving me utterly exhausted. Saturday night came, and, for the first time, found me not only without a sermon, but not even with an idea. All efforts were vain. My brain was confused, and I could not stand up two minutes without reeling. I prayed, and went to bed at half-past eight. It was some hours before I could get to sleep.

"At two o'clock I awoke—weak, lonely, disconsolate. I began to murmur. 'Nobody knows me,' I murmured aloud. 'Who knoweth the things of a man, save the spirit of man that is in him?' instantly flashed on my mind. Then, that whole chapter (1 Cor. ii.) passed before me, clear, consistent, beautiful, till its important climax in the fourteenth verse. I forgot every trouble; my soul was full of love. I had a sermon, complete in every part, with introduction and application; and the particular persons before me (as I usually do) whom it would benefit. I was bright and happy. The clock struck four. I thanked God for His revelation to me, and turned to sleep. In the morning I awoke so refreshed that I laughed aloud. Other things so engaged me that I did not have time to think of my sermon again till I went into the pulpit. I preached it commencing with 'Nobody knows me!' and next Sunday I expect to baptize one who in it first grasped the evidence, that she was indeed born of God. This week I feel quite myself again, and am ashamed of my weakness.' . . . .

After a visit of two or three days to Kennebunkport, he writes:

"The morning after my return, I bounded down to our little prayer-meeting; and everybody seemed so glad, so thankful, that I was made doubly happy. Each prayer, and there were many, thanked God that 'He had brought back our dear pastor.' Three came to tell me they had found the Saviour while I had been gone, and I have heard of one or two more . . . . . And I have felt, since coming back, how strong is the attachment between myself and these dear people. I do not know but my church is in danger of becoming my idol; I wonder at my blessings, and deliberately conclude that I am the happiest man on earth. . . . . Last evening we had a *perfect* prayer-meeting; not the slightest thing was out of joint."

"*March* 31.

"DEAR R——:

"I want you to spend next Sunday with me. It will be a day of days—a day of a *lifetime.* About thirty persons are to be baptized. . . . . I want you here—to rejoice with me—and to give me some one to talk to.

"The interest still prevails, and if I am not mistaken, increases. The Lord is being pleased just now to bring us some efficient men, and to convert some who were in peculiarly desperate case.

"Crowded out, at last, of our lecture-room on Tuesday evenings, we last evening opened the house above; and, to my surprise, it was instantly filled: but, in outward activity, I fear I am neglecting heart piety. Pray much for me, my dear brother:—I am far from the right state. Come—do come . . .

"Yours, ever,

"K."

The Tuesday evening lectures continued to be held during the remainder of this year, in the main audience room of the church, and were fully attended. An effective course of lectures on the parable of the "Prodigal Son," was given:—"The Soul's Patrimony;" the "Soul's Wandering and Waste;" the "Soul's Want and Hungering," etc. etc. Later, there was a course on the "Converts of the New Testament," which furnished peculiarly fruitful themes, and was much blessed.

Of the Sabbath referred to in the preceding letter, the "day of days," he says afterwards :

"You can imagine how great a day it was. This is the largest number ever baptized into the church at one time. The crowd was immense—hundreds going away. One gentleman told me he could not get near the steps," etc.

"*May* 5, 1858.

"DEAREST MOTHER,

"I cannot repine at any of the losses I am experiencing, such as the delights of correspondence, social intercourse and general study, so long as so great gains are vouchsafed to me by my heavenly Father. I feel that I ought only to be overwhelmed in gratitude and adoration, that I, who am so utterly unworthy, should be made the instrument of so glorious achievements of Almighty grace. I say 'Almighty,' and well, for I have had of late a fresh sense of God's omnipotence as manifested in the regeneration of souls. Last Sunday, in baptizing twenty-four new candidates, I preached on this theme, 'Christ, the *power of God*' being my text. We had a delightful baptism, the group comprising all classes, especially an unprecedented number from the Sunday School ; I was only sorry there were not more —not from any ambition of numbers (I abhor ambition of that sort), but because the work seemed so delightful to me, the converts so happy, and the great throng of spectators so eager, and so deeply affected.

"In the afternoon I addressed the converts from '*Loose Him and let Him go*'—and gave the hand of fellowship to thirty-eight persons. The line extended across the front and partly down either aisle, and passing from one to the other with a few words to each, I found this a delightful service. We have not had a better day. The evening meeting for prayer was the most crowded yet; and though Satan is busying himself among us intensely, I cannot lose my courage, nor think of an abatement in this marvellous work. I do not dwell on the discouragements. Last night I had a very solemn audience while speaking on that part of the Prodigal Son's story, in which he says, 'I will arise and go to my father.' I dwelt chiefly on the simple words, '*I will*,' and felt, in a degree, as I sometimes do, that every word was given me directly from the Lord. . .

"Your loving son,

"K."

"*May* 12.

——"On Sunday I had unusual assistance in preaching on passages at the beginning of Hebrews—representing the superiority of Christ to all other religious teachers. Indeed, I liked it so well that I am going on next Sunday with 'Better than the Angels.' I find I get no such satisfaction on any other theme as in preaching on Christ. When I speak of him and him only, his inspiration seems imparted to me, which carries me beyond myself. . . Besides this, I have of late enjoyed some very good times in *direct conscious pleading* with the impenitent, when I felt the Lord Jesus standing in the pulpit side by side with me. I pity ministers who do not *enjoy* preaching."

May 31, after a few days of illness, he describes another remarkable experience in preaching.

——"Some of the good people doubted my ability to preach, and especially to preach twice. But how the Lord did magnify Himself! I fairly feasted on preaching yesterday! My heart swelled with thankfulness for the privilege, and I felt like bounding in upon my audience with the glad gospel 'like a youthful hart or roe.' I had resolved to give homœopathic doses that day, but found it impossible to stop short of full measure. The people were startled into unusual solemnity in the afternoon. Just as I was about to rise for preaching—and the house was brim full—a tall man stood up in the front part of the house, and asked me if he might be allowed to speak a word to this congregation. 'Speak on, Sir, speak,' I told him. He said that he wanted to confess before them that he was a sinner, a great sinner. He cried to God to have mercy upon him. He looked to *Him*, and begged the people to pray in his behalf. What a preface, and what an introduction to my sermon! I repeated what the man had said, that all might hear, and proceeded to speak from the words '*How shall we escape if we neglect so great salvation?*' It was a very solemn afternoon. God seemed very near to us. . . . . .

"It is astonishing how much good a hearty '*preach*' will do a man. It has set me up more than all the medicine I swallowed last week."

"*5th of July*, 1858.

"Dear Mother:

"It occurs to me to congratulate you upon the passage of another of your *birthdays*—which we are now celebrating in delightful style. Yesterday I preached a Liberty, Anti-(spiritual) Slavery sermon from the words, '*If the Son shall make you free, ye shall be free indeed.*' We had also a pleasant baptism of six happy candidates. In the afternoon my cold heart was a little melted while meditating on, '*Unto you therefore who believe He is precious.*' Seldom has a sermon done the preacher's soul more good.

"It was a great satisfaction to have L. with us. She came Friday afternoon, tired and lean. Saturday we had a delightful forenoon among the artists, visiting their studios, and carrying away (on memory's canvas) many forms of beauty that will be a 'joy for ever.'

"To-day we are in pure enjoyment of 'the glorious Fourth.' We made an early escape from the rising hubbub of the city by a beautiful steamer up the East River to Harlem, and thence two or three miles by row-boat through placid water to Melrose. Here we are spending the day. . . . .

"Just after dinner we took to our boat, with a precious cargo of eight souls, and rowed through the beautiful Harlem River, under the magnificent High Bridge, to the 'Spuyten Duyvil' Creek and Hudson River. . . . .

"Yours, "K."

In the summer Mr. Nott took the customary minister's vacation. He hurried away from the sultry city down to cool Kennebunkport, by the sea-side, and here for six weeks, free from the burden of heavy care, was at full liberty to "recreate." But his ideas of what constituted recreation had become peculiar. A very few days of lobster catching and mackerel fishing, and of rambling along "the sounding shore," sufficed; and he was then observed, through the greater part of twelve hours, thoughtfully pacing the floors at home, roaming "from attic to sitting-room, and sitting-room to attic." What was suspected to be ennui, was sober and practical meditation, for at night he announced his plan. York County was large, was behind the age, and religious interests were torpid. Why would not an attempt at re-evangelizing the wide field be delightful? The attempt was sure to be so, whether immediate results should occur or not.

His scheme, then, embraced these elements: First, to hire a respectable horse and chaise. Second, to send handbills, after the manner of electioneering politicians, all over the county, announcing the coming of a religious "stump-speaker." Third, to go into every town and hamlet, wherever he could obtain a gathering, in meeting-house or school-house, and preach to the people with the endeavor to arouse them to greater religious activity.

The announcement upon the handbill was so contrived as to offer a pretext for the visitation; it read as follows:

REV. A. K. NOTT,

FROM NEW YORK, WILL PREACH

In . . . .

On . . . .

AND GIVE SOME ACCOUNT OF

THE GREAT REVIVAL

IN THAT CITY.

The project was carried out in the same spirit of enterprise in which it was conceived. The following letters give incidents of the tour:

"ALFRED, *Aug.* 17, 1858.

"DEAR FATHER:

"My preaching tour is fairly inaugurated, and I may say, successfully. I had a very pleasant leisurely ride over the wooded plain, which lies between these high-lands and the sea. Horse and I frequently stopped by the road-side, or made incursions into the bushes to gather the berries which grew plentifully by the way. On reaching the hills which embosom this quiet village, the scenery rises before one quite finely. With some delay, I at last found Bro. D—— in the meadow, who immediately left his mowing, and started out with me to scour the parish. This we did so effectually, scattering the notices in every direction, that when evening came the meeting-house was well filled. All the ministers in the place were kindly in attendance, and a choir to sing for us. The people listened with commendable patience to what I had to say, though I was not so interesting as I meant to be. Now may God add His blessing to this humble attempt to advance His Kingdom! . . . .

"I go on this morning to the Gore, and to Bro. W——'s at Waterboro. I am hoping for a personal blessing in this work, which I need certainly as much as any whom I exhort. My heart catches an occasional gleam of interest, which is all too transient. I seem to live *two* lives, instead of *one hid with Christ.* '*Unite* my heart to fear thy name!'

"York County needs a stirring revival through its country towns, and if, despite my utter unworthiness, I can be employed in the slightest degree to promote it, I shall greatly rejoice. Pray that I may be purged from sin and freshly anointed for the mission.

"Thus far the Lord has opened the way for me as completely as I could wish, and I can set up *one* 'stone of help.'

"And so with much love to each and all,

"I remain," etc.

"ALFRED, *Aug.* 18, 1858.

"DEAR MOTHER:

"I had a various day yesterday. . . . Bro. D—— and I drove to Waterboro', to Bro. W——'s, who was unfortunately away from home. One disadvantage was that our prospects for dinner were alarmingly diminishing. But we were sent on to 'the Major's,' who took up our matters heartily, and arranged both for our dinner and the meeting.

"A part of this road passes the most beautiful spot I have found. Shaker Pond lies among rich meadows and rising hills, and along its bank the road winds, bordered on one side by the meadows and water, and on the other by the huge rocks and oaks that cover the hill-side. Here the Shakers, with an evident taste for fine scenery, many years ago pitched their habitations. Their palmiest days are past, only two 'families' remain, and these so crippled that they are obliged to hire help to carry on their farms. We talked with a number of their queer, venerable people, and were permitted to look through their seed-garden, and some portions of the buildings. The latter are patterns of homeliness in the ugly sense. I could not find any young people, though they say there are some. It is now practically little else than an asylum for decrepid old age and helpless vagrant childhood. They are constantly entreated to take children from Portland, and do so; but when I asked whether such remained when they grew up, I was told that it was impossible to keep them. An itching for 'the world' and the trial of their own fortunes drives the ingrates from their sober home. To hold them by any obligation would be contrary to the principles of the order. They assemble in the Hall on Sunday, when people flock from far and near to 'Shaker Meeting;' and on week-day evenings they hold stated meetings among themselves. It is only a half life. Requiescat in pace! . . . .

"*August* 19.

"Yesterday I had a long ride to Buxton: mostly

over a high plain, through pine forests, whose rounded cones scolloped the roadside. . . . .

"To-day I am at Limerick, a snug little village which surprises you prettily as you surmount an overlooking hill. S. and his meeting-house live on this hill, and the surrounding landscape bounded by the White Mountains, is magnificent. . . . . Here I am making a pleasant halt, and have arranged my programme for the future: which is, Saturday evening, Limerick; Sunday, A.M., Parsonsfield, P.M., Effingham, evening, Freedom; all of these three churches being destitute of pastors. Afterwards Cornish, etc., etc.

"I hope you and L. are jubilating. Do you find Tennyson? I carried it off, and sip from it every day along the road, while sober pony jogs on with the reins hitched to the chaise." . . . .

A few days later:—

"KEARSAGE HOUSE, N. CONWAY, N. H.

"DEAR C——:

"Though half-starved and hardly recovered from shivering with the cold, I seize the first hour to send a missive homeward. We, that is Evans and I, have been riding all the morning in a cold mountain wind, that has cut through and through.

"One of the most interesting times I have yet had, was on Friday eve at Bar Mills. We found the schoolhouse to which we were directed, just in time to begin the service, but learned that another preacher had possession there. So we turned back to another, where we came upon a most miscellaneous gathering. I really doubted whether they would allow us to go on in quiet, but they listened with the most eager attention, and begged me to come again.

"It was very curious that Evans and I should arrive in Portland the same day and meet so providentially. I was greatly pleased, and of course I dragged him into my chaise, to share with me the remainder of my fortunes. . . . .

"A full house greeted me on Sunday at Limerick. It was a blessed Sabbath morn. The hills seemed to bring us nearer Heaven, and the very breath of God rested upon them. We rode seven miles to Parsonsfield, where I preached in a queer old-fashioned house. No people have appeared so much to feel what was said as they. The old men bowed their heads and wept, and bade me such a good-bye, saying, 'Shan't I *never* see you again? *God bless you*,' with voice choked by emotion, so that I felt reluctant to leave them. They are destitute and desolate. This was a blessed visit.

We passed on to Effingham, four miles, and across the State line. Here is a sweet little cluster, with one pretty meeting-house, and a people of unusual refinement. As they were already waiting, we went in at once, and had a pleasant service. Especially did the singing surprise me. Such a choir is seldom found in country or in town, and I was particularly appreciative of good church music at the time, having for so long had none or worse than none at my services. We stopped at Judge D——'s, and at half-past four held a second service, when Evans preached.

"At its close we came on to Freedom, arriving just at service time, half-past seven. We found one meeting-house, but no symptom whatever of a meeting. The notices had failed to arrive. I took a youth into my chaise, rushed around the village, thrusting notices into every house and into every man's face;—the bell was struck, lights carried into the desolate old house, and in fifteen minutes half the population was gathered together and I preached.

"This N. Conway is a glorious place, in air and scenery at least.

"Good bye," etc.

KENNEBUNKPORT, *Aug.* 26, 1858.

"MY DEAR R——:

"It is through—done, and I am at home again. Like the cable, a preaching tour has been proved possible. It has been successful in every item, so constantly has a good providence opened the way for me. Of course it is 'bread on the waters:' the results for others must be left with God. I at least have been blessed in it, and am in better mood for preaching than when I left. . . . . My experiences, which have been of every sort, we will talk over. I have preached every evening, save one, and three times on each of the two last Sabbaths, making sixteen sermons, in as many different places, besides Dover, and the 'Wildes neighborhood,' making twenty in all since leaving New York. I am every way the better for all this. To-morrow evening I am to speak at Biddeford. Think I shall spend Sunday at home," etc. etc.

CHAPTER XXVII.

SECOND YEAR IN NEW YORK—PERFECTED CHARACTER—EXPERIMENTAL PREACHING—SUNDAY-SCHOOL LABORS, ETC.

THE first letter written in the new year contains the following touching passage:

"*September* 17, 1858.

"I am waiting for a something—a *power* from on high. And *first*, FIRST, I must learn to pray. I humbly confess, that I have never been, for any great length of time together, a *praying man*."

The humility of this language finds its commentary in that exclamation of the Apostle Paul's, "Not as though I had already attained, ... I count not myself to have apprehended . . . but . . . I press toward the mark."

One cannot help reflecting, how exalted must be the privileges really accessible to the child of God on earth, how boundless in their range must be the enjoyments, knowledge, and power attainable in communion with God, when a Christian, distinguished for a prayerful life, sees so much unfathomed in the *idea* of prayer and untasted in its bliss, that he feels he has never prayed! "I must learn to pray!"

With this spirit, self-depreciating, aspiring, trustful, hopeful, the young preacher began the last year of his service to God on earth.

It is evident now to those who then remarked a change in him—the sudden ripeness of his character, which, so fully formed before, and beautiful for every excellence, seemed now all at once to have acquired its final mellowness and bloom; the perfection of certain Christian graces, the most rare, and commonly the last to mature. His advanced self-conquest, his gentleness, and, above all, his *love*—the *ἀγάπη*—the thirteenth of Corinthians realized—love, "envying not, vaunting not itself, not puffed up, seeking not her own, thinking no evil, bearing all things, believing all things, hoping all things"—this loveliness of love, which made "his character and life," especially in the last year—(says one)—"the most Christ-like I ever knew;" to those who observed these things, and, withal, the new spirituality and experimental depth of his preaching, and his increased zeal to be "always abounding in the work of the Lord;" it is evident now, that a new heavenly anointing, a fresh equipment of divine grace and energy had been granted him, as a mark of his Father's love, and in order that he might worthily run the brief remainder of his race. It is something not carelessly to be said, but many have said that, had the prescience been bestowed by which he should have foreseen the grave and crown so near he could not, under the awfulness and glory of the thought, have labored more purely, watchfully, and faithfully than he did.

A change—corresponding to that observable in his character—was felt also (as intimated above), in his preaching. With ripening self-knowledge and growing consciousness of personal intimacy with Christ, there must always be, in the heart of any one, a proportional abandonment of self, and conscious realization of the absoluteness of the soul's dependence upon the free gifts of God through the efficacy of the peculiar work of Christ. Naturally, therefore, at the epoch of Kingman's experience of which we are speaking, he apprehended the importance and majesty of the *great doctrine of grace*—God's Sovereignty, Christ's Godhead and Vicarious Atonement, the Holy Spirit's Creative Work—with greater clearness than ever before, as the sole pillars of Christian faith and hope, and the basis of all that can with any shadow and pretence of meaning be called religion. These became, then, more the staple of his preaching. And with these, the *inculcation of the duties of holy living* assumed new prominence; for practical holiness and sound doctrine are certainly joined by blood relationship—both in the Christian's apprehension and in reality.

"I am now preaching," he says, "in the forenoons, upon the Holy Spirit and His Work. Some of the themes I select are these: The Love of the Spirit; The Spirit of Truth; The Spirit the Life-Giver; The Fellowship of the Spirit; Christians the Temples of the Holy Ghost; The Spirit the Comforter, the Intercessor, etc. In the afternoons I am preaching *practical piety*. Both these classes of topics interest me much, and do the people good. Especially do my people love to hear of the Holy Spirit. O, here would we tarry, till endued with His power!"

The first sermon of the year was an "Anniversary Discourse," commemorating the goodness of God in the previous year. It was entitled, "The Review of God's Gracious Providences humbling to His Children," from Deut. xiii. 2. The introduction happens to be extant in his own hand; we quote most of it:

"A stranger who should have stepped into this house one year ago and again to-day, would see no wide contrast in the scenes presented to him then and now. The same sacred old walls are about us. Each pew remains unaltered. People fill the seats as then. The same psalm has just been read, the same hymn of praise has been sung. The same voice would fall upon his ear. As then, an open baptistery (may it never be closed!) awaits the obedient convert.

"And even to you who have always been here, most is familiar. A few faces you miss. Many new ones, but not *strange*, because the love of Christ shines through them—greet you. Probably there are very few churches in this fluctuating city which know so few changes as this. . . . Fathers and mothers in Israel! we thank God for your presence to-day! We rejoice that your aged eyes have seen the salvation of the Lord! But we cannot spare you from us yet. May God preserve you to lead the way to glory!

"And I—if for a moment it may be permitted me to speak of myself—stand before you to-day with feelings different from those of a year ago. I approached with trembling, an untried, imperfectly comprehended responsibility. I knew I could not stand upon the heights and from above you shout, 'Come on! Follow me!' But I said to myself, 'The way is dark—and there are many rough and miry places—I can run along by their side and hold the lantern'—for, Thy word is a lamp unto my feet and a light unto my path . . . . If from that word, poorly as I have been able to hold it up, a ray has sometimes flashed upon your path, then—'Not unto us but to Thy name be the glory!' . . . .

"But there is a Spirit who, invisible, makes His own eternal record of all scenes enacted on this world's stage. The angel who hovers over us to-day, and whose eye penetrates the inner sanctuary, marks *infinite* changes. . . . If you would know what changes there have been, unveil those secret shrines where altars to Jehovah have been erected. Tell us of faith's early dawn, of pardon, joy, of consecrating vows, of communion with Heaven. Open the Lamb's Book of Life, and—see! new names recorded there! Tell us of the angels' jubilee, answering our rejoicings!" . .

In the following letters he relates another of those "wonderful experiences" with respect to special sermons, of which we have had two or three samples:

"*Oct.* 18.

"I usually find some call to preach on Wednesday evenings. Last week I was at the Bloomingdale Church for an installation sermon, when I was moved to preach on 'The Supernaturalness of Successful Preaching'—a thought that has interested me of late.

"In Broome Street I am still preaching on the Holy Spirit. A week ago I spoke on Inspiration, and in the afternoon considered the Last Day—'*I saw the dead small and great stand before God*,' etc. And here I have to record a gracious experience. The week had been absorbed in public meetings, and I was in great apprehension for Sunday. Besides my mind seemed distracted, my heart dull. On Friday evening I noticed that the brethren prayed for me *unusually*, and it so touched me that I spoke of it. Sunday morning I was unfruitful. In the afternoon I said to myself 'Somebody has been praying for me,' I felt it. The moment I stood up to preach and had uttered my text, the Holy Spirit seemed to drop right down, as if visibly, on the whole assembly. I was quite overcome by it. My tongue was thick in my mouth, and I could not speak. I could have fallen down prostrate, so great was the oppression upon me. But at last, apologizing, I proceeded, and we spent as solemn an hour as Broome Street has ever seen, I think. The same feeling continued in the evening. Every one seemed transformed. At the close of the meeting a lady was found in great distress for her sin. The next day I found three new converts, and I have met others since. It was *this* which led me to preach on the '*Supernaturalness*,' etc. Since then I am more encouraged for the church. A spirit of faith and activity is animating a goodly number." . . . .

We subjoin a plan of the discourse mentioned—all that is extant. The sermon itself was undoubtedly—from the reports of listeners—a remarkable one.

"Lo! I am with you alway—even to the end of the world."—Matt. xxviii. 20.

"Tarry ye in the city of Jerusalem until ye be endued with power from on high."—Luke xxiv. 29.

SUPERNATURALNESS OF SUCCESSFUL PREACHING.

Int. Remarks on a preacher's experience. Customary to enumerate *human* qualifications for successful preaching, assuming, as of course, spiritual power, or reserving it for a climax. Pursue the reverse plan.

The differences among men—as (1) regenerate and unregenerate; (2) preachers and laymen; (3) in respect of degrees of success in different persons, and the same person at different times.

Allude to the few *successful* ones. What is the secret of success? the question of preachers and of people.

The Theme.—(Retrace the steps by which a truly successful preacher has arrived at his position and show by what power he maintains it.)

I. In regeneration he was, by a *supernatural* act, separated from among men.

II. Separated by a *supernatural* call to preach, and designated to a definite mission.

III. *Supernatural* truths are the substance of his preaching.

IV. He is borne on by *supernatural* motives and impulses.

Obj.—(1.) That this implies Inspiration. (2.) That it ignores natural powers and means.

Conclusion.—(1.) The need of more spiritual power in the preaching of the word.

(2.) The means of obtaining it (a) by ministers, (b) by churches.

(3.) Appeal to impenitent.

October 13*th*, 1858.—Installation of Rev. R. L——, Bloomingdale.

Mr. Nott's labors beyond the bounds of his own parish were extensive and varied. His zeal knew positively no limits; the difficulty was to confine his undertakings within the bounds of prudence. He rarely failed on Wednesday evening to preach somewhere, in a suburb of the city, some village on the Hudson, or country town on Long Island. "Spurgeon," said he once, "preaches twelve times a week, and thrives on it. That cannot be the way for all; but the more I study myself and watch the leadings of God's providence, I am persuaded that He has called me to be emphatically *a preacher*—that is my great commission. I meditate deliberately resolving to undertake all the preaching I can possibly find to do. Why may I not as well spend and be spent in this manner as another? As for material, if the Holy Spirit have really set me apart for such a work, He will feed my *mind* through my *heart*." Whatever his theory, in practice he seldom declined an opportunity to preach; when he did, it was with the same reluctance and regrets that an enterprising merchant feels when compelled to turn his back upon a fascinating speculation.

Into the "new measures"—the new applications of the art of preaching—initiated and pursued with such success in the time of the "great revival," he threw himself with all his ardor. Still, a man could not do everything, and he lamented mournfully when he discovered that Broome Street Church and Chatham Square Theatre conflicted in their demands, and that he neither possessed strength enough nor could control hours enough to till properly the home field, and yet lead expeditions into every foreign territory.

But in one direction his restless energies found the opportunity for unrestricted exercise. Here duties to his church set up no bar—for here he was simply master-workman, leading, urging, guiding his church-members to work—the pioneer, the marshal of them all—striking out new paths continually, and as rapacious for new conquests, as Alexander. The field, in which his piety and zeal so fortunately found scope, was that of Sunday-schools. Twice, in his student days, he had been a missionary of the Sunday-school Union; he was still the servant of the cause.

A gentleman connected with the Sunday School Union in New York, kindly writes thus:

"N. Y. S. S. U., 375 BROADWAY,
July 23d, 1859.

. . . . "I am desirous that justice should be done to the memory of Kingman Nott, in regard to his *love and devotedness in the Sunday School cause.* I therefore write a line to call attention to the point. He really *believed* in the institution, and he and his people *worked* through it. Would that every pastor did the same, and was not content with merely *patronizing* it.

"I well remember his zeal in that cause on his first arrival in this city. . . . A committee of his church had been appointed to secure a place for a Mission school. Some weeks had elapsed, and no room had been obtained. His anxiety for the work led him to apply to me for assistance. That afternoon we went out together, and in less than one hour we had obtained the refusal of two rooms in Canal street.

"In two or three Sabbaths the large room was filled to overflowing with a noble school, and soon after another mission school was opened in Brooke's Assembly Rooms. Later still in his life, his heart was drawn out in practical sympathy for the great desolation of the Fourth Ward. Had his valuable life been spared, I doubt not that he and his people would have there started a Sunday School. May his mantle fall on his successor! * * *

"R. G. PARDEE."

The last mission school mentioned, is still in successful operation. The majority of the children gathered in are, nominally, Catholic;—in reality, Pagan.

The "Fourth Ward Mission" established since the death of Mr. Nott, is one of the most prosperous and useful benevolent institutions of the city. It owes much to the impulse given to the cause by his labors and example.

The circumstances of the origination of the second mission school, furnish a special illustration of his tact and enterprise. A new school was needed—the old was overflowing: but a suitable place was not easily to be had. In the neighborhood of Broome street Church there is a large hall with convenient ante-rooms, used for a dancing school.

Upon this building Kingman cast a scheming eye. Contriving in some manner to obtain an introduction to the proprietor, he resolved, keeping a utilitarian end warily in view, to prosecute the acquaintance. He called one day; was politely conducted through the apartments, admiring, as he went, their adaptation to the uses for which they were fitted up. At last, turning with his frank smile and a shake of the hand to the pleased proprietor, he said: "A project has occurred to me—a fine one: it will be the easiest thing in the world for you to be doing some good with these fine rooms: suppose you and I set our wits to work to gather in these ragged, ignorant, neglected children, who swarm in your vicinity: you supply the rooms—I'll supply the teachers." His engaging and persuasive manner was irresistible. "I will do it," said the gentleman; "you shall have the rooms for the mere cost of warming them; and I'll aid, in every way I can, to bring in the children."

"And now," said Kingman, as he related this the same day to the writer; "now I'll not rest till we have *one thousand children* within that building!" He had great projects when he died. But he was no day-dreamer; if his imagination devised grandly—imagination was only the pioneer of the will, energy, and ability, that could execute: imagination formed no archetypes which his creative faculty was not able to realize in the actual.

CHAPTER XXVIII.

PREACHING—ACADEMY OF MUSIC, ETC. ETC.

WE now resume the quotation of letters, though the selections must be few. Most are occupied, as heretofore, with accounts of sermons and "wonderful Sabbaths."

"*December* 15.

"Death has been busy among us, and if you were to visit Broome-street Meeting-house, you would see many pews newly shadowed with mourning. It is a constant sermon to the preacher. Yesterday, I preached on the *Transfiguration*, and said that one purpose of this manifestation was to strengthen and cheer Jesus in the prospect of death; for I cannot doubt that he was oppressed by fear of death, and shuddered on the brink of the dark river as truly as ourselves—else he would not have been, in all points, tempted like as we are" . . . .

"*Jan.* 1859.

"MY DEAR C.

"I am so ashamed not to have written home this week, as I have hoped each day to do, that I pause at noon this busy day, and insert this letter between two sermons.

"I am going to preach to-morrow, first on Baptism, in answer to the written request of a gentleman who wishes light. . . . . I shall aim to treat it gently, simply, and above all, scripturally, taking as my code and standard the accompanying tract [containing simply the scriptural passages relating to Baptism], six hundred copies of which are to be distributed in the pews, and will need little comment from me. Next I shall try to preach on Pride the Sinner's Hindrance, from Ps. iv. 10, in which, after remarking that all the separation between God and men is now in the opposition of the human heart, I shall show that *Pride* is the stronghold of that resistance, and opposes God in three ways:

"1. Denying the existence of a Supreme Being.

"2. Denying the fallen state of the heart—or denying

"(a) That it has no self-redeeming power—or

"(b) That it is responsible for its condition.

"3. Objecting to the plan of salvation by the Gospel. And shall conclude by entreating my hearers to submit to God *in every particular*, as the only hope of salvation. . . . .

"I have heard something of Miss Newton's Memoir, and shall look into it. I am now reading 'The Higher Christian Life,' which would interest *you* very much indeed. Have been dissipating recently in Hugh Miller, whom I enjoy very much, and feasting on Ruskin, of whom I must have spoken, for I was greatly carried away with him.

"We had a precious, powerful day of prayer last week, which gave us one bright convert, a gentleman in middle life, well known, and added an impulse to our social meetings which is wonderful." . . .

"N. Y., *Feb.* 6.

"Next Sunday I am to take my turn at the Academy

of Music, and I ask your prayers that I may suitably feel the great responsibility belonging to the task, and have grace given me to discharge the service to the saving of souls. The preacher at the National Theatre is about to desist from his labors there for the present, and seems desirous to have me assume the post. This I am not prepared to do, because I could not abandon my Sunday evening meeting, which is so blessed, and because I either could not do justice to three sermons on the Lord's Day, or should injure my health in doing it. But I feel a great yearning for the souls there gathered, and shall be willing to stand in the breach at least at intervals."

"SAME DATE.

"Yesterday was one of our best days. A crowd, that occupied every procurable seat, and stood in the door-ways, listened patiently to a sermon on '*If ye love me, keep my commandments*,' and witnessed in solemn stillness the ordinance of baptism, in which seven happy converts put on Christ. One was a person converted through the influence of one of our young converts. . . There followed, in succession, an Episcopalian, a Lutheran, and a Quakeress. Of these, the first is the mother of a little girl, baptized a month ago; the next, a German woman, whose experience, like others I have heard from simple countrymen and women of her nation, is a transparency through which shines the work of the Holy Spirit, unmodified and unobstructed. . . . . Is not this an interesting company? . . . . To-day another has come to speak to me of a timid hope in Jesus just found; and a dear S. S. scholar tells her glad pastor how she loves the school, and has learned to pray—so that 'when she does not pray, everything seems to go wrong all day long.' . . . .

"Our three Sunday Schools are hard at work, and doing well, and the mission children are improving somewhat. But they are a vicious race. We have a large band of Tract Visiters, busily and perseveringly going from house to house, though not seldom martyrs to rudeness and ill-treatment," etc., etc.

"N. Y., *Feb.* 28.

"DEAR C——

"I perfectly agree with you that it is not in any way wise to preach three times on a Lord's day, but extraordinary circumstances may sometimes demand the attempt, and so yesterday I followed my day's labor by a sermon to the wild animals of the National Theatre in Chatham Street. The building was filled full, and mostly with young men and boys of the roughest type. I went with a sermon in mind, but as soon as I came upon the stage--greeted with a 'Hi! hi!' and saw the motley and uproarious crowd I had to do with, I let all thoughts of the sermon go, and catching up the parable of the Prodigal Son, tried to interest them in that, and succeeded in keeping most of them inside the house and tolerably attentive.

"The service was short, and hastening back to Broome-street, I found a full room of those who had been praying for us. My people stand by me nobly, and have voted to pay all the expenses of the service as often as I may officiate there; and yesterday one man, a member of the congregation only, told me I might draw on him for the expense of a service as often as I pleased.

"To-night we have our church meeting, and hope to hear new experiences." . . . .

Mr. Nott's sermon in the Academy of Music on Jesus and the Resurrection, is well known through the printed report in "The Pulpit and Rostrum." Its powerful effect upon the vast audience could scarcely be exaggerated in description. The immense room was densely filled, even to the aisles and passages and the upper "tier." One gentleman was told by the doorkeeper that "he had shown the last man in who could possibly find standing-room." At a moderate estimate, four thousand (?) persons were present. Mr. Nott spoke as usual without notes; his voice penetrated with ease the farthest recesses; his youth, attractive appearance, engaging manner, and above all his simplicity, and directness, and the inspiration of the theme, irresistibly held all suspended on the speaker's words. Breathless silence reigned to the close.

He writes thus of it:

"*Feb.* 24.

"I did not preach the 'spiritual sermon' at the Academy, but the 'Resurrection.'

"The other smacked too much of the seminary and the recitation-room. I like the Academy and would gladly preach there every Sunday. I knew the ground of my sermon pretty thoroughly; was calmed into solemnity, as all seemed to be, by the imposing spectacle of so vast a throng (it was the largest audience assembled within walls ever preached to in America), and though just a little tamed by fright, I went through what I had to say quite smoothly, with ease, and was very sorry at the end of an hour or more to stop. That evening, should it never be renewed, will always be delightful to remember. But I am feeling great anxiety to hear of more definite results from it than the solemn attention yielded for the passing hour. Can it be, I ask myself, if the gospel was *faithfully* proclaimed to such thousands, that God will not bless it to the conversion of *one* among the number? There is a magnetic power in a vast throng—is it all dissipated upon their scattering? I cannot feel quite happy over the occasion, until permitted to hear some one say, 'There God met me!' I begin to wish for lungs of brass and a frame of steel, so as to throw myself into the great preaching movement," etc.

"N. Y., *April* 20, 1859.

"Dear Mother:

.... "Bright, beautiful days we have had this week—days which are calling out all the beauties, animate and inanimate, which New York can present. Broadway is brilliant; the houses are turned inside out for 'cleaning,' and the Broome-street congregation are fast shedding their feathers from grave to gay. But I apprehend that levity, whether of dress or manner, has as little place among our people as with any congregation of similar size and class. The reverse of the old proverb about a 'prophet's' own country is in my case true; for I get more honor at home than abroad, finding larger congregations and better listeners here than anywhere else.

" Last Sunday was a glorious day with us, the Lord seeming to help me preach more than for some time past, as indeed there was need He should. I preached in the morning on the Covenant—as made in David for Christ and his people (2 Sam. vii. 13–15)—a noble theme; and again on '*The redemption of their soul is precious, and it ceaseth for ever*,' which made us all solemn. Now where do you suppose I got those sermons? I had an appointment, that was made some weeks previous, to preach on Thursday evening of last week at Cold Spring—a little harbor village on the upper side of Long Island, thirty or forty miles from New York, where there has lately been a little reviving. The day came, but with it a violent storm of rain. I went in the rain, but the people had given up the expectation of having a service. But when it was found I had really come, a small congregation assembled, and I preached to them the sermon I had been preparing for my own people. As in apostolic days, they then besought that these words might be spoken to them again, on the following day, and urged me to remain until noon, and preach at ten o'clock, promising me a congregation. I thought it would be as good a way as any to prepare for Sunday, and consented. Next morning was bright and clear, and I was up early, and out upon the sea shore before breakfast. The country air, the water, the grass, the May-flowers, and the birds seemed very delightful to a city-bound mortal, and I felt fresh and vigorous. So I blocked out a new sermon, and had the altogether novel sensation of preaching on a week-day forenoon, in a quiet little village, to a very fair congregation, who seemed to be solemnly impressed.

. . . . "Now for the sequel :—Stepping into a house near by, where I was to lunch and take the stage, I was introduced to two ladies, acquaintances of the family, who had dropped in a moment on their way from church. Pretty soon I remarked that they had been differently introduced, one as 'Sister,' the other as 'Miss.' Finding thus that one of them was unconverted, I turned and invited her to tell me the true state of her feelings upon the subject of religion. In an instant, before I could be aware of it, she had sprung from her chair at my words, and fallen on her knees in a flood of tears, sobbing out the answer,—'Oh, Sir, I'm *very* wretched!' For several minutes there was silence, till she entreated me to pray for her, and we all knelt down while I tried to do so; then I talked with her. When I asked whether this was of long standing with her, she replied, '*That sermon*, this morning!' Her convictions seemed to be deep and genuine, and her heart ready at once to yield to the Saviour. It was a most happy occurrence to me, and I came away in a maze of gratitude.

"There are several new cases of interest with us. . . . One is that of a lady who had attended here only a little, but came to hear the lecture on *Dr. Cone*, and under that was seized with a strong desire for a better and a holy life, which grew upon her until she has been led to Christ! This is like the dead man raised, by touching the prophet's bones! The memory of the just is blessed! It does seem as though *no word* were to be spoken here without a blessing. Pray much for us. May God pity Kennebunkport!

"Your affectionate Son."

The latter part of April and the first of May were marked by incidents then apparently unimportant, but connected with their sequel they possess a large and a sorrowful meaning. Who ever knows what may be the final result of the most trivial actions of his life?

From different quarters of the land, moved by some inexplicable impulses; without concert, and each almost without a plan, seven or eight of Kingman's dearest relatives came up to New York, as if some invisible messenger had summoned them, to look upon his living face for the last time. They saw him, talked with him, drank in the light of love from his eyes, and dispersed, to meet next around his bier!

If there be no *Providence*, events have no cause, and the necessary persuasions of our own consciousness are a lie!

A letter written after his death by a sister who was one of his visitors at this time corroborates what was said (page 327) of the loveliness of his character, as it impressed his associates.

"It seems to me that K. changed wonderfully those last two years. The vast responsibilities of his great work mellowed and softened his character. Gentleness and humility became peculiarly apparent in his whole demeanor. And what wonderful *evenness* and calmness of spirit he possessed—which resulted from heavenly peace. His mind and heart were not at the mercy of the circumstances and events of the day—ruled by them—but *these* were subject to his serenity of soul.

"I think it was wonderful how humble he grew under the very circumstances, that would have exalted *most* beyond themselves.

"When I was in New York in May, he said (in reference to some remarks of mine) almost in a whisper and with tears in his eyes. 'I'll tell you in truth—I do not feel that I am good enough for God to send me such a great blessing. There is a great work to be done in my own heart, and I see it more plainly every day.' A—— H—— saw him in May, and she said again and again, 'His face is *heavenly*.'"

"I never shall forget how I sat and gazed at him when he sat in the desk, at an evening prayer-meeting—father beside him—and his face 'shone like an angel's.' I thought then that I had never seen a countenance so expressive of the *purest* peace and joy—it was too pure for earth—it had no alloy in it—it *was* heavenly."

During the "May Anniversaries," his father and many friends were with him. Among the pleasant scenes of friendly intercourse, one of the most delightful was furnished by a quiet "Festival," which he gave in honor of his Rochester friends. Professors and former pupils mingled here. A brief address made by his father, is held in tender remembrance by many. Its theme was—" I am passing away—my work is nearly finished—my son rises up to wear my armor."

CHAPTER XXIX.

HIS LAST ACTS AND WORDS—DEATH.

THE logic of events is often, to appearance, faulty. An expected, and, so far as visible data are concerned, a legitimate sequence fails to occur, and instead—an issue that blankly negatives, if that were possible, the plain facts that preceded! A sudden calamitous event frequently stuns with its illogicalness, before it overwhelms us with its woe. Thus, indeed, the *heart* is spared; more hearts would be broken but for this; a blow falls first on the reason, and amazes it with the sense of contradiction; reason staggers to and fro—back to what she *knew*—forward to what *seems*—not believing both are real—doubtful which is the lie; reason must recover, and be able to comprehend the sorrow, before she can wholly reveal it to the heart.

To what did all things point, in the condition of Kingman Nott—that happy spring of 1859—to what did all things point, but to long life, and growing transcendent usefulness? So many fortunate traits; so complete a character; so great and various abilities; such power of persuasion, attraction and command; a spirit, so purified; withal, such vitality, such far-anticipating vigor; for what had these gifts been communicated, for what had such a being been constituted and disciplined, why this care in the preparation of an instrument, unless for some long-continued, perhaps toilsome but noble service?

Yet the youthful pastor, in the full vigor of his powers, usefulness, and hopes, was now hastening—not to higher achievements—but to the grave. Nothing foretokened it; his step was elastic, his path broad, smooth, and prosperous to the verge. Yet, had he no presentiment? Already what he wrote in college has been quoted:—

> "I have often thought that my career might be brief. Often have I in imagination gone through the parting scene. And if death should call me away before you, dear mother, be assured it cannot take me by surprise."

In a memorandum book of 1859, a book that was but little used, the following affecting and solemn entry stands almost alone. The date is his *birthday*—the last.

"TUESDAY EVENING, *March* 22, 1859.

"One cannot help sometimes thinking whether he is likely to live to an old age, or be cut down early. I am not fitted to die now, shall I ever be more so? I hope I may. At any rate, I must be reminded that I am now fairly into the heat of the day, and the night will soon come. Already my life's work seems short in prospect. It will *very* soon be all over—and *for ever!* How insane to trifle! I ought to be more earnest and single-hearted. God forgive the past—and for the future make me better—holier—teach me to pray—*and to preach!*"

There is a sad interest, as the termination of his course approaches, in observing narrowly his conduct and his bearing. We know, though he did not, that he was doing his last deeds and speaking his last words. Were these becoming? Were they what he would have wished? Were they such as must deepen the tenderness of our recollections, and soothe sorrow with the consolation that there was nothing, till the very close, to wish unchanged?

His last words are contained in a few remaining letters, of which we transcribe two or three—exhibiting his earnest joyousness, his grateful appreciation and relish of all the kind gifts of God, and the cherished plans which occupied his last days on earth.

The first is addressed to his father, after the return of the latter from the "Anniversaries."

"NEW YORK, *June* 6.

"MY DEAR FATHER:

"I am afraid you will think I did not much appreciate your visit, if I (apparently) so soon forget you. But it is the old cry—bewilderingly busy—too much so to write, but not too much so to think, to remember and to love. I feel constantly grateful for your brief stay with me, when I find what a treasure the recollection of it is. I hope that your future pilgrimages to New York may be many and frequent.

"I was amused to find *your* pen, as in your last letter, proffering condolence for the loneliness of my estate, and I said, 'Is Saul also among the prophets?' Did I seem to you so very lonely? At least, I can boldly say, that the idea could only have been inferred—that no complaint has been caught from my unwary lips. No; I don't think that I am given to any sentiment in this matter. I have never taken up the lyric,

"'It is not that my lot is low,
That bids the silent tear to flow;
It is not grief that makes me moan,
It is that *I am all alone!*'

"I *invariably* feel that if ever a mortal had reason to be grateful for his lot, I, above all others. Daily contentment attends my busy round, and more than contentment—an active *satisfaction.* Daily I murmur (my only murmur!) 'The lines have fallen unto me in pleasant places—yea, I have a goodly heritage.' And when I walk about Zion, and tell the towers thereof, and mark her bulwarks, joy possesses my heart, and I say, 'All my springs are in Thee!'

"And as for going to a lone home at night, I obviate that difficulty by going so late and so tired, that I 'thank God for sleep,' and am speedily beyond all cares. And in the morning, I do not think I ever begin a day without at a glance seeing each hour *filled* in prospect, until bed-time again.

"But then I live with people all the while. There are always a special dozen or so at a time, whom I carry about in my heart; usually religious inquirers, and with whom I am carrying on *mental* conversations even when no one is near. I find, as my pastorate lengthens, that my burdens increase, but this weight is a pleasant pressure. I have been trying to gain the confidence of people, and now begin to receive the penalty of any success I may have had, by being called upon to *share* all sorts of sorrows or of joys. It surprises me to discover how *dependent* the mass of people are. How very few ever learn to go alone! And if one does, he is compelled to spend more than half his strength in supporting the tottering," etc., etc.)

A second letter is written from the Highlands.

"THE LOCUSTS, AT NEW HAMBURGH, ON THE HUDSON,
June 10, 1859.

"DEAR C——:

"I must write you a word from this most beautiful place. I am in the midst of the finest scenery I ever saw. So much natural beauty is seldom seen around a mortal. I came up here, yesterday, on invitation from my friend ——, to enjoy the hospitalities of his country-seat for a day or two, and nothing but duty would drag me away from here to-morrow.

"On Wednesday night I preached at the Presbyterian church, at Tubby Hook, for the benefit of several of my own parishioners, who live near there. This is at the upper end of Manhattan Island, on the high borders of the Hudson. Mr. H. took me in the morning to the Deaf and Dumb Asylum, etc., etc. Then we drove up to Yonkers, where a great many New Yorkers reside—then the cars for this place.

"I write in an elegant library, which looks down the

river, and up, and across it. Yesterday we drove out, and visited some of the most beautiful of the estates on the river. Such loveliness I had not imagined. I want to tell you about there, and about the people some time; do not fail to remind me. At evening, we walked out by moonlight, and this morning had a grand horseback excursion, in which I got along famously, till my horse fell, and threw me off—unharmed. This afternoon we take a boat-row and to-morrow (if I stay) Mr. —— and myself go in saddle to visit Idlewild, etc.

"I have just retreated for the ostensible purpose of making a sermon, but found it necessary first to relieve my excitement, by at least this trifling effusion to you. Beautiful—beautiful region! Delightful friends, too—I wish you were with me to enjoy it all. I know you would be enthusiastic.

"But I must to work. So in much love to all—good bye.

"Your affectionate brother,

"KINGMAN."

The following letter makes reference—near the close—to a sermon, one of the last he ever preached, and which is said to have made an unusual impression.

"NEW YORK, *June*, 1859.

"DEAR MOTHER:

"I think it must be as long a time since I wrote you as anybody, so here I am once more, your dutiful son. And I am before you in good condition. Last spring I was going through with my *acclimation*, but this season I am in superb health and spirits, so as almost to begin to question the necessity of vacating New York at all during the summer. At any rate, if you see it announced that the Rev. Mr. Nott, D.D., has joined the clerical squadron of European tourists, *don't* think of adding that it is for his health he goes.

"I had a good quiet time last week, with the unexciting varieties of my *pastoral* life. For instance, on Wednesday, went to prayer-meeting at eight; made part of a sermon; looked over twenty odd Rutgers' Institute compositions, by the young ladies, selecting the best for a premium; attended the Spingler Institute commencement, where one of my lambs graduated; conducted a funeral at one; went home to dinner; another funeral at two; made four or five calls in different parts of the town; home to tea; officiated at a wedding at eight; and finished with a musical soirée at the Spingler, and a call on Dea. and Mrs. ——, to congratulate them on the successful completion of their daughter's education. Went to bed, and do not recollect whether or not I felt *lonely*.

"Last week was also distinguished as witnessing my long contemplated visit to L. New Haven looks fresh, and so does our L——.

"We had another perfect day for the Sabbath, and I preached to full houses. In the afternoon my own up-town people fall off very much, but their places are supplied by strangers and those of other churches. I enjoyed one sermon unusually well, from the words—'*If it were not so, I would have told you.*' Ah! I wish that I might oftener revel in such experiences! But they are only very occasional. Only once or twice since being a pastor, have I been lifted quite so high. Sometimes I feel that such occurrences become more occasional; sometimes I indulge a hope that the future may secure them to me more frequently. I am quite sure that I have yet to learn how to make and how to preach sermons. May the Great Teacher instruct," etc.

The next is the last letter to his father :—

"*June* 27, 1859.

"DEAR FATHER :

..... "Two or three new inquirers presented themselves to-day. I hope there may be prayer and faith enough in us—the church—to pray them into the kingdom. But I fear we are falling behind in this regard. I fear there is not a universal and longing desire for the conversion of souls. How strange that the mass will tire even of this, and appear almost content to *rest*. . . . .

"I preached at Nyack last week for Dr. Devan's church. This week I am going down to Long Island a day or two to preach. This island is our Aroostook, our Sehard, I might almost say. For summer vacation I am balancing between three weeks of labor in evangelizing that region, and the same period of quiet retirement, with study and meditation, at home (i. e., Kennebunkport). I certainly *need* to '*go apart*.' My heart's desire is to receive in *some* way a *fresh anointing* for my work. One looses hold of many strings that slip through his fingers in a year's time, and needs to gather up anew," etc. . . . .

The anticipated summer vacation was at hand. His plan had been matured. He had decided to occupy most of the time with a missionary tour on Long Island. One more Sabbath intervened—July 3d—the first Sabbath in the month, the day for baptism and communion. On the succeeding Monday he was to take the outside steamer for Portland, intending a visit of a few days to his father and family; and then meaning immediately to return and enter upon his projected labors. He anticipated with great exhilaration the whole,—the short sea voyage, the visit, the tour.

He began, truly, to be in need of rest. Upon Sunday he was ill; a vacation would doubtless restore him to full strength and elasticity, but his vigor had certainly now become much impaired. On Sabbath morning, near church-time, a deacon called. He had not risen; he lay weak and pale, but was cheerful, and lightly ridiculed what he called his unmanly, and of course temporary prostration. "Oh I can preach," he said; "I shall preach." "No, no, you must not leave your bed to-day, we shall insist." He answered by endeavoring to rise, but fell back—too weak to stand. (Another minister, Rev. Dr. Church, was applied to at the last moment, and preached in the morning.) A favorite sister, L., who happened to be visiting him at the time, sat by his bedside during the forenoon. He talked much, speaking chiefly of sermons he intended to preach, and of plans for doing good. "I need an occasional break down," he said once; "God prostrates me sometimes, to remind me of my dependence on Him: I forget it, and trust too much in my own strength."

Though obliged to succumb in the morning, he had absolutely determined that no degree of physical disability should altogether prevent his sharing in the interesting public services of the day. Sheer force of will prevailed against infirmity.

By his order a carriage came to take him to the church in time for the baptismal service, after the morning sermon. He lay for a time upon a lounge in the study, helpless as a child. Then the baptizing robes were put on him. He walked almost totteringly across the threshold of the church door, trod more firmly up the aisle, was erect as a soldier the instant he stepped upon the platform, where an *open baptistery* greeted him; the natural color began faintly to flush his cheeks; his eye kindled. He went down into the water, and for the last time officiated in the ordinance of baptism. In the afternoon he preached a short sermon, and administered the communion, aided by the Rev. Dr. Hill, who had long been one of his congregation. At the close of the service he said, "Now I am a well man." From that hour he seemed to grow strong again. It was a marked victory of the spiritual part over the material. What can we not do when, in the next world, our bodies are spiritual too?

The intended embarkation for Portland the next day did not occur. The reasons which he saw for the postponement are told in the following letter. God's reasons were soon made manifest.

"DEAR BRO. HILLMAN:

"It was not until Saturday afternoon that I reluctantly dropped my plan for a sea-voyage this week, finding that my invited guests all seemed to fail me. You were left alone, and I hardly dared to hope you would feel like undertaking it.

"I feel *just* like it to-day, and believe I should start off with you alone, if it were not for *unfortunate engagements* which I allowed to be pressed upon me as soon as I relinquished this, and which now *bind me beyond all release.*

"I shall go as soon as I can, and I hope you will not fail to take my sea-board home in Maine during your summer travels.

"The Lord go forth with you, my dear brother.

"Sincerely yours,

"*Tuesday.* "A. K. N."

The original letter bears the following endorsement: [*Rec'd after his burial, July* 11*th*, 1859.]

According to his custom of preaching in country places on Wednesday evenings, he had accepted an appointment for Wednesday July 6th. This was the "engagement . . . which bound him beyond all release."

Upon the New Jersey side of that narrow frith which, on the west of Staten Island, connects New York harbor with the ocean, at the distance of about twenty miles from the metropolis, stands, close on the shore, the old village of *Perth Amboy.* It was here that Mr. Nott, consenting to invitations repeatedly and kindly urged, had arranged to preach.

It was with no slight difficulty that he contrived to keep his word. Obstacle after obstacle opposed. The eagerly anticipated excursion to Portland must be put off. His best friends, meeting him here and there, said, "Do not go; you are not fit; you cannot bear the trip; to preach will make you ill." Persuasions, in some instances importunate, were added to deprecation. His physician positively forbade his departure. Invitations came to go elsewhere, from friends ignorant of his intentions; one in particular, most urgent, and which he declined with the greatest reluctance and disappointment. Finally, his sister L. says this:

"Several times, when he was so weak, I begged him not to go to Perth Amboy, and told him he would certainly be unable to preach the next Sabbath if he was not careful. He said, with such earnestness as startled me, 'L. we know not what a day may bring forth.' Several times he repeated this, and I overheard him saying it to himself."

His "engagement bound him beyond all release," because it was with the bond of a divine decree!

Tuesday was a busy day. There were many calls, and engagements to fulfil with his sister and other friends. Throughout the day there was, for some reason—partly, no doubt, from his physical languor, an appearance of unusual sweetness and seriousness in his demeanor. When alone with his sister he was thoughtful. "Once," she says, "in the midst of conversation Kingman paused, with a startled look—'*God is angry with the wicked every day—how fearful!*' he said, then pursued the conversation."

On Tuesday evening he lectured as usual. The day and the day preceding had been so crowded with occupations as scarcely to have allowed time for the smallest preparation. After supper he made haste, in company with L., down to the study. Before he had opportunity to secure the door there was an interruption—then another—and only a few moments remained before the time for lecture. "Now, L., keep perfectly quiet," he said; and seizing his Bible, opened to a passage, fastened his eye upon it for a moment, and then, rising suddenly, ran as fast as he could—on tiptoe—round and round the table, with his hands clasped to his forehead, and then all at once exclaiming "*I have got it—let us go*," walked quietly into the lecture room, and spoke with his accustomed connectedness, fluency, and power. The incident proves, doubtless, a highly excited state of the brain.

On Wednesday morning a pleasant company, consisting of himself and his sister, with two intimate and dear friends (whose goodness of heart and active kindness are deserving of most grateful remembrance) went, by steamboat, to Perth Amboy. The passage ordinarily occupies two hours, and the scenery is more charming than can be described. Kingman seemed even more than usually appreciative of whatever was beautiful, and spoke many times of his love of the water. "Next to being a Christian minister," he said, "I would like to be a sea-captain."

His sermon that evening was essentially the same he had preached in other places, the text being from 1 John ii. 1, "If any man sin, we have an advocate with the Father, Jesus Christ the righteous."

L. remarks: "A stranger in the congregation said, 'That young man prays as if he was almost in Heaven!" He read, for singing, the hymns,

"While thee I seek, protecting power;"

and

"In the cross of Christ I glory."

He said that these were two of his favorite hymns, particularly the last, and that he always selected these when he preached away from home, and found a book that contained them.

Accounts agree in representing that the sermon was extraordinary in earnestness and power. He seemed to preach under a presentiment. His mind and heart overflowed with vivid thought and emotion. He continued speaking a full hour, scarcely able to break off his earnest exhortations—nay, entreaties. He closed; he glanced lovingly and lingeringly upon the assembly, as though still reluctant to bid farewell; he gave the benediction—and his last work on earth for God was ended; the last message had been spoken; his mission was completed, and the account sealed till the Last Day.

The next morning dawned bright and beautiful. It had been his purpose to return immediately to New York, but he willingly yielded to the persuasions of friends to remain through one day, in the hope of rest, pleasure, and new strength. In the forenoon he joined a sailing party, and went down the bay. His happiness was exuberant. "Never," says a companion, "did I see him so full—so overflowing with enjoyment."

The party returned and landed. "I saw that young man when he came from the boat," remarked an old fisherman afterwards; "he was *worn out:* I saw his look."

All proceeded to the house of the kind friends whose hospitality he was enjoying. A cheerful company was gathered in the parlor reading, talking, playing. Mr. Nott had just entered, coming from his own private room, where afterwards a Bible was found open upon the table, showing what his employment had been. Presently a young lad came gaily to the door, and looking around, said, "Who would like to go and *bathe?* Who will go?" "I will most certainly—I never refuse an invitation of that kind!" said Mr. Nott, laughing, and springing eagerly to his feet. At that instant the performer at the piano was playing a familiar, touching melody: Mr. Nott listened, paused, then walked slowly to the instrument, and leaning upon it, joined softly in the song. It was this:

"My days are gliding swiftly by,
And I, a pilgrim stranger,
Would not detain them as they fly—
Those hours of toil and danger!

"*For oh! we stand on Jordan's strand,*
Our friends are passing over:
And just before, THE SHINING SHORE
We may almost discover!"

The pianist left the instrument, and Mr. Nott, with one friend and the young lad, went from the house. L. looked after them, smiling, "We shall see you again in a few minutes, I suppose—and no doubt much refreshed!"

A steep bank terraced, and planted with shrubbery and flowers,—flowers to the last, for him to whom they were such a delight!—descends abruptly, in the rear of the house, to the water's brink—a fence alone dividing the garden from the narrow gravelly beach which the tide washes. A little bathing-house stands just within the enclosure. Kingman and his friends were soon arrayed in their bathing-suits, and ran gaily to the stream. A slight indentation on the shore, with a wharf projecting at one side, forms here a miniature harbor, where small vessels anchor and boats are fastened. Mr. Nott struck boldly out ; he swam easily and well, and with vigor not soon tasked : but he chose not to go into the main current, contenting himself near the shore, with the most leisurely movements and quiet enjoyment of the luxurious coolness of the water. His friend, after a very little time, became tired, and returned to the bathing-house. The lad soon prepared to follow. Mr. Nott said, "I am not ready yet; do not wait for me." The youth looked back and saw him lying on the water, calmly floating, looking upward, and absorbed in contemplation of the sky, over which light clouds, tinged variously with the rays of the afternoon sun, were passing. The lad saw distinctly his face; its look of tranquil enjoyment and wonder, and heard him say, "How beautiful the sky is!"

Five minutes later he looked again,—and the bather was not in sight. Perplexed; then fancying he had swam to the wharf, and might be ascending it, the youth hastened thither—vainly! Then supposing he might be concealed by the boats that were anchored in the cove, he called his name; but there came no answer. In great terror the lad hurried to the house, and not alarming all, called one or two. These ran to the bank, took a boat; they knew where he had last been seen, and, rowing to the place, they found where his body lay. His face was still turned upward to the sky; it was as placid as when last seen. Thus he rested! The vision of the beautiful sky was exchanged for the vision of Heaven!

The depth of the water was a little less than his own height. He might have stood there, and breathed the air. It was a visitation of God—God had called him home.

What was the immediate occasion of his death, can only be surmised. If cramps had seized him, he might have cried for assistance, or would have struggled. He had evidently sunk without a stroke of hand or foot. He lay as he might have been lying on the surface of the water. Probably—in a condition of greater exhaustion than he knew, and with a brain of late too often excited and over-strained, the sudden chillness of the water had caused a congestion, with which he died instantly.

The body was borne to the house. L. soon knew. Alas! her farewell had not been a final one; those were not "last words!"

Soon, at her request, despatches were sent to his friends.

His father, at Kennebunkport, was in his study; his mother, singing at her household work.

His eldest sister—lightly chattering with her little children and directing their sport.

Two sisters, in a town remote from home, were

engaged in the pleasant employments of their school.

A brother, at a Theological Seminary, was in the recitation-room, where the final public examination of the course was just commenced.

Upon each, thus busy, light-hearted, and hopeful, fell—at nearly one and the same hour—the thunderbolt! Thus it is in life; tragedy unpreluded: the events of another sphere vague in their greatness, and terrible—abruptly intervening among the easy, natural, quiet, recognizable sequences of this!

On Friday, July 8th, these friends, summoned from different quarters, were hastening to meet in New York. The morning of the same day the steamer from Perth Amboy—her flag at half-mast—ran up the bay, with her little company of heavy-hearted ones,

"And her dark freight—a vanished life."

The sad news had already reached the city and had touched with lively sorrow the hearts of multitudes. Far beyond the circle of his own church and his personal intimacies, there were thousands who felt the shock as if they had lost a dear and valued friend. His personal influence had been so widely extended, it had been so powerful and pure, that when his star shot from the zenith, all who ever saw its ray mourned the extinction of a beautiful, tender, and inspiring light.

If such was the universal feeling, even where only

his name had gone, what was it among the religious population of the city—what was it in his church? "We have no words to describe the effect of the news," remarked "The Examiner"; "every Christian man whom we met, without respect to the denomination with which he was identified, referred to the event with those tearful expressions of grief that are common to a great personal bereavement."

Words, truly, have no power to describe grief. It would be only an impertinence, then, to dwell longer on the present theme. But the affecting tributes to his memory by hundreds of mourners who seemed broken-hearted, the extraordinary strength of *personal attachment* immediately developed to view on the part of the entire membership of his church, and a very large number of his congregation, are almost passing credence—attachment, too, which they who now mingle with his people, must feel was so genuine and so much a part of their life that it suffers no perceptible decay with time,—these it was fit thus to indicate, though they cannot be described.

His body lay, on Saturday, at the house of Dr. Bigelow, on Sixth-street, where his contented home had been. Hundreds thronged the steps, the passages, and the silent room where his loved form was placed, all day. Poor women, to whom he had never spoken but perhaps a casual word; children, who had sometime met the smile of his kindly eye, or felt the affectionate touch of his hand, converts, old pilgrims, came, and many with sobs, to look once more upon his face, or kiss his lips.

It is a fact, that, to many, in gazing upon his face, grief was almost smitten back to its source in the heart, by the wonder, solemnity, and all the effects of the "powers of the world to come," that filled the soul from the serene beauty of his countenance. Death had conquered him, but—it was unmistakable—he lay there a conqueror. Death, which seemed at first to stand terrible, triumphant, exulting, sneering, by the bier, shrank away, vanished; was among the things of transient, disappearing, unimportant *time*, while *eternity* rushed around and transported the beholder instantly to the realm of the *real, the enduring, and the changeless.* In the look of his face could be seen what *life really is*, not its manifestations—its weak, struggling phenomena here in mortality, but in its essence. It was seen that life in essence is holy and partakes of the eternal; that all else is death, and that to what is *else* death is limited.

And there was not one, also, that did not feel that *Christ Jesus lives*, and is exalted, and has a kingdom. The signet with which he presses the brow of his dead, bears the stamp of his love, his victory and his promises.

The funeral took place on Sunday. It was in his own church on Broome-street. There was no sermon. Addresses were made by Rev. Dr. Cuyler, of the Dutch Reformed Church, Rev. Dr. Williams, Rev. Dr. Adams,

Presbyterian, and Rev. Dr. Robinson, who had been his dearly loved and revered instructor in Theology, at Rochester. "The Examiner" says, "The large meeting-house was filled to its utmost capacity, and the street in front of it was thronged by multitudes who could find no admission. The number present, in and outside the house, is variously estimated at from five to eight thousand. There is no doubt that at least six thousand persons were there. The most impressive testimony to the excellence of the deceased, was the heartfelt grief manifested by the thousands who sought the opportunity to look once more upon the placid face of him who there slept in death. Hundreds of these passed before his remains in uncontrollable sorrow. It was a scene never to be forgotten."

The coffin was borne to the church from the residence of Dr. Bigelow, in Sixth-street; the pall-bearers, Rev. Messrs. Somers, Dunbar, Weston, Danforth, Sarles Evans, Norton, Pendleton, Pelts, walking by its side. It was affecting to see the venerable Dr. Somers, and the veteran yet still vigorous Dunbar, holding the pall over the remains of their young brother who had fallen in the early morning of his earthly career.

The long procession on foot which followed the coffin, rendered a more appropriate and touching tribute of affection, than any pompous show of sorrowful trappings could have done.

A more detailed account of the funeral services

and of the remarks made on the occasion is here copied from the *New York Chronicle*:—

"The body was borne up the aisle to the front of the pulpit.

"On the coffin lay a couple of wreaths of immortelles and other flowers. The hymn beginning

> "Brother, thou art gone to rest;
> We will not weep for thee,"

was sung in solemn strains as the coffin was carried up the aisle. Rev. Dr. Hill, Secretary of the Home Mission Society, opened the services by appropriate remarks.

Rev. Theodore L. Cuyler, of the Dutch Reformed Church, then read a portion of the Scriptures, and addressed the congregation.

"He said he hoped no one had come to listen to studied addresses or eloquent orations, but that they had assembled to pay with their hearts the tribute of grief. The pulpit, where so lately he stood, all health and strength, is now too early empty, and that coffin too early full. Said the speaker: How that beloved young man came among you, what he did for you, and how he has left you, are the three things which I shall briefly present to you. But two short years have passed since he came among you, fresh from the halls of learning, to take the weighty responsibility of a church in a great metropolitan city. For one as young and inexperienced as he, it was certainly no easy task, no light struggle for him to stand before a congregation where such a preacher as SPENCER CONE had ministered and uttered his brilliant truths. We little dreamed that the time was soon to come, when he would cease from his labors and be called home to his reward. But his work was done—he has more than fulfilled the brightest hopes of his kindred, friends, instructors, and brethren, who on this spot so lately gave him the right hand of fellowship, and welcomed him to his field of toil. During his ministry, no church in the city has enjoyed greater prosperity.

"The fame which he has already gained—and it is no ordinary thing for one so young as he—the fame he has won and the affection he has drawn to him, was pure, legitimate and deservedly sacred. He sought no notoriety by illegitimate means, he sought not the public; the public sought him, and hung upon his lips to hear the words his Master gave him. The fame which attended him was that which attends God's truth, earnestly, clearly spoken. Such was his ministry, with you his glory was; he preached Christ, he loved Christ, and pointed souls the way to Christ; and the hundreds who have already welcomed the cross of Christ are the seals of his ministry. Could he open those pallid lips and speak to us from the realms of glory, he would say to us his brother ministers, Preach Christ alone, and him crucified. But four days ago he left us—last Sabbath he was with you, taking part in a service most dear to a preacher who loves his flock—the commemoration of the great act of his Saviour and of ours. His words were those then of a dying man, and his sublime utterances of the truth yet ring in your ears. He went from you, but he bade none of you good bye; there was no bitter pang at parting; you expected to-day to see him in his accustomed place. He parted from you, and soon he parted from friends nearer still to him, yet bade them no good bye; he parted from one who had been his playmate from childhood, and bade her no good bye. He went on to his last hour of suffering with no eye upon him but his God's, and no arm beneath him but his Saviour's. Over his last hour hangs, to-day, a pall of unbroken mystery, placing it beyond mortal ken; yet, who can doubt that in that last struggle with death, his soul rose from his sinking frame, to legions of angels awaiting him, crying, 'Oh, Death, where is thy sting? Oh, Grave, where is thy victory?' [Here sobs and weeping were heard in all parts of the house.] His record is on high; his memory is in the hearts of his beloved people. I would not, to-day, exchange the crown which rests upon that brow, for the crown of empires. To-day is he welcomed by those who have gone on before, and who now join with him in singing the praises of him who died, that man might live."

Tears were shed freely by many during the remarks of young Mr. Cuyler. Rev. Dr. Armitage offered a prayer, during which the weeping still continued throughout the house. Rev. H. J. Weston, of the Oliver Street Baptist church, then read the 749th hymn, which was sung. Prof. Robinson, of the Theological Seminary at Rochester, next addressed the audience. He spoke in substance as follows:

"My heart is too full for articulate utterance. I am to-day too much of a mourner to speak to you otherwise than in broken catches, of one whom I have intimately known as a cherished pupil, a dear friend and a Christian minister. This is no time for formal preaching. With this church I can say, the waves and the billows have gone over us. Summoned from duties, from festivities even, I may say, of which our young brother was once a joyous participant, I have come merely to speak to you from the feelings of my heart—to join with you in an humble trust to God that He will show us why He has so afflicted us, and to mingle my utterance and my prayers with yours over this bier. Stunned as well as blinded, I can do but little else than grasp for a few of those great truths upon which, in times of affliction like this, we lay hold and feel strength. Our young brother is not here, for God has taken him—it is a simple but a great truth—God has taken him. God is a sovereign, He hath done it in His wisdom; it is not a misfortune; it is not an accident; it is but a part of the purpose of our God, as much a purpose as was the beginning of his existence. God gave, and at the appointed moment He hath taken away: let us lay hold upon that truth, that is an act for good of a sovereign God. Every circumstance accompanying that death seemed to point it out as especially an act of God. It was not the result of carelessness or the neglect of any one. In consequence of an invitation extended months ago, he went over to

New Jersey last week, to preach a sermon in the evening. He did preach a long and faithful discourse, praying, as a brother present says, with unwonted fervor and devotion. The next morning he went on a fishing excursion, and it was only by the most trivial incident, an inquiry at dinner for bathing dresses, that the company went out bathing during the afternoon. While out with his companions, playfully diving and sporting in the water, with no eye to witness it, no outcry, no commotion of the water, he sank so quietly, so peacefully to rest, that no one knew it until he was gone. God took him, not by accident, but in His own sovereign way He said to him, 'Thy work is done, come up higher.' I have felt, then, that it is well for us, here, at this moment, bowed down as we are, to lay hold with an unrelenting grasp upon this truth, that God is a sovereign infinitely wise and good, who even chastiseth us for our benefit. It is a wise providence. Oh how difficult for us to believe that it is a wise providence, that it is for the best that he should go, as he did, and when he did, I know that to our weak faith this seems almost like a dagger. Even the Bible itself, speaking as it sometimes does in paradox, seems hard for us to believe; how difficult then, for us to feel that our dear brother should be taken away from us, as who can say that the day of death is better than the day of one's birth? Our brother lived briefly, and he lived well, and now his work is done. Not two years since, I, with another brother, placed my hands on his head in solemn ordination. He then bade fair for a long and most useful life; and how difficult for us now to see the wisdom of God so taking him away." The speaker then referred to the extraordinary command possessed by the deceased over his faculties, and remarked, "He was not a genius in the ordinary acceptation of the term. His was the genius of patient, untiring labor. He possessed a rare combination of excellent qualities, and was especially known for his cheerful, earnest and devoted piety, and his life of Christian activity commenced while he was yet at college. At that early period of his life he was noted for his endeavors to save his companions from the ways of sin, and took every opportunity of addressing those who would hear him, on the riches of the Redeemer's grace. Had he known from his earliest years, when he should lie still and cold in the mighty frost of death, he could not have devoted himself more zealously to the service of his God. Ever since his ministry in the First Baptist Church, he has not confined his energies solely to that field, but has been in the habit of visiting, preaching, and exhorting, on the outskirts of the city, and in the neighboring villages, whenever men would come to hear him, or he could find a pulpit open to him." In his remarks the speaker paid this tribute to Mr. Nott's efficiency. "He did not preach a single sermon here, or in the surrounding towns, from which he has not subsequently heard, as having been blessed by God with the conversion or awakening of some soul, and it is rare for a young man to, as he did, add to his church within two years, over two hundred members." In conclusion, the speaker said, "We mourn not so much him as the hopes of usefulness buried with him; but neither he nor the hopes buried with him are for ever lost to us; they shall come again and shall meet us at the judgment seat of Christ. He has gone to a higher sphere—let us prepare to follow him."

"Professor Robinson was followed by Rev. Dr. Adams, of the Presbyterian church, who cited, as a sort of parallel to the case, the death of Rev. Mr. Spencer, of Liverpool, who was drowned while bathing in the Mersey. He said, "Let us be still and know that this is God. But last Sabbath a preacher of the gospel, now he lies before you, preaching yet more eloquently than ever from those cold and pallid lips. Ah, could he but now open them, and break the silence of the grave, what might he not tell us of the glories which have burst so suddenly upon his view. The best tribute of your affection is your remembrance of the many great truths he has uttered to you, and your faith in them."

"Dr. Adams then offered prayer, after which the 1284th hymn was sung. There being a general wish to see the deceased once more before his consignment to the grave, an arrangement was made by which the persons in each section of seats in the body of the church, and afterwards those in the galleries, were allowed to pass in order before the coffin, as it stood in front of the pulpit, and cast a glance on the beloved face.

After all who were in the house, except the clergy

and immediate friends, had viewed the remains, and left the church, the large crowd who had waited over two hours outside the church, unable to obtain admittance because of the throng, were allowed to enter and pass round before the coffin. This occupied some time, during which the utmost silence and solemnity pervaded the church, notwithstanding the vast numbers going in and out. Last of all the various ministers went forward and took a last look at the body of their young brother. It was five o'clock before the exercise closed. The procession then formed and moved to the cemetery in Second street. The people gathered around, and after singing, the pall was removed and the coffin, with a single lily lying at its head, was lowered into the vault. The father of the deceased, Rev. H. G. Nott, then gave the benediction as follows :

"Blessed are they who die in the Lord : Yea, saith the Spirit, they rest from their labors, and their works do follow them. He being dead yet speaketh. May the love of Jesus Christ, through whom he preached the resurrection and life now be given. The love of God, our Father in Heaven, and the fellowship of the Spirit abide with us all, and for ever. Amen !" all responded.

In the following December the remains were removed to Greenwood, and placed in a lot then first provided by the First Baptist Church. A granite obelisk, erected by the Broome-street congregation, and inscribed with the names of all their pastors, marks the place where he now lies.

In place of any extended remarks of our own, it may be fitting that we should quote from some of many discriminating and genial tributes which the life and death herein feebly pictured, called forth. Dr. Church in the *Chronicle* observed that, among other characteristics.

"Mr. Nott was always remarkable for the perfect availableness of his powers on all occasions. His reasoning was a sort of intuition, and his faith, perception. Thoughts and truths found in his mind a congenial soil, instantly springing up in appropriate words and gesticulations. His voice was full and commanding, and his utterance perfectly easy and natural. His person was short and light, but his countenance was lively and expressive, beaming with the sentiments of a fervid soul. He always in the pulpit had perfect command of himself and his subject, and his hearers were never apprehensive of a failure from his youth, inexperience, or any cause.

"One thing we will say of his people, that their treatment of their young pastor is a model for all churches in similar relations. Their sorrow at his loss is not embittered with the memory of unkindness to him while he was with them. It has been, throughout, one of the happiest unions of pastor and people with which we were ever acquainted. The deacons were always tender of his health, careful of his reputation, judicious in their advice, and the most faithful of Aarons and Hurs to sustain his uplifted hands. Though short, how sweet the memory of such a pastorship! "*That* will never die, but will remain for ever an occasion for gratitude and of adoring praise.

"Brother Nott," he continued, "had no partizan connexions since he came to New York, and his union was as perfect with brethren of one party as another; for literally he knew no man after the flesh. Hence all alike feel that one of themselves is gone, and over his grave we all meet in the most cordial sympathy and good will. So let us remain evermore."

A writer in a New York daily journal found a place in the midst of heated political discussions and partizan warfare to write thus on the day after his death:

"In briefly analyzing his character we observe a combination of qualities that, as we reflect upon them in their relations to each other, extort from us for Mr. Nott the appellation of a model man. A bright example, worthy the imitation of all young men. He was the moving spirit of the social circle; was tenderly attached to his family relations and his friends; and in the Sabbath School, where he would be found sure as the Sabbath came, and in the Society meetings of the Church, he always displayed the same genial disposition. Yet he was never light nor trivial, but always conducted himself with a dignity of bearing, and displayed a gravity and common sense in conversation, which would be expected only in one who was more advanced in years.

"Especially did he always keep in view the object of his mission, and never let pass unimproved an opportunity to enforce personal religion upon those unconverted persons with whom he came in contact. He was noted for his kindness to the poor and the afflicted, and the weak always found in him a heart to sympathize and a hand to help.

"His intellectual attainments were of a high order. 'An educated Christian' was an expression he often used, in speaking of what individuals should be. No words could more accurately delineate his own character. They are an epitome of himself. And an educated Christian is the highest form of character. His sermons displayed an originality which was the subject of frequent remark; they were characterized by sound doctrine, and beauty of language and of thought, and were delivered with a grace and fervor which did not fail to secure the attention, to convince the judgment and to win the heart. His own fervent piety shone out on every occasion. In conversation and at the baptismal service he had an appropriate word for every individual, and was endeared alike to persons of various tastes and dispositions.

"His last ministrations were noted for piety and zeal. He preached Christ. He was handsome in person, was manly and independent in spirit, yet humble and gentle as a child. The members of his Church and congregation are in great grief at their loss, for he was beloved by every one, and was just entering on a brilliant career of usefulness. It was remarked that on Thursday he went into the river singing, and just before the water covered him, asked his friends to observe how beautiful the heavens were. How suggestive! Singing in the river and the heavens beautiful. He passed through the river of death singing, and went to realize how glorious the heavens are."

Dr. Bright, in the *N. Y. Examiner*, in a copious and eloquent sketch, (July 14, 1859) remarks as follows:

"It was regarded by many as a perilous undertaking for one so young to stand in the place of such a man as Dr. Cone; but it is no exaggeration to say that he proved himself to possess, in extraordinary measure, the ripe wisdom, the ready tact, the clear-sighted discrimination, the sterling integrity, the warm-hearted nature, and the pulpit power, necessary to make him a highly successful pastor and preacher in any position. We gave him a large share of our heart the first time we heard him preach, and every subsequent sermon that we heard from him, or interview we had with him, did but increase our respect and love for him. His preaching was without notes, and it is said that he rarely, if ever, wrote a discourse before delivering it. But if the half-dozen discourses we heard from him, in the ordinary ministrations of the pulpit, may be accepted as samples of his style of elucidating and enforcing gospel truth, he must have been an earnest and prayerful student. His conceptions of a subject were never commonplace, but always natural and comprehensive, his language chaste and simple, his illustrations apt and striking, and his elocution easy and impressive. He seemed to us, when standing in the pulpit, like an intelligent man with rare conversational ability, illuminating every thought that occurred to him, and making it the property of every hearer, however young or illiterate he may have been. Hence he invariably had the fixed attention of his large congregation, and we have the testimony of more than one of the most discriminating of his hearers, that he preached so well at no previous time as in the last three months of his life.

"The brief ministry of Mr. Nott was productive of remarkable results. The first sermon which he preached in Broome-street led a soul to Christ, and at every monthly communion of the church, the hand of fellowship was given to some newly converted persons that had just been baptized. From the first Sunday in September, 1857, to the first Sunday in July, 1859, the last of his Sabbaths on earth, his people seemed to be constantly gathering the fruits of a *present* revival; and it was surprising, as we are told by one of his deacons, to observe how large a proportion of the 205 persons he had baptized in the twenty-two months, traced their first convictions of sin, or their subsequent deliverance, to the sermons or exhortations of their pastor. His heart was in what he said, and it seldom failed to make other hearts feel its power; and the consciousness of his dependence on God was so deep and abiding, that it was no uncommon thing for the family with whom he boarded, to hear his voice in earnest prayer after midnight. "He walked with God;" and such was the influence of his blameless and joyous life, that we have been told by an intelligent member of his church, who knew him intimately, that the example of Mr. Nott, in his every-day intercourse with his people, was worth more to the church than all that he received for his services as their pastor.

"Our departed brother was not satisfied with the numerical increase of his church. He brought all the enthusiasm of his generous nature into the service of developing its missionary life. Fruitful in devising wise measures, he labored, with an assiduity that knew of no repose, to bring the church and their work as near together as possible, and to have as much of it done as possible. He had the most exalted conceptions of the church as an evangelizing organization, and regarded it as a part of his mission to demonstrate how *much* direct missionary work a church might accomplish. He has told us that he did not believe any other pastor had so good a people to work for and with, and that he found a boundless satisfaction in the thought that he was so completely one of them. He knew that he had their confidence, and he asked no more than to be their helper in unfolding and nurturing the truly aggressive character of a Christian church. Few pastors of maturer years could have died leaving behind them the records of nobler beginnings in that direction, than are now to be found in the mission schools, the tract districts, and other beneficent enterprises of the First Church.

"Mr. Nott possessed, to a remarkable degree, the power of adapting himself to the diversified duties of a pastor. Other men might have been able to do some things better than he, but we can name no man who did a larger number of things so well. We have seen him as the presiding officer of one of his church societies, and as the conductor of a prayer-meeting. We have heard of him as the sympathizing friend in sickness, and as the counsellor of the anxious inquirer. We have listened to him as he stood in the pulpit, on the platform, and on the floor. But we have not seen or heard of the first instance in which he did not develope some quality, of mind or heart, that gave him special fitness for every class of ministerial duties, and for those duties among all classes of men. The sermon which he preached, as one of the series, in the Academy of Music, Sunday evening, February 13, 1859, about "Jesus and the Resurrection," riveted the attention and electrified the hearts of as large and cultivated an audience as could be gathered in any house in the city of New York. The demand for its publication was instant and universal. But the preacher on whose lips thousands hung with ever swelling emotion on that memorable occasion, could and did make ineffaceable impressions on the hearts of children, and the most grovelling and ignorant of men. He loved to carry and to open the treasures of the gospel to the poor, and he seized every opportunity to do it. His vacation of last summer was spent in a missionary tour in destitute districts of Maine, and August of the present year was to be given to a like work on Long Island. He intended to take the whole length of the island, preaching Jesus, from evening to evening, in every accessible place.

"What Mr. Nott was in his social life, will best appear from the following letter, written at our request, by a member of his own church, who had rare means of estimating his worth as a friend:"

"What you ask of me is at once a very grateful and a sadly painful task. Whatever of egotism you find in the few lines I send, will, perhaps, be excused, as almost unavoidable, if I would write clearly and to the point.

"I first saw and heard Mr. Nott in the pulpit, in November, 1857. I became personally acquainted with him in April, 1858. He baptized my wife and daughter in May, and myself in August of that year. The personal intimacy between us has existed scarcely more than a year—yet it seems as though the attached friendship of a lifetime was compressed into these twelve months. Many intimacies, more or less close and constant, and highly valued, have been my privilege in the course of somewhat peculiarly varied scenes in the last twenty years. But no other man has ever so gently, yet so irresistibly drawn out towards him, by the cords of love, all the best and deepest sympathies of my nature, as did this great-hearted young apostle.

"His mode of elucidating religious truth was to me peculiarly interesting, even as an intellectual exercise; for I could but admire his ever-ready, fluent, earnest eloquence—his dignified bearing and self-possession—his happy choice of language—and the winning, sympathetic tones of his voice; and above all, the manly sincerity and truly Christian spirit that breathed through all he said. If ever my own inmost consciousness has been touched and enlightened by divine truth, it has been through the words which fell from his lips.

"But this is not what you desired of me. Ten thousand others more competent can worthily testify of his public ministrations. The intimacy with which he honored me and my family during the last year of his life, gives me the privilege of remembering, with peculiar and earnest satisfaction, the characteristics of his social intercourse;—the qualities which marked and endeared him to us as a man, as a friend, as a pastor, in the freest and most intimate everyday relations. I can hardly trust myself to express, in full, the warm admiration, respect, and love which every day's knowledge of him served to strengthen and increase.

"Of the facilities for a few hours' change of air, and relaxation which my house (a few miles out of town) afforded him, he frequently availed himself. His coming was always hailed with delight by the *little* children as well as the oldest. Very few persons had so happy a faculty of winning the confidence and love of children. I am sure that those of four, six, and eight years in my family, are as vividly and keenly grieved in knowing that they 'will never see Mr. Nott again,' as they could be if he had been their own brother.

"In every way did he seem to win and secure the entire *confidence* of all who knew him best—confidence in his intelligence, his judgment and discretion, and in the *purity* and sincerity of his Christian character.

"He was always genial, hopeful, buoyant; often almost boyishly joyful—while there was ever an undercurrent of earnestness; and though we might be sure that there was nothing of bigotry or asceticism in his nature or his faith, yet it was always apparent that he never forgot his own dignity as a man, his principles and his hopes as a Christian, or his responsibilities as a pastor. It was this remarkable union of winning, joyous, hopeful sympathy, with keen intelligence and discrimination, peculiar *tact* (a rare quality), and vigorous earnestness in all his ministerial duties, which specially characterized our most valued friend.

"I never knew any one who seemed to *live* so *thoroughly* as he. All the sources of pure enjoyment in the physical universe seemed to inspire him. He bounded along, exhilarated with the very sense of existence. He keenly enjoyed the invigorating influence of free air on the hills and fields. He had, too, a discriminating love of Art; while all these large capabilities were chastened and regulated by simple, unaffected, cheerful, manly piety.

"It so happened that at many different times, in summer and winter, he has been with us, as one of the family, in our simple recreations and employments—on the ice—clearing the snow—rowing on the water—walking to breathe the pure air of the hills—talking over some book or topic of mental culture. Always *one of us*, sharing heartily in our enjoyments, we should have looked to him for still heartier sympathy in our sorrows, if they had come. In the studies and employment of the children, he always showed an appreciating interest, and I think they would have confided to him their inmost thoughts even more freely than to their parents.

"Of the large flock under his charge, as a church, and individually, he always spoke as though his whole heart was with them. If, perchance, he would hear a word slightly deprecatory of any brother, the pastor never failed to defend, or find excuse, for the absent. In no instance did I ever hear him speak otherwise than kindly and fraternally of one of his charge; many he would warmly appreciate and praise. In this spirit of Christian charity and brotherly love, he seemed to imitate more closely (I say it reverentially) the Divine Master himself, than any one I have been privileged to know. While his own faith was firm as a rock, and clear as crystal, he breathed the very spirit of that charity and love which 'endureth all things, hopeth all things.'

"For myself, while I looked up to him as a pastor, a teacher, and a guide, I loved him as an own brother. One in whose discrimination of character I have great confidence, says that no other person she ever knew, *combined* so many admirable characteristics as our pastor. In very few characters, indeed, do we find perfect symmetry. Human perfection is unattainable, of course. Yet we are commanded to strive after it; looking to the Master as our model, as well as the end of the law for righteousness. The infirmities of poor human nature are too deep-rooted to be eradicated by our own wisdom or strivings. But since the beloved disciple himself leaned on the bosom of his Lord and Master, I believe sincerely that no mortal frame has ever enshrined a purer and nobler spirit than that of my dearly beloved friend, KINGMAN NOTT."

"Brief as was the public career of our deceased brother, he was so well known and justly esteemed beyond the limits of his own denomination, that we asked a Congregationalist friend, who had often been associated with him in works of beneficence, to give us his impressions of Mr. Nott. He writes as follows:—

"The death of the youthful and beloved Nott, is the bereavement not of a family, a society, a denomination, or a community, but of the church of Christ. As a member of *that* church, endearingly associated with him in the last few months of his life, by no narrower tie than the all-embracing love of which he was so rare an example, I cannot, I must not keep back the sorrowful tribute which in every branch of the household of faith belongs to his memory. In a day when 'the unity of the Spirit in the bond of peace,' has suddenly received a development so unprecedented and prevailing—in a day when the spirit of redeeming love is going forth in the Redeemer's followers with such an expansive energy, I knew not the man who seemed, on the whole, quite even with him in the advance. He threw his person forward, *with* his views and convictions, into the van; the whole thinking and acting man was there, indivisible—with a courage that electrified his fellow youth, while a discretion worthy of age, and a commanding decision superior to precedent and prescription, secured the respect of veterans, in his boldest positions. His great gifts, as they appeared from my point of view, were such as these. That combination of the generous and uncalculating courage of youth, with the calmness of a great heart and an imperturbable judgment, which is best expressed in one word as VALOR, and constitutes the born leader of men. Thus, in his eloquence, he was master of an electric energy which could carry away with it all minds but the one, calm and self-possessed, which alternately reined and let loose the fiery element at pleasure. So, too, the unbounded breadth and liberality of his Christian sympathies, which endeared him to his brethren of every denomination with a love in which more partial relations could only have been swallowed up and lost, had they existed, was a thing of which he was the master, not the slave. It was no lax effluence of an easy good-nature, liberal for want of earnestness, and open for want of self-continence; but was as well defined and strictly contained by the principles he embraced and professed, as it was unconfined by any prejudice or jealousy, denominational or personal. He could give his heart without surrendering his judgment, independence, and responsibility. His principles, instead of confining, served rather to contain, concentrate, and preserve from diffuse waste, the great wealth of his catholic sympathies.

"Again, his stamp as a Christian hero was aggressive. Rather than the quiet inheritor of a post of routine duty, to keep things as they are, he was, in his church, and among the churches, like the youthful Napoleon of a new order, promptly assuming the offensive, and surprising friend and foe with the decision and rapidity of his movements. Far as a man could possibly be from the desire of notoriety and prominence, he was forward in every good word and work, and in every united movement of the churches, and was already marked as a destined standard-bearer of the embattled tribes of the spiritual Israel. His favorite theme, and the subject of his public and private discourse respectively, on the last two occasions that I saw him in life, was the eternally 'aggressive' love of God, self-originant, self-energized, unattracted, SOVEREIGN, as the very spirit of the church which is begotten in His image. Upon this he founded his theory of church-life, and by this infinite motor, he sought everywhere to impel the energies of the church universal toward the final triumph of redeeming love.

"One more grand quality of the young leader so prematurely stricken down in the first promise of his career, I cannot omit to mention. His holy magnanimity towered out of sight of any supposed interests or dignities of his order. He never seemed to remember them, unless to repudiate every consideration of the kind. The true dignity of his office was lowliness—its greatness, to be 'servant of all.' Stripping himself of all established pretensions, and renouncing all authority, save for the Divine Word of which he was a bearer, he strove constantly to make the ministerial office as lowly and unassuming as its Author. He was eminently a man of prayer, with all his practical energy, and hence the spirit of Christ was thus brightly exemplified in his chosen position and bearing. True, he was but human; he was but young:—but while the sorrow of the hour dispenses imperatively with the office of criticism, these very facts enhance the praise and love we pay to him who has entered into rest."*

* With reference to other characteristics, a few lines are here quoted from one or two other sources. A near relative says:—"Kingman never could harbor resentment or unkind feeling. There was no dark corner in his heart for retaliation, or bitterness, or wounded pride. His was the Bible rule, 'answering not again.' He was sometimes misunderstood, and perhaps he was thought to be deficient in sensitiveness. He was not indifferent to unkindness, but with the shield of brotherly love and unselfish charity he warded off all that was opposed to those influences. Many instances of this spirit in him are well remembered, and other incidents which proved that he not only exercised this virtue of Christian forbearance as a *principle* and a rule of life, but that with it he always sustained a peculiar dignity and self-respect. Always kind in manner, he could at times still give a severe and just reproof. An instance of discourtesy towards him by some fellow students, while in college, was thus met by mingled kindness and justice, and the parties became fast friends." . . . .

Mrs. Bigelow, with whose family Mr. Nott found a cheerful home during his entire residence in New York, writes much of him that is most interesting to his family and friends. A paragraph or two only is quoted:—"We always knew his elastic step as he entered our dwelling, and all was cheerful and happy where he was; his ever joyous countenance at once dispelled any sadness that hung over us. He always had a smile and a kind word for every one; all, from oldest to youngest, delighted to be in his company.

"We miss him everywhere, but most at the family altar, where his earnest, heartfelt prayers, will not be forgotten. His whole soul was in his prayers.

"Sabbath mornings he always seemed peculiarly happy; his countenance *shone;* he enjoyed so much of heaven, that it was imprinted on his face." . . . .

But the fond memory of friends would lead us to unreason-

"We have thus," adds the *Examiner*, "aimed to place before our readers a simple, truthful statement of the manner in which death came to the youthful pastor of the First Baptist Church, and of what they and the Christian world have lost in that sad event. But while thousands of Christian hearts, in all lands, will have tears to shed over his precious memory, and warmest supplications to pour forth to God for the church and family who have been so severely smitten, no one must forget that he who has been suddenly and mysteriously taken away from the circles which he loved and adorned on earth, once exclaimed, as if his far-reaching and all-appropriating faith had given him a new and seraphic vision; "Oh, then, what a glorious morn will the resurrection morning be! Methinks I see the glad procession coming up!—a multitude to which the throng I behold to-night is but a drop in the vast ocean, whom no man can number! I see them coming up in robes of white, with crowns of everlasting joy upon their heads, and palms of victory in their hands. I hear their shouts of gladness as they cry, 'Victory! worthy is the Lamb that hath redeemed us!' Fathers and mothers grasp children long lost. Husbands and wives, separated many centuries, fall again into each other's arms. I hear a voice which calls my own name! I start as did

able limits in such quotations. Eulogy, as such, is needless and unprofitable. Our aim has been to present succinctly such personal characteristics as afford a lesson and an example.

Mary, when Jesus gently uttered that word—'Mary!' That voice! * * * * I had dreamed of it all through my life, ever since my boyhood. I know it—and the child is clasped in the arms of its mother, who cries out, 'My son!' and the child looks up and whispers, 'Mother!' in the old familiar strain, and rests again in the bosom that gave it life. I behold these reunions; no one comes alone or empty-handed, but all go up with arms full and laps laden with treasures which the grave and the sea had buried, but which now are all restored for ever with the coming back of Jesus."

THE END.

www.ingramcontent.com/pod-product-compliance
Lightning Source LLC
LaVergne TN
LVHW020118110826
845151LV00001B/196

* 9 7 8 1 4 2 5 5 4 2 0 3 0 *